FREEDOM and FLOURISHING

FREEDOM and FLOURISHING

Being, Act, and Knowledge
in Karl Barth's *Church Dogmatics*

Robert Leigh

 CASCADE *Books* • Eugene, Oregon

FREEDOM AND FLOURISHING
Being, Act, and Knowledge in Karl Barth's *Church Dogmatics*

Copyright © 2017 Robert Leigh. All rights reserved. Except for brief quotations in critical publications or reviews, no part of this book may be reproduced in any manner without prior written permission from the publisher. Write: Permissions, Wipf and Stock Publishers, 199 W. 8th Ave., Suite 3, Eugene, OR 97401.

Cascade Books
An Imprint of Wipf and Stock Publishers
199 W. 8th Ave., Suite 3
Eugene, OR 97401

www.wipfandstock.com

PAPERBACK ISBN: 978-1-4982-9916-9
HARDCOVER ISBN: 978-1-4982-9918-3
EBOOK ISBN: 978-1-4982-9917-6

Cataloguing-in-Publication data:

Names: Leigh, Robert, author.

Title: Freedom and flourishing : being, act, and knowledge in Karl Barth's Church Dogmatics / Robert Leigh.

Description: Eugene, OR: Cascacde Books, 2017 | Includes bibliographical references and index.

Identifiers: ISBN 978-1-4982-9916-9 (paperback) | ISBN 978-1-4982-9918-3 (hardcover) | ISBN 978-1-4982-9917-6 (ebook).

Subjects: LCSH: Barth, Karl, 1886–1968 | Theology, doctrinal | Knowledge, theory of (Religion).

Classification: BT203 L45 2017 (paperback) | BT203 (ebook).

Manufactured in the U.S.A.   11/06/17

Scripture quotations are from New Revised Standard Version Bible, copyright © 1989 National Council of the Churches of Christ in the United States of America. Used by permission. All rights reserved worldwide.

For Claire and Isabella

CONTENTS

Acknowledgments | ix

Abbreviations: Works of Karl Barth | xi

Introduction | 1

Part A: Being and Act—Karl Barth's Actualistic Theology of Freedom

1 Freedom in the Early Barth: Being and Act | 17

2 "Being-in-Becoming": The Development of Barth's Actualistic Theology of Freedom | 55

Part B: Divine and Human Freedom in Asymmetrical Reciprocity in *Church Dogmatics* IV/3

3 Divine and Human Freedom in Asymmetrical Reciprocity: Being, Act, and Knowledge in *Church Dogmatics* IV/3 | 107

4 The Participative Logic of *Church Dogmatics* IV/3: Placing Barth in Conversation with Hegel | 145

5 Called to Liberty: Human Flourishing in *Church Dogmatics* IV/3 | 177

Conclusion | 217

Bibliography | 231

Index | 243

ACKNOWLEDGMENTS

While I take full responsibility for the arguments in this book, it could never have come to fruition without the support of many people, whom I would like to thank sincerely. This book developed out of my doctoral research at Selwyn College, University of Cambridge. First and foremost I owe an unspeakable debt of gratitude to David Ford, who guided me through my theological education with wisdom, patience, generosity, and—above all—joy. It is profoundly humbling to have served my apprenticeship under the tutelage of someone whose daily life is a testament to the freedom Barth's life-work envisions. His friendship is a blessing that I cherish.

I would like to thank the Arts and Humanities Research Council for the scholarship that financed my doctorate, as well as the Faculty of Divinity and Selwyn College, Cambridge, for making possible several formative research trips. I would especially like to extend my deepest thanks to Canon Hugh Shilson-Thomas, Dean of Chapel and Chaplain at Selwyn College, for helping me and my family to feel at home in Cambridge during my years of study and afterwards.

I am grateful to Eberhard Jüngel, Jürgen Moltmann, Hans-Anton Drewes, George Hunsinger, and in particular to Bruce McCormack, all of whom generously agreed to meet with me to discuss my project, and without whom I could not have adequately understood the significance and complexities of Barth's thought. I am grateful also to Ian Torrance for granting me access to the wonderful resources of Princeton Theological Seminary whilst undertaking research at the Center for Barth Studies. Many thanks also go to Sarah Coakley, Tom Greggs, John McDowell, Peter Ochs, Micheal O'Siadhail, Janet Soskice, Daniel Weiss, and Simeon Zahl, with whom I have held numerous enlightening conversations, and from whom I have learned a great deal. I am especially grateful to Nicholas Adams, who has been a continuing source of inspiration and encouragement, was kind enough to share unpublished manuscripts of his own work throughout my research, and examined my doctorate with Paul Nimmo. I am grateful for the advice that both Nick and Paul gave me during my time in Edinburgh and Cambridge, and after my doctoral examination, which has helped enormously to improve the quality of my work.

A number of friends and colleagues have commented perceptively on various drafts of this book, and I am especially thankful to Cosmio Ajmone-Marsan, Stephen Bovey, Diane Saywack, Bryce Wandry, and Grant Woolner for their intellectual rigor and assistance. I am also indebted to my philosophy and theology students whose insightful questions have made me a far sharper thinker.

Several friendships, in particular, have been profoundly important for the development of my ideas: Sean Turchin, Matthias Grebe, and Giles Waller have been steady companions, and have all engaged thoughtfully with various drafts of this book. One friend, however, stands out for the wonderful support and guidance he has given me: Ashley Cocksworth has been a loyal friend ever since we first discovered Karl Barth's thought together in New College, Edinburgh. He has been a generous and affirming "first reader" of my research, and I could not have written this book without his conversation, enthusiasm, wisdom, and advice.

I am grateful to my parents, Mira and Douglas Leigh, and to my parents-in-law, Liz and Tony Salmon, who have provided me with all sorts of care and encouragement over the years.

Above all others I am thankful for my wife Claire, whose love, patience, kindness, generosity, and joyfulness are the primary signs in my life that the kinds of freedom and flourishing I have tried to describe in this book are not mere possibilities, but realities to be seized gratefully. It is to her, and to our daughter Isabella Grace, that this book is dedicated.

ABBREVIATIONS

Works of Karl Barth

I/1	*Church Dogmatics*, vol. I, part 1. 2nd ed. Edinburgh: T. & T. Clark, 1975
I/2	*Church Dogmatics*, vol. I, part 2. Edinburgh: T. & T. Clark, 1956
II/1	*Church Dogmatics*, vol. II, part 1. Edinburgh: T. & T. Clark, 1957
II/2	*Church Dogmatics*, vol. II, part 2. Edinburgh: T. & T. Clark, 1957
III/1	*Church Dogmatics*, vol. III, part 1. Edinburgh: T. & T. Clark, 1958
III/2	*Church Dogmatics*, vol. III, part 2. Edinburgh: T. & T. Clark, 1960
III/3	*Church Dogmatics*, vol. III, part 3. Edinburgh: T. & T. Clark, 1960
III/4	*Church Dogmatics*, vol. III, part 4. Edinburgh: T. & T. Clark, 1961
IV/1	*Church Dogmatics*, vol. IV, part 1. Edinburgh: T. & T. Clark, 1956
IV/2	*Church Dogmatics*, vol. IV, part 2. Edinburgh: T. & T. Clark, 1958
IV/3	*Church Dogmatics*, vol. IV, part 3. Edinburgh: T. & T. Clark, 1962
IV/4	*Church Dogmatics*, vol. IV, part 4. Edinburgh: T. & T. Clark, 1962
ChrL	*The Christian Life: Church Dogmatics IV/4 Lecture Fragments.* Edinburgh: T. & T. Clark, 1981
KD	*Die Kirchliche Dogmatik*, 4 volumes in 13 parts. Zürich: Evangelischer Verlag, 1947–1967
Romans II	*The Epistle to the Romans.* London: Oxford University Press, 1933

INTRODUCTION

For freedom Christ has set us free.

—GALATIANS 5:1

In his eulogy for Karl Barth, Eberhard Jüngel said that "Barth's lifework . . . was nothing less than an essay in the theology of freedom."[1] Given the ubiquity of the concept of freedom in Barth's theology, such a statement might appear somewhat platitudinous. Yet there is a sense that Jüngel has offered us *the* hermeneutical key to unlock the most basic thrust of the *Church Dogmatics*. His point is that, despite the complexity, originality, and subtlety of Barth's writing; regardless of the multiple inter- and intra-textual refractions, recapitulations, and renewals he weaves into his deep engagement with centuries of Christian and Western intellectual history; and notwithstanding the grandeur and vision of his theological architectonic, in the last resort, every page of Barth's work strives to communicate one very simple and dearly cherished motif: Jesus means freedom![2]

Yet Barth is also absolutely insistent that theology consists, first and foremost, of faithful exposition of the biblical witness in service to God and the Church.[3] He would therefore resolutely refuse the idea that freedom—or any other concept—could function as a master concept in his thought.[4] The themes and leitmotifs central to the *Church Dogmatics* gain their prominence in Barth's exegetical lexicon only to the extent that they serve to make sense of the Bible's stories and its testimony to God's glory and wisdom. And Barth is adamant that the meanings of those stories themselves must never be assimilated apologetically into a general philosophy or doctrinal scheme,

---

1. Jüngel, *Karl Barth*, 20.
2. I borrow this motif from Timothy Gorringe, who employs it as the title of his chapter on Barth's soteriology in *Karl Barth against Hegemony*, 217–67.
3. Ford, *Barth and God's Story*, 11–13; and Frei, *Types of Christian Theology*, 39–46.
4. Gorringe, *Karl Barth against Hegemony*, 271.

derived in abstraction from what the New Testament says about the person of Jesus Christ.[5] Timothy Gorringe observes that in his final radio interview Barth insisted the last thing he had to say as a theologian and as a political animal was not a concept, like grace (or freedom!) "but a name: Jesus Christ. *He* is grace, and *he* is the final thing . . . and what I have sought to do in my long life is . . . to highlight this name and say: *there* . . .!"[6] It may seem curious, then, that Jüngel should insist that Barth's writings are fundamentally about *freedom*, a concept that features more centrally in classical and modern politics, philosophy, religion and intellectual culture than it does in the Bible itself. Why, then, is Barth so particularly fascinated by freedom? It is because the idea of freedom invokes something of the very tenor of the Bible's entire witness to the *Heilsgeschichte*, and to the name Jesus Christ. Barth insists that "in the Bible [the theologian] learns about the free God and the free man, and as a disciple of the Bible he may himself become a witness to the divine and human freedom."[7]

Essentially, to say that Jesus means freedom is to characterize divine and human agency—and their intersection—in terms of a gift. This was the central point of Barth's 1953 lecture on evangelical ethics, titled "The Gift of Freedom,"[8] which serves as an excellent way into Barth's theology. On the one hand, freedom captures the sheer super-abundant gracefulness of God's covenantal self-identification with humanity in the incarnation. On the other hand, it attests to the absolutely joyful liberation God offers human beings in and through personal encounter with Jesus and His Holy Spirit.[9]

For Barth, every chapter of the Bible is a reminder that God does not have to be *this* God, the God of humanity; and yet God freely chooses not to be God without us. God's sovereign lordship and absolute *aseity* is therefore simultaneously the *freedom* of one who loves supremely, and the *love* of one who acts absolutely without external compulsion. God's infinite qualitative distinction from—and ontological priority over—humanity consists in the fact that it is God who decides to create; God who preserves creation; and God who upholds the covenant as the space in which creatures may flourish. The freedom that characterizes God's agency is anything but the abstract aloofness of the monadic God of classical metaphysics. The Bible, Barth concludes, has no interest in a purely immutable God who is free to

---

5. Ford, *Barth and God's Story*, 48–49.
6. See Gorringe, *Karl Barth against Hegemony*, 280.
7. Barth, "The Gift of Freedom," 88.
8. See ibid., 65–95.
9. Ibid., 78–79.

remain completely self-contained, and utterly transcendent.[10] To conceive of God's freedom in this manner would be to divorce freedom from the love revealed on the cross; it would be to imagine God's freedom in distinction from the gift of that freedom, and thereby to view God's lordship merely as the infinite possibilities of one who elects not to exercise God's omniscience and omnipotence, for fear of risking that very freedom. At no point, then, does the Bible confuse the divine prerogative with divine isolationism.[11]

By contrast, to speak of human freedom is not to refer to a capacity for action, or to safeguard a contra-causal account of self-determination by proving the existence of some inner recess of subjectivity as the foundation for ethics and politics. Rather, it is to speak of the gift of liberation through personal encounter. In the Bible, it is as humans are attracted into the presence of God that they are liberated to become most fully what they already are: participants in the drama of God's life.[12] In other words, the human does not enjoy the freedom of God, the freedom of sovereignty. Human life is given; God's is not. The human is free to the extent that she is given the chance to glorify God through a life of humble, obedient, and grateful service. And Barth is adamant that any construal of human freedom as the possession of a choice to reject the gift of the covenant is a futile illusion, for godlessness is an ontological impossibility in light of God's exercise of the divine freedom not to be God without us.

The gift of freedom portrayed in the Bible is therefore captured in the form of a narrative about the sheer gracefulness of the loving God who wills to take creation into God's own life, for the sake of God's own glory, and quite without necessity or on the basis of any merit of creation—but who really does grant a genuine and deep partnership to creation, and therefore enables it to flourish in a radical sense. Where is this dynamic of freedom and flourishing primarily located in the Bible? For Barth, three biblical stories in particular capture the profound astonishment and deep gratitude of their authors in light of the radical divine initiative to which they witness. These stories are the creation saga, in which God creates *ex nihilo*, revealing the "Yes of God the Creator" for a reality which is distinct from God and which has no reason to be, other than the "overflowing of [God's] inward glory";[13] the crucifixion, in which God reveals the sheer depth of utterly

---

10. Ibid., 67. Barth goes on: "God's freedom is not merely unlimited possibility or formal majesty and omnipotence, that is to say empty, naked sovereignty . . . [I]f conceived of as unconditioned power [God] would be a demon and as such His own prisoner" (ibid., 67).

11. See ibid., 67.

12. See ibid., 77.

13. III/1, 15. See ibid., §§41–42.

undeserved divine love for humanity in the obedience and humility of the Son;[14] and the resurrection, in which humans are regenerated beyond the pride, guilt, sloth, misery, stupidity, inhumanity, anxiety, falsehood, self-assertion, and perversion revealed of them in the crucifixion.[15]

In and through these acts of divine initiative "God's freedom is and remains above and beyond human freedom."[16] The creation and preservation of the relationship between God and humanity is capable of being generated by God alone. But while the interaction of God and humans is therefore marked by an absolute asymmetry, the *fact* of the gift of freedom in these three moments of super-abundant divine self-giving also means there is a reciprocity between the covenant partners. God and humanity are free with respect to each other, which is to say their respective freedoms are not jeopardized by, but are grounded in, committed relationship with one another. The consequence of this construal of mutual freedom is profound: the freedom of humanity to flourish at the heart of the drama of God's life is itself integral to the freedom in which God determines God's own identity. "God's own freedom and its realisations is the source and object of every Christian act of recognition and confession."[17] In other words, God's self-determination assumes the genuine historical predicates of one whose story unfolds in organic relationship with a created order that is permitted a distinct ontological integrity of its own. And this daring vision of the

---

14. IV/1, §59

15. IV/1, §60; IV/2, §65; IV/3, §70. I am indebted to Giles Waller with whom discussions about Luther on creation, crucifixion, and resurrection proved instructive in developing this insight about Barth's biblical location of divine and human freedom. I also note the centrality of these three narratives to Ford's interpretation of Barth's exegetical method in the *Church Dogmatics*. While Barth insists that these stories refer to real historical events, it is part of his "realistic narrative" approach to hermeneutics not to read them realistically in the sense of taking them to be historical reconstructions of the events themselves, but as realistic portrayals of the human witness to God's initiative for, and assessment of, humanity. (Ford, *Barth and God's Story*, 51–52) For instance, by definition no human could experience the creation. And no witness was present at the resurrection itself: the biblical testimony is to the empty tomb *kerygma*. (Ford, *Barth and God's Story*, 109) Yet the stories are written from the perspective of ones who really believe that the narrative concerned (whether creation saga or resurrection *kerygma*) identifies the Yes of God the Creator or the positive verdict of the Father in and through real historical events, and which therefore claim what is revealed in these narratives to be supreme reality, not reality in the sense of mere historical reconstruction. (Ford, *Barth and God's Story*, 53) That supreme reality is the free, sovereign love of God for humanity, and the humble obedience of the creature who flourishes in service and gratitude, as actualized in the person of Jesus Christ.

16. Barth, "The Gift of Freedom," 71.

17. Ibid., 71.

provocative and attractive freedom of God opens up a genuine space for authentic human agency and contingency.

If Barth is to avoid synergism (the idea that it is necessary for humans to co-operate with God in order for God to fulfil or complete the reconciliation of the covenant, and so in some sense to achieve their own salvation) while defending a conception of human freedom worthy of the name, his eschatology and theology of mediation will surely play a vital role in his soteriology. Barth must establish the manner in which God resolves eschatologically not to be God without humanity, while resisting the notions that humanity is coerced into fellowship, or that everything is resolved in Christ on their behalf, so that individual humans and communities have no genuine role to play in the covenant. Just how is it that God attracts humans into the truth, light, and life of Jesus through the Holy Spirit? In what does the freedom and vocation of the Church for service to God's glory consist? Barth explores these themes in *Church Dogmatics* IV/3, the final completed and largest book in his systematic theology, by way of a novel exposition of Jesus in his prophetic office as the mediator of the covenant.

It is strange, therefore, that *Church Dogmatics* IV/3 has yet to enjoy any significant scholarly appreciation. John Webster complained, in 1998, that "Like much of Barth's work, what he has to say here has yet to win an audience" and that "this section of Barth's work has had almost no impact on either Christology or theological hermeneutics since its publication."[18] Two decades later, this remains true. The criticisms of *Church Dogmatics* IV/3 will be rehearsed in detail below (see Chapters 3 and 5), but, to anticipate, typical complaints against Barth's treatment of the *munus propheticum* (the prophetic office of Jesus Christ—the portrayal of Jesus as the one who announces the Gospel) include the following charges: soteriological over-objectivism (the idea that God achieves salvation ontologically in Jesus without any participation on the part of human beings, to the extent that their agency, repentance, witness, and confession bear no significance for the state of the covenant); Christomonism (the view that Barth focuses solely on the person and work of Jesus Christ, to the exclusion of all other relevant considerations of God and humanity); pneumatological abstraction (the criticism that given Barth's supposedly exclusive concern with Jesus Christ there is no role for the Holy Spirit in his theology); and the divorce of theological epistemology and ethics from ontology and soteriology (the complaint that the subjective processes by which humans are awakened to knowledge of the Gospel, and to action in light of this knowledge, are

---

18. Webster, "Eloquent and Radiant," 126–27.

accidental and irrelevant to God's works because of Barth's absolute emphasis of the saving reality of God's grace).

In this book it will be argued that a number of commentators have failed to apply an adequately participative account of being, act, and knowledge to Barth's theology of mediation in IV/3 in line with his "actualistic" method and ontology as it developed after the doctrine of election in *Church Dogmatics* II/2.[19] As I shall demonstrate in the chapters below, to refer to Barth's "actualism" is to observe that it is an integral feature of his mature theology (the works developed after Barth began to re-conceive the doctrine of election from 1936) not only that he construes the being of God and the being of humanity primarily in terms of dynamic act and event, but, as Paul Nimmo observes, that we cannot understand the doctrines of revelation, predestination, creation, reconciliation, vocation, justification, sanctification, and glorification outside the history of God's works, fulfilled in and through Jesus Christ and the Holy Spirit.[20] Following Bruce McCormack's landmark study of Barth's theological method,[21] the most convincing readings of Barth have recognized that his actualism is not only a motif for interpreting Barth, but that it is a structural feature of Barth's theology that "the beginning of all the ways and works of God, and therefore of the identity of God, is the self-giving of God in Jesus Christ."[22] Barth's actualistic ontology begins to emerge in *Church Dogmatics* II/1 with the insistence that God "is not an other than He is in His works,"[23] but the radical Christocentric application of this ontology to his doctrine of God does not find its fullest expression until *Church Dogmatics* II/2, where Barth explicitly names Jesus Christ not only the elected man but also the electing God.[24] In other words, from II/2 onwards Barth maintains explicitly what until this point had only began to emerge implicitly in his ontology: that the incarnation, death, and resurrection of Jesus Christ are acts "in the course of which God determines the very being of God."[25] An actualistic reading of IV/3 after this manner would acknowledge that if one wishes to do justice to the revelation of reconciliation and to the participation of humans in the history of God, one cannot divorce the noetic aspects of salvation (our knowledge

---

19. It should be noted, with Nimmo, that "actualism" is not a term Barth ever used himself. Rather, it is used by scholars of Barth to draw attention to some of the key aspects of his ontology and theological method. Nimmo, *Being in Action*, 5.

20. Ibid., 6–7.

21. McCormack, *Karl Barth's Critically Realistic Dialectical Theology*.

22. Nimmo, *Being in Action.*, 7–8.

23. II/1, 260.

24. II/2, 103.

25. II/1, 8.

of reconciliation) from the history of God's eventful self-determination in Jesus Christ.

The genius of IV/3—often obscured in readings of Barth's doctrine of reconciliation—is that it offers a dynamic integration of knowing with being, being with action, truth with witness, individual with community, and divine initiative with human flourishing, in and through the prophetic action of Jesus Christ. Consequently, the mediatorship of Jesus Christ and the history of the Church in the "time between times" are viewed as integral to the very actualization of God's self-election to a life of love. It would be paradoxical to suggest that God could achieve a restoration of covenant relations without drawing human beings into active participation in that covenant history. The claim of IV/3 is that God's salvation is not only entirely graceful and unmerited, but that it is deeply attractive, energizing humans to take up their responsibility for the glorification of God through joyful service. Perhaps it is for this reason that in IV/3 Barth seems to write with the kind of freedom of a theologian whose entire oeuvre (a work of *Church* dogmatics) climaxes in an ecclesiology, eschatology, and pneumatology marked by a profound sense of the joy that the living Jesus and Spirit radiate in their brilliance and eloquence.

In order to demonstrate how this part-volume builds on Barth's earlier works and goes beyond them in ways that have not yet been appreciated, I argue that readers of Barth ought to reconceive the way in which the objective and subjective categories are usually taken to operate in Barth's mature theological epistemology. His use of the terms "object" and "subject" (which translate various pregnant German words such as "*Objekt*," "*Gegenstand*," "*Sache*," and "*Subjekt*") is, as with most German-language thinkers, both complex and inconsistent. On the whole, to refer to objectivity is to treat of questions of being, essence, and "thinghood" (hence ontology); to refer to subjectivity is to refer to questions of activity, knowing, and understanding (hence epistemology). Yet at times Barth will distinguish between the objectivity of God's being *in se*; God's being in history as an object in the world; God's inner, triune subjectivity; God's revelatory subjectivity, and so on. The way the object-subject relation (being, act, and knowledge) functions at certain points for Barth must be derived from the context of the texts in which it features; and if there is a good deal of ambiguity about what Barth means when, for example, he describes God as object or subject, or when he insists upon the objectivity of the subjective aspect of salvation, this is not surprising: he is not himself always explicit about how he intends to use such terms. In other words, there is no clear demarcation between ontology and epistemology in Barth's theology, and he is not particularly interested in clarifying his use of technical terms philosophically, which can make interpreting his works a difficult task.

One of the main purposes of this book is to explore the complex interplay between being, act, and knowledge in Barth's texts, building on the "actualistic" interpretations of Barth given by contemporary Barth scholars such as Bruce McCormack, Paul Nimmo, and Paul Daffyd Jones, in order to clarify how in IV/3 Barth embeds the revelation of salvation into the very structures of God's historical self-determination in Jesus Christ. It is argued that whereas Barth's earlier texts reveal an axiomatic concern to protect the sovereign freedom of God over against the world, the later works pursue a more integrated vision of God and humanity in their Christocentric freedom for one another. This culminates in IV/3, where, the study finds, divine reality and human flourishing are construed as being ordered in asymmetrical reciprocity. It belongs to the very act of God's self-election to covenantal relations that humans are awakened to the Gospel through the mediating work of Jesus and the Spirit, and given their share of responsibility for the joyful glorification of God. Hence in IV/3 Barth is able to offer the most daring language about human participation in the life of God perhaps of the whole *Church Dogmatics* when he affirms that "God allows everything to depend on this recognition and confession. What a risk!"[26] The gradual emergence, in Barth's works, of a theology of revelation that expounds mediation and human witness in terms of a divine *risk* is shown to operate on the basis of an increasingly holistic integration of the structures of being, act, and knowledge within his actualistic Christology.

Facilitating a reparative reading of *Church Dogmatics* IV/3, this book draws on the philosophy of Hegel to investigate the structures of Christian thinking, asking: what kinds of thinking are displayed in interpretations of Barth's soteriology that neglect IV/3? How does Barth's mature work reflect a transformation beyond some of the more quasi-Kantian strands of thinking operative in his earlier works?[27] And, to what participative patterns

---

26. IV/3, 431.

27. By the term "quasi-Kantian" I simply mean to suggest that Barth's interpretation and use of Kant does not necessarily represent the best possible reading of Kant (hence it would be unfair to name some of the more problematic areas of his thought "Kantian" *per se*), but that it was nevertheless a particular engagement with Kant's object-subject schema that had a significant impact on the development of Barth's conceptualization of being, knowing, and acting within his emerging theology of freedom. In later years, Barth seems to characterize the object-subject and divine-human relationships in rather different terms, suggesting he had mitigated the influence of his earlier reading of Kant on his theological ontology and epistemology. I make use of Hegel's texts as a set of logical tools to display this shift in Barth's thinking, and to help readers of Barth diagnose certain problematic patterns of thought that hinder engagement with his

in Barth's mature theological method might Hegel's logic help to draw our attention?

It is my suggestion that Barth's theology of mediation conceives the relationship between the objective and subjective categories in "triadic," rather than "binary," terms.[28] That is to say, Barth takes terms such as object and subject, being and knowing, and truth and witness as pairs of terms which are distinct, but which may not be adequately characterized in separation from one another. The truth of the covenant embodied and expressed in Jesus Christ is necessarily distinct from its contemporaneous reception in the world. But, for Barth, to think of Jesus Christ's truth in abstraction from its expression and reception would not really be to have grasped that truth at all.

A surprising number of scholars have missed how basic this point is to Barth's Christology, accusing him of obliterating the importance of the Church and the Spirit in the revelation of salvation. Such readings, it is suggested, fail to account for the place and value of IV/3 within Barth's soteriology because they assume a false opposition between the objective and subjective categories. That is to say, some commentators pursue a binary, rather than triadic, approach to some of the key pairs in Barth's work, taking two or more terms (such as reconciliation and revelation, for example) as being capable of being understood in abstraction from the other, when for Barth they are not. And then they find—rather unsurprisingly—that Barth is unable to resolve the supposed disjunction between them. Pairs of terms such as reconciliation and revelation are to be interpreted triadically because what is to be understood is not only each distinct term, but the centrality of the interrelation of the two to an adequate definition of each.

The consequence of a binary, rather than triadic, interpretation of Barth's understanding of the contemporaneous mediation of reconciliation is the corrosion of an appreciation of the reciprocal nature of divine and human agencies as embodied in the Jesus Christ. When commentators posit a false opposition, in Barth's works, between reconciliation and its revelation,

---

works, and not in a "genetic-historical" sense to imply that Barth makes the transition from a set of "Kantian" to "Hegelian" intellectual commitments. Such a claim would be a gross mischaracterization of Barth's theological method, and would undermine the enduring significance of Kant's thought to Barth.

28. I borrow the term "triadic logic" from Nichiolas Adams's excellent study of Hegel's logic, *The Eclipse of Grace*. Pairs of terms are triadic, not binary, because in a pair one is dealing with three terms, not two: the distinct terms within the pair, and the relation of the two that makes them a *pair* and not two separate things. (Adams, *The Eclipse of Grace*, 9). "Pair-talk is triadic" because "a pair is not two things that happen to be in relation" but two terms "where each is what it is because of its relation to the other" (Adams, *The Eclipse of Grace*, 9).

a further false opposition or binary opens up between the freedom of God and the freedom of humanity, when in reality, for Barth, divine freedom and human flourishing cannot be understood in separation from each other. This book suggests that where commentators find that the Jesus of IV/3 (the prophet and mediator of the covenant) prohibits rather than grounds either the divine freedom or human flourishing, it is a sign that they have not offered the most affirming and generative reading of Barth available given a generous appraisal of the resources within his texts.

Throughout the book it is argued that once the false opposition between key pairs of terms such as being and knowing, object and subject, truth and witness—characteristic of many interpretations of IV/3—has been overcome, the false opposition between the freedom of God and the freedom of humanity will also be repaired. And this triadic reading of the freedoms of God and humanity in IV/3 will prove instructive in the contemporary debate over Barth's doctrine of election and its implications for accounts of divine and human agency. In sum, it will be seen that Barth's re-conceptualization of the prophetic office of Jesus is the keystone in his thoroughly participative doctrine of salvation, for it is in IV/3, more explicitly than in any other of Barth's texts, that divine freedom and human flourishing are construed in a deeply integrated pattern of asymmetrical reciprocity.

Outline of Work

The book has five chapters, divided between two main parts. Part A (Chapters 1–2) explicates the development of Barth's actualistic theology of freedom, outlining his interest in freedom, and indicating the kinds of questions he is wrestling with when he employs the term to describe certain patterns of divine and human agency. This section lays the foundations for a close reading of *Church Dogmatics* IV/3 in Part B (Chapters 3–5) by tracing Barth's emerging sensitivity to the integration of the objective and subjective categories through the development of a Christocentric, actualistic, and historicized theological method.

Chapter 1 demonstrates that it is his dissatisfaction with various nineteenth and early twentieth-century attempts to repair the concept of God after Kant that motivates Barth's own desire to retrieve the living God of Scripture. It is argued, however, that his early attempts to do so are impeded by a persistent sense of disjunction between God and the world. The earlier Barth's desire to protect the sovereignty and lordship of God causes him to posit something of a metaphysical gap between the triune being of the

Godhead and the divine economy, with the result that he one-sidedly emphasizes God's freedom *from* creation over God's loving freedom *for* the world. Barth's indebtedness to a quasi-Kantian epistemological criticism served to remind liberal theologians, in the wake of their desire to reclaim the historical immanence of God, that God is not a given object in the world, immediately available to human cognition. However, whilst Barth wanted to counter the theological abstractions resulting from Kant's Copernican shift, his anti-liberal stress on the absolute transcendence of God's being served to perpetuate theologically the object-subject disjunction inherited from his reading of Kant, thus compromising the persuasiveness of his alternative to liberal theology.

Nevertheless, although the trinitarian doctrine of revelation in *Church Dogmatics* I tends, to some extent, to isolate God's being *in se* from God's historical economy (thereby upholding a sense of the God-world dualism prevalent in the commentary on *The Epistle to the Romans*), an important transition takes place: here, Barth begins to think of the divine ontology in less abstract and more relational, historicized and Christocentric terms, and this lays the foundations for the future of his theology, which is better able to integrate key terms such as being and acting, and being and knowing, within an historicized framework, and thus to emphasize the freedom of God and humanity for each other, as actualized in the history of Jesus Christ.

Chapter 2 traces the development of Barth's theological actualism after the first volume of the *Church Dogmatics*, finding that Barth continues to fluctuate between stressing the non-objective transcendence of God, and stressing the historical relationality of the divine being, and that this dialectic leads both to the most important advances in his works, and to the most perplexing ambiguities in his texts. Nevertheless, it is demonstrated that Barth's increasing willingness to integrate the objective and subjective categories helps to overcome the dualistic and competitive theological elements in his earlier works. The history of human knowledge of God (God's self-giving life *ad extra*) is not accidental or posterior to God's eternal essence, but is taken up into the event of God's "being-in-becoming."[29] God's "thinkability" occurs precisely because God comes to Godself by coming to humanity in Jesus Christ.[30] In this chapter we see that Barth's doctrine of election (*Church Dogmatics* II/2) in particular has significant implications for the theology of divine and human freedom, since the history of Jesus Christ is seen as determinative of God's very being. And this means

---

29. Jüngel, *God's Being Is in Becoming*, 75.
30. See Jüngel, *God as the Mystery of the World*, 37.

that, contrary to his earliest theology, God's freedom must be defined in utterly relational terms as God's sovereign and eternal self-determination for fellowship with humanity. This chapter engages critically with the trinity-election debate in contemporary theology, arguing that Paul Molnar and George Hunsinger fail to recognize the radicality of Barth's integration of divine reality and human flourishing within an actualistic ontology, and that they thus perpetuate a sense of competition between God and the world that Barth increasingly sought to resist.

In the second part of the chapter I investigate the shape of human flourishing in light of the doctrine of election, where Barth's Christocentric theology of human freedom is distinguished from general philosophical attempts to offer a metaphysical response to the problems of causal and theological determinism. It is the developments in Barth's ontology traced in Chapter 2 that throw into relief the second part of the study, which argues that by *Church Dogmatics* IV/3 Barth is committed to a refusal to think God's reality and human life in abstraction from the name Jesus Christ, through which the two are reciprocally related.

Part B examines the fruition of Barth's actualistic, participative theology of divine and human freedom in IV/3, finding that in this part-volume Barth has largely overcome the dualistic tendencies that haunted his earlier texts. Where the earlier Barth perpetuated an object-subject split, which led to a disjunction of God and the world, the mature Barth integrates the objective and subjective categories in a far more holistic manner, somewhat reminiscent of Hegel. By uniting the history of divine being and human knowing in the actualistic theology of mediation, IV/3 reveals a shift in Barth's theological conception that facilitates a more generative theology of divine and human freedom.

Chapter 3 provides a close theological interpretation of the "God-man" Christology of IV/3, arguing that Barth's moves in this work reveal a desire not only to expound the utter unity of God and humanity in Christ the mediator, but also to signal Barth's commitment to integrating the doctrine of revelation with his divine ontology in a more thoroughgoing manner than in earlier works. For this reason, it is argued, IV/3 presents the most participative account of divine and human freedom of any of Barth's texts, and is therefore worthy of greater attention than it has received to date.

The chapter contends that the mutual implication of Christ's objective and subjective functions as mediator in IV/3 underwrites Barth's vision of God and humanity existing in asymmetrical, covenantal reciprocity. Taken together, both the objective mutuality of Christ's divinity and humanity, and the eloquent and radiant form of this covenantal life-act, serve to indicate that Christ does not only live the divine-human unity objectively and vicariously in and for Himself. It is also a function of His objective actualization of the covenant that He lives in an expressive, contemporaneous form, giving human subjects the freedom for active participation in, and qualified co-operation with, His truth. Here the revealing work of Jesus Christ is explicated as an integral function of His reconciling life-act, so that the noetic or subjective aspect of Barth's soteriology is ingredient in, and not accidental to, his soteriological objectivism. Contrary to typical readings of Barth's doctrine of reconciliation, it is not simply that Christ achieves the unity of God and humanity in His own being, and subsequently communicates dogmatic knowledge of this as if it were a brute fact simply to be accepted epistemically by humanity. This book contends Barth is working with a rather different soteriological epistemology, where the emphasis is on a covenantal truth that *occurs* between God and humanity in the contemporaneous self-mediation of Jesus Christ's life-act, rather than a view of truth that takes its ontic actualization *illuc et tunc* ("there and then") and noetic communication *hic et nunc* ("here and now") to be essentially separate moments in the covenant history. This triadic unification of the objective and subjective aspects of salvation undergirds the sheer depth of fellowship that Barth envisages between God and humanity, because it takes human history, participation and flourishing to be ingredient in God's own covenantal freedom. God shapes God's own identity in and through a history in which we have an authentic—and not merely apparent—share. The reciprocity of Christ's divine-human life-act therefore becomes a genuine covenantal reciprocity, insofar as Christ's subjectivity draws other humans into participation in the drama of His living truth.

This is not to obscure Barth's anti-Pelagianism (his resistance to any theological down-playing of humanity's radical need of God's grace or the complete impossibility of humanity's achieving salvation, either partially or wholly, for itself), prevalent in IV/1 and IV/2, but simply to say that the principle of salvation by Christ alone cannot be equated with Christomonism (the obliteration of all agents other than Jesus Christ). Jesus Christ does not live His saving life-act in ontological isolation, but in an utterly communicative and inviting form. The covenant is consummated solely by Christ, but it is a function of the mediator's truth that it is lived contemporaneously in a manner that serves to attract human subjects into the heart of His life, and therefore into the covenantal history in which God's own being is in becoming.

Chapter 4 places Barth in conversation with Hegel, using the latter's critique of the Kantian tradition to demonstrate the kinds of thinking that are most fruitful for a Christian theology of freedom. By alluding to certain resemblances that IV/3 bears to some of Hegel's diagnostic and reparative insights for theology after Kant, this chapter sheds light on the nature of the transition that has taken place in Barth's method in relation to his conceptual heritage. The argument is not "genetic-historical"; it is not suggested that Barth explicitly pursues a Hegelian theological conception. Reference is made to Hegel's attempt to repair Christian thought after Kant simply because his investigation into Christian logic helps to explain that the most participative and generative types of Christian thinking refuse to force a static binary between being and knowing, but refer to the mutual implication of the two triadically through the category of event. By alluding to the parallels between Hegel and the mature Barth the study draws attention to the way Barth himself has overcome the somewhat dualistic and competitive aspects that are evident in his early work.

This investigation into the mode of Barth's theological conception helps, in Chapter 5, to overcome the popular complaint that Barth's ethics is Christomonistic, robbing the ethical agent of her moral accountability. Contributing to this line of argument is the construal of Barth's pneumatology as overly-noetic, so that the function of the Spirit is merely to help human agents "find out" what has happened on their behalf. On this reading, there is no space for a Spirit-led Christian freedom in which the human agent is liberated for authentic participation in the life of God. Nevertheless, once one begins to understand that for Barth there is a far more fluid relation between the objective actualization of divine-human covenantal reality and the subjective participation in this event by human agents, it is possible to reclaim Barth's reconciliation ethics as providing a genuinely participative account of human freedom.

In its two parts this book offers a broad survey of Barth's life-long fascination by divine and human freedom, demonstrating that, over the course of his long theological career, Barth was increasingly attentive to the radicality of God's prophetic call to humans to take up their own part within the drama of super-abundant divine love. If Jesus means freedom, then it belongs to His saving reality and to the very identity of God not only that He wins salvation for humanity, but that He mediates the divine-human truth embodied in His name attractively and joyfully, drawing humans into the depths of the covenant, and liberating them for a life of love and joy. *Church Dogmatics* IV/3 represents Barth's culminating witness to the intensity, eloquence, and radiance of the One who reciprocally grounds the freedom of God and the flourishing of humanity by declaring: "I am the way, and the truth, and the life. No one comes to the Father except through me" (John 14:6).

Part A

BEING AND ACT
Karl Barth's Actualistic Theology of Freedom

1

FREEDOM IN THE EARLY BARTH

Being and Act

The most recent developments in theology appear to me to be an attempt to come to an agreement about the problem of act and being . . . At the heart of the problem is the struggle with the formulation of the question that Kant and idealism have posed for theology.

—Dietrich Bonhoeffer[1]

Introduction

This chapter explores the origins of Karl Barth's interest in the concept of freedom. Below, Barth's early theology of freedom is placed within the context of the conceptual tradition out of which he emerged. The main contention of Chapter 1 is that Barth was rooted in an intellectual tradition for which being and act were of central importance. The way Barth handles being and act in various texts, as well as related pairs of terms such as object and subject, being and knowing, and reconciliation and revelation,

---

1. Bonhoeffer, *Act and Being*, 25–27.

determines to a significant degree how his theology of freedom operates. It shall be demonstrated that in the theology prior to and including *Church Dogmatics* I, Barth began to establish an "actualistic" theological method and ontology, by which is meant (at the most basic level) that being is conceived primarily in terms of action or event. Whilst his actualism would not come to full fruition until II/2, where Barth explicitly integrates the self-determination of the triune Godhead with the history of the incarnation through a radical interpretation of the doctrine of election, as his work developed in the years before 1936 Barth realized with increasing clarity that being, act, and knowledge are mutually implicated in the name Jesus Christ. The gradual emergence of this theological actualism in the early works therefore has profound implications for the Christocentric theology of freedom that culminates in IV/3. Indeed, once Barth's actualistic method had come to fruition in II/2, he began more consistently to insist that one cannot comprehend God or humanity in a-historical terms that seek to divorce a theological or anthropological ontology from the history in which being becomes determinate.

In Barth's earlier works, however, he was not yet able to integrate being and act, and being and knowing, with the same sophistication he achieved in later volumes of the *Church Dogmatics*,[2] and this hinders his earliest visions of divine and human freedom. The younger Barth rightly stressed the ontological priority of God over humanity, and sought to resist the domestication of the divine that he detected in a number of natural theologies. But his critical and cautionary tone in the texts before II/2 does not resonate in the same way that the joyous voice of IV/3 does. Barth's early epistemological concern to protect the transcendence of God betrayed an inability to do full justice to the historical predicates necessary to an adequate theological ontology, and this needed to undergo revision in the *Dogmatics*' later volumes. Critical engagement with the younger Barth in Chapter 1 therefore throws into relief the main body of the work, which demonstrates how the development of Barth's actualistic theological ontology facilitates an increasingly generative theology of freedom, climaxing in IV/3.

To anticipate, I shall argue that the earlier Barth had not yet satisfactorily transcended the thought-world of his neo-Kantian liberal heritage. Barth was dissatisfied with various theological attempts after Kant to recall that God is not simply an abstract other existing over against the world. He felt that liberal theologians had variously and unduly stressed the immanence of God, and he reverted to a quasi-Kantian critical epistemology to remind theology of God's otherness. It was precisely Barth's indebtedness

---

2. See Nimmo, *Being in Action*, 12.

to Kant, however, that meant he could not satisfactorily repair the lasting, damaging effects that certain responses to Kant had had on theology, thus restricting the fruitfulness of his alternative to liberalism. Barth's attempt to safeguard the freedom of God by means of emphasizing the divine non-objectivity in the revelatory economy reveals a one-sided theological emphasis of act over being, and subjectivity over objectivity. This served to uphold the distinction between God and humanity, and between the eternal Godhead and historical economy; but it did not also provide a firm ontological basis for the relationship and unity between God and creation. Thus, a sense of competition or dualism between God and the world arose in his texts. At this stage of his career, Barth had not yet integrated God's eternal being with God's historical act in such a way that God's humanity in Christ can be said to have ramifications for the very identity of the triune Godhead. In sum, it is seen in this chapter that Barth's early attempts to conceive divine and human freedom stand in need of further development, although it is precisely Barth's early efforts to unite being and act, object and subject, that reveal an emerging actualism and therefore foreshadow later advances.

Locating Barth within the Being-Act Tradition: Kant, Liberal Theology, and the Barthian Revolution

The origins of Barth's interest in divine and human freedom cannot be divorced from the wider context of his attempt to establish a "new starting-point"[3] for theology in reaction to the anthropocentrism of the "liberal" tradition.[4] In this section we must examine the neo-Protestant background to Barth's early theology, and ask how this in part shapes his use of the concept of freedom. The purpose here is not to rehearse Barth's reaction to liberal Protestantism exhaustively, but rather to establish a claim basic to

---

3. See Torrance, *Karl Barth: An Introduction to His Early Theology*, 33ff., and McCormack, *Karl Barth's Critically Realistic Dialectical Theology*, 129ff., on Barth's "new starting-point."

4. In 1960 Barth described his liberal heritage as a tradition "in the succession of Descartes, primarily and definitely interested in human, and particularly the Christian, religion within the framework of our modern outlook on the world, considering God, his work and his word from this point of view, and adopting . . . an anthropocentric theology" (Barth "Liberal Theology," 213). Axt-Piscalar observes that "the term 'liberal theology' is not a straightforward one"; in this study, I use the term in the sense that Barth and other contemporaries endorsed, "to describe the entire nineteenth-century theological program and to disparage it as a falling away from true Christianity and the true theology of the Word of God" (Axt-Piscalar "Liberal Theology in Germany," 468).

this investigation: that the being-act, object-subject pattern is imperative for the function of freedom in Barth's thought.[5]

Establishing the precise nature of Barth's engagement with the object-subject, being-act question proves challenging, however. Although Barth's theology is strongly influenced by his post-Kantian philosophical heritage, Barth himself is "[disinterested] in clarifying theological concepts philosophically."[6] There is no doubt that Barth must be understood within the context of his university training, which "threw him into the prevailing philosophical and scientific discussion pursued within the tradition of the eighteenth and nineteenth centuries so that he was forced to think within its universe of discourse."[7] Yet we must also recognize that Barth became "deeply uneasy" about the "prevailing *Weltanschauung*" of neo-Protestantism,[8] and that as a biblical theologian he therefore sought to adopt the imagery of the "The Strange New World Within the Bible"[9] that he and Eduard Thurneysen had discovered through intensive scriptural study.[10] Barth's deliberately eclectic use of philosophy sought to establish the priority of Scripture over philosophy, and thus to distance his theological approach from a Protestant tradition he considered unduly beholden to philosophy.[11] Barth was reticent about engaging systematically with philosophy throughout his career. Hence, when, in 1955, a student asked Barth "can the theologian take philosophy seriously?" Barth responded "It is really not my business to accept philosophy . . . philosophy can never answer the ultimate question."[12]

Nevertheless, despite his refusal to form fixed philosophical commitments, Barth is by no means neutral towards or uninterested in philosophy. As Diller reminds us, it would be a mistake to take Barth's warnings about

---

5. In his essay "Fate and Idea in Theology," Barth set his theology in the context of modern philosophy, and identified the object-subject relation as "the basic problem of all philosophy" ("Fate and Idea in Theology," 25).

6. Reuter, afterword to Bonhoeffer, *Act and Being*, 163.

7. Torrance, *Karl Barth: An Introduction to His Early Theology*, 33.

8. Ibid., 33.

9. Barth, "The Strange New World within the Bible," 27–50; see also Torrance, *Karl Barth: An Introduction to His Early Theology*, 34–35, and Busch, *Karl Barth*, 101.

10. Barth and Thurneysen had considered further study of Kant and Hegel in their attempt to break from liberalism. Choosing not to pursue this avenue, however, the pair found themselves "compelled to do something much more obvious. We tried to learn our theological ABC all over again, beginning by reading and interpreting the writing of the Old and New Testaments, more thoughtfully than before" (Barth, "Nachwort," 294). See also Busch, *Karl Barth*, 97; and Macken, *The Autonomy* Theme, 24.

11. See Dorrien, *The Barthian Revolt*, 91–92.

12. Godsey, *Karl Barth's Table Talk*, 20.

the usefulness of philosophy for the theologian as "a blanket interdiction" or to read in his unease with the prominence of philosophy "a posture of isolation" towards the modern German-language conceptual traditions.[13] For Barth, "we may read philosophers (and we should!) without accepting their presuppositions. We may listen respectfully (I have a holy respect for a *good* philosopher!). We can learn much from philosophy."[14] Moreover, as Rudolf Bultmann was keen to point out (albeit in overly polemical terms) in 1928, Barth was just as indebted to philosophy as his contemporaries, despite his attempts to achieve the "emancipation" of theology from philosophy.[15] It is therefore illuminating to consider the philosophical impulses underneath Barth's biblical hermeneutics. One of the key indicators of where especially to investigate Barth's relation to his contemporary intellectual milieu is when he tends to use non-biblical, or uncommon biblical terms. Freedom is one such term, but being and act, and object and subject are also strong indicators in Barth's texts that despite his self-description as a biblical theologian he is wrestling with inherited conceptual problems. It is therefore necessary for theologians to have a sound grasp of Barth's philosophical heritage and its impact on his genesis.

Throughout this chapter, it will be particularly useful to draw upon the resources of Jüngel and Bonhoeffer, who were more explicitly concerned with the relation of Barth's biblical theology to philosophy than was their mentor himself. Bonhoeffer and Jüngel help us to locate Barth's exegetical orientation within the wider context of the modern Protestant thought-world. Jüngel's *God as the Mystery of the World* traces the origins of the modern theological *aporia* back to the legacies of Descartes and Kant, providing analysis of the intellectual tradition out of which Barth and the modern theological fascination by divine freedom emerged. Bonhoeffer's *Act and Being* engages with theology's "long and deep involvement in continental philosophy's epistemological object-subject paradigm, which theology has employed precisely as a means by which to explicate its categories of *transcendence* and *revelation*."[16] It is therefore particularly well-placed to assist our investigation into Barth's early theology of freedom and the handling of the object-subject, being-act relation.

---

13. Diller, "Karl Barth and the Relationship between Philosophy and Theology," 1.

14. Godsey, *Karl Barth's Table Talk*, 19.

15. See "Bultmann to Barth, 8th June 1928," in Jaspert, *Karl Barth/Rudolf Bultmann Letters, 1922–1966*, 38; and "Barth to Bultmann, 12th June 1928," in ibid., 42.

16. Floyd, introduction to Bonhoeffer, *Act and Being*, 11.

Kant

My investigation begins with Kant, whose philosophy "has unparalleled significance for the theology and philosophy of the nineteenth century and beyond."[17] Kant had a particularly important impact on the young Barth studying theology in Bern, who "was earnestly told, and I learnt . . . that all God's ways begin with Kant and, if possible, must also end there."[18] Indeed, Kant's *Critique of Practical Reason* was "[t]he first book that really moved me as a student."[19] Three interrelated elements of Kant's philosophy are of particular interest to us: the "Copernican Revolution" in epistemology, the claim that the concept of God is an ideal of pure reason, and the definition of human freedom as autonomous self-legislation.

As Hegel would later reflect, Kant's philosophy was driven by the same principle that had inspired the storming of the Bastille; but what the French did by force, the Germans would do by reason.[20] The basic aim of Kant's work is relatively simple: it seeks to demonstrate that whilst we live in a natural world whose objects are external to us, we are not merely determined by this objective world.[21] Rather, human subjects are capable of determining themselves through the application of reason. Reason has theoretical and practical dimensions, and tells us that although the world we perceive clearly manifests natural laws of causality, yet freedom from manipulation by forces external to the self is both an intelligible possibility (the demonstration of which is the task of the *Critique of Pure Reason*) and actually achievable (the argument of the *Critique of Practical Reason*).[22] In short, for Kant "Freedom consists in our ability to move ourselves to action rather than being pushed around by forces external to ourselves."[23]

Kant's transcendental idealism attempts to acknowledge the active role of the subject in the account we give of knowledge of things, and thereby to highlight both the fallibility of human reason, and the centrality of

---

17. Adams, "Kant," 3.
18. Busch, *Karl Barth*, 34.
19. Barth, cited in Webster, *Barth*, 3.
20. See Dews, *Idea of Evil*, 17. See also, Hegel, *Lectures on the History of Philosophy*, 425.
21. Kant is committed to empirical realism and transcendental idealism. The former, countering the skepticism and subjectivism of post-Cartesian empirical idealism, affirms the reality of the empirical world outside us (see Beiser, *German Idealism*, 1–4). The latter, repairing transcendental realism, "names the view that the conditions for our knowledge are our ideas, rather than objects in the world" (Adams, "Kant," 5).
22. See Allison, *Kant's Theory of Freedom*, 1.
23. Pinkard, *German Philosophy*, 52.

subjectivity in descriptions of reality.[24] In a departure from his rationalist and empiricist forebears, Kant's suggestion is that the task of philosophy consists not in trying to account for how the external world *really* exists, independently of us (either through the foundational auspices of reason or of sense experience) but in articulating how the world comes to be known by us. Or, as he puts it at the conclusion of the Transcendental Aesthetic, "how are synthetic *a priori* propositions possible?"[25] Since "Thoughts without content are empty, intuitions without concepts are blind,"[26] it is impossible to think of the world in abstraction from the guiding principles of reason by which world is known *qua* world, or of thought in abstraction from its application to the manifold of experiences.

For Kant, there is no immediate knowledge or "pure intuition" of objects as things-in-themselves (*noumena*), but only knowledge of objects as appearances (*phenomena*), that is, an object considered "as it appears to us when we judge sensible intuitions by means of concepts."[27] In order to cognize something as a *phenomenon*, an intuition (incoming sense data represented in perception) must be subjected to a concept (the rules that guide the way we unify or schematize intuitions) to form a judgment ("an object-related unity of representations under a concept").[28]

Kant's claim that all knowledge is mediated is specifically important to theology because "no theology after Kant can respectably present itself as other than the outcome of such fallible processes of judgment."[29] Theologians after Kant are required to account for the object-subject relation in theological epistemology, and thereby to explain the role of the human subject in the acquisition of knowledge of God. As we shall see below, Barth's early theology arises in reaction to various accounts of how knowledge of God is possible, and his understanding of revelation and description of divine freedom is shaped—both positively and negatively—by the way in which he engages with Kant in his theological epistemology. It is the epistemological question posed by Kant that will principally shape the way Barth attempts to safeguard the freedom of God over against the fallible subjectivity of human religiosity. Yet it is also Barth's influence by a particular reading

24. See Adams, "Kant," 11.
25. Kant, *The Critique of Pure Reason*, 192.
26. Ibid., 193–94.
27. Adams, "Kant," 16.
28. Allison, *Kant's Transcendental Idealism*, 85. For Kant's understanding of sensible intuition, concepts, and judgments, see, for example, Pinkard, *German Philosophy*, 26–33; Bowie, *Introduction to German Philosophy*, 18ff.; Allison, *Transcendental Idealism*, 78–84.
29. Adams, "Kant," 11.

of Kant (which divorces the subjective from the objective) that leaves him unable, in his earlier theology, to overcome a sense of disjunction between God and the world.

God appears in Kant's theoretical philosophy as an ideal of reason. "Kant is deeply interested in how the manifold of perceptions is unified by the thinking subject,"[30] and God is discussed primarily within this context. God is not to be thought of as a living reality existing in the world, but is the ideal of reason by which the unity of the sum total of objects in the world can be thought. In Kant's Transcendental Dialectic, God is the realization and hypostatization of the ideal of pure reason, the personification of transcendental freedom, whose regulative function is to give respite to reason.[31] Transcendental freedom means the conditions under which something is not dependent upon any prior causality in order to determine other effects in the world. It is a ground of causality "through which something happens without its cause being further determined by another previous cause, i.e., an *absolute* causal *spontaneity* beginning *from itself* a series of appearances that runs according to natural laws, hence transcendental freedom."[32] It is a kind of cosmological spontaneity that does not accord to the rules of cause and effect, but is itself the ground for such rules.

Here Kant falls under Jüngel's theological indictment levied against a tradition concerned with satisfying the principle of sufficient reason which states, in various forms, that there is no effect without a cause.[33] Since there cannot be a regress *ad infinitum*, reason assumes that there must be something that exists as the first cause without itself being caused (though Kant is not interested in divine ontology or the proposition of adequate reason *per se*, but simply in what it means for "persons to attribute cause and effect in their thinking"[34]). "God is supposed to be the name for the 'final reason of things,' which as such is the 'necessary being' ('*Ens necessarium*'), the absolutely necessary Existing One."[35] God is now defined as the "final ground" or "*ultima ratio*" of all things, and as a "hermeneutical necessity," that which is

---

30. Ibid., 12.

31. Kant, *Critique of Pure Reason*, 559. "The ideal of the highest being is . . . nothing other than a *regulative principle* of reason, to regard all combination in the world *as if it* arose from an all-sufficient necessary cause, so as to ground on that cause the rule of a unity that is systematic and necessary according to universal laws; but it is not an assertion of an existence that is necessary in itself" (ibid., 577). See Allison, *Kant's Transcendental Idealism*, 396–422, on "The Ideal of Pure Reason."

32. Kant, *Critique of Pure Reason*, 484.

33. See Jüngel, *God as the Mystery of the World*, 29ff.

34. Adams, "Kant," 6.

35. Jüngel, *God as the Mystery of the World*, 29.

necessary in order to understand the world as world.³⁶ Kant names God the *ens realissimum, ens originarium, ens summum,* and *ens entium.*³⁷

Adams identifies the theological consequences of Kant's reference to God as a regulative principle for reason. Kant shrinks

> the scope of "God" to the *ens realissimum,* and then [glosses] the latter as the unity of all possible objects and their predicates ... When this unity is named "God," ... and when the scope of this term shrinks significantly, certain important theological questions become meaningless, and it is the accompanying disappearance of the question of the relationship between nature and grace that should motivate the theologian's most serious complaints.³⁸

After Kant, theologians were tasked with retrieving such questions about God in a manner that did not limit the conception of God to the infinitely abstract "ultimate reason of things." It is in part Barth's dissatisfaction with certain nineteenth and early twentieth-century attempts to repair the concept of God that motivates his own constructive endeavors to reclaim the living God of Scripture. For Jüngel, Kant epitomizes an Enlightenment tradition that increasingly rendered God an unthinkable, abstract entity—a logical necessity, but not a living, graceful reality. When God is reduced to an unconditioned, "hermeneutical necessity," an ideal of reason used to explain how the subject thinks of reality, meaningful speech about God ceases, for "The Unconditioned is ... an inappropriately abstract category, because it is much too ambivalent to be able to speak for itself [*Das Unbedingte ist ... eine unangemessen abstrakte, weil viel zu ambivalente Kategorie, um für sich allein sprechen zu können*]."³⁹

Jüngel turns to Hegel's critique of Descartes and Kant in order to make sense of the incoherence of post-Enlightenment theology, and to assess the grounds for repairing contemporary theology beyond the *aporia* he identifies. He says, "The tragedy of the Enlightenment which Hegel perceived consists of a reason which "recognizes something higher above itself from which it is self-excluded"—a formula which one should remember."⁴⁰ By

---

36. Ibid., 30.

37. See Kant, *Critique of Pure Reason,* 553–59.

38. Adams, "Kant," 15.

39. Jüngel, *God as the Mystery of the World,* 35 = Jüngel, *Gott als Geheimnis der Welt,* 44–45.

40. Jüngel, *God as the Mystery of the World.,* 70, citing Hegel, *Faith and Knowledge,* 61. Hegel describes the unspeakability of God in the Cartesian and Kantian traditions in his *Lectures on the Philosophy of Religion* of 1821: "The following distinction is made

positing faith as that which is opposed to reason, philosophy ultimately criticized reason, because the necessity of an absolutely unknowable God meant that reason relied upon something it could not access. "In this way reason deprived itself of the possibility of comprehending rationally its noblest subject. God cannot be known anymore. And thus 'the better part of reason' has been translated into something 'beyond reason.'"[41] Kant's famous dictum, "I had to deny *knowledge* in order to make room for *faith*"[42] indicates that any speech about God as a living reality in the world is fundamentally un-reasonable, and faith must seek understanding to no avail. Having borrowed the concept of God as the absolutely infinite from the metaphysical tradition in theology, now the Cartesian and Kantian traditions in philosophy find it impossible to marry faith and reason: "The 'old' antithesis of 'faith and knowledge' is now encountered within philosophy in such a way that critical reason restricts knowledge to the finite and thus makes room for faith with reference to the infinite."[43] God must remain in the rational heavens, "over us," "superior" to the created order, and therefore an abstract, non-relational entity.[44]

Jüngel helps identify one of the tasks of post-Kantian theology as the refusal to limit the scope of the term "God" to that which is necessary as a regulative ideal for the unity of apperception. Jüngel insists, "Necessity . . . is a category which does not reach too high for God but which does not reach as far as God. The proposition 'God is necessary' is a poor proposition. It is not worthy of God."[45] The necessary God is not a God who can exist in the world, who assumes the name Jesus Christ, who can take finitude into God's own life radically on the cross. The task of post-Kantian theology will be to recall that God is not simply an abstract being existing over against the world, but is one who exists in and for the world. It will be important to recall this later, because the earlier Barth will struggle to strike an appropriate balance between the transcendence of God's eternal being and the worldly immanence of God's historical act as he describes the sovereign freedom of the biblical God.

---

by modern presuppositions: we have (a) concrete, empirical humanity—a union of reason and sensible [nature]; (b) *only* a concept [of God], beyond which one cannot go, [so that] the contradiction with (a) [remains] unresolved" (Hegel, *Lectures on the Philosophy of Religion*, 73).

41. Jüngel, *God as the Mystery of the World*, 69.
42. Kant, *Critique of Pure Reason*, 117.
43. Jüngel, *God as the Mystery of the World*, 69
44. Ibid., 103.
45. Ibid., 25.

Finally, I turn to Kant's definition of human freedom. Kant's first *Critique* concludes that rational subjects cannot experience freedom within the causal order. "We rightly regard events in the world of objects as the causes and effects of other such events. If persons are such objects, their actions too are rightly regarded as causes and effects," and hence we cannot be said to be free.[46] But Kant's theoretical philosophy, which maintained that freedom was at least an intelligible possibility, though not something we can experience within the natural world,[47] creates a space for his practical philosophy, in which he details the nature of human freedom. To put it in Kant's own words, "the moral law thus determines that which speculative philosophy had to leave undetermined, namely the law for a causality the concept of which [viz. freedom] was only negative in the latter, and thus for the first time provides objective reality to this concept."[48] In the first *Critique* Kant showed that if there is freedom it must be freedom *from* causal determination; in the second *Critique* he must therefore defend an account of morality in which the human will is not determined by any sensible conditions, but is determined solely by itself. Reath characterizes the second *Critique*'s vision for human freedom, describing Kant's aim as being "to establish the reality of transcendental freedom, according to which the will is a capacity for spontaneous activity, or a kind of causal power, which is independent of determination by empirical conditions."[49] Taken together, the first two *Critiques* show that there is a link between two apparently disjunct realms: those of "the starry heavens above me and the moral law within me."[50] Kant is now claiming, then, that we both experience the deterministic world of natural causality through theoretical reason, and can influence the world through a causality of our own by practical reason.

Kant states that a truly free will is determined "solely by the [moral] law . . . not only without the cooperation of sensible impulses but even with rejection of all of them and with infringement upon all inclinations insofar as they could be opposed to that law."[51] A will determined by empirical impulses derived from the world cannot be truly free since it is dependent upon principles external to the moral law for its determination. Thus it follows that for Kant the kind of freedom begotten of the moral law would

---

46. Adams, "Kant," 20.
47. See Allison, *Kant's Theory of Freedom*, 23–24.
48. Kant, *Critique of Practical Reason*, 42.
49. Reath, introduction to Kant, *Critique of Practical Reason*, x.
50. Kant, *Critique of Practical Reason*, 133.
51. Ibid., 63.

seek to eliminate any justification of human actions based on inclinations.[52] Kant's ethics is therefore deontological: it appeals to the intrinsic value of a moral duty, and not to the consequences of certain actions as justifying the means.[53] Kant rejects hypothetical imperatives—maxims that command action based on the principle, *if* I want X then I *must* do Y.[54] He endorses categorical imperatives: maxims which determine the will, irrespective of the effect, purely on the basis of the necessary sufficiency of the law itself.[55] Thus a categorical imperative is a maxim which commands an action based on the principle, I *ought* to do X. Kant claims that we can discern when the form of a maxim is sufficient in and of itself on the basis of the "fundamental law of pure practical reason," which reads: "So act that the maxim of your will could always hold at the same time as a principle in a giving of universal law."[56] That is to say, an action is morally justifiable when one can will that the law upon which it is based would be universal and unconditional. Only according to this deontological moral principle can human beings act with complete self-determination, and therefore in the actualization of freedom.

Liberal Theology

This brief introduction to Kant's philosophy sets the conceptual scene for a discussion of freedom in Barth's early works, and will be of continuing use throughout the study as we consider Barth's location within the being-act tradition. Barth's struggles against liberal theology can be read as an attempt to redirect the theological response to nineteenth-century philosophy and theology in view of Kant's epoch-defining works.[57] It is in light of Barth's break from nineteenth-century neo-Protestantism that we must consider his location within the being-act tradition, for "Barth did not . . . confront the Enlightenment directly. Between him and it lay his more immediate resource and *bête noire*, the German 'neo-Protestant' theology of the nineteenth century."[58]

Perhaps some of the most theologically restrictive features of the legacy bequeathed by the Enlightenment (especially Kant) to nineteenth-century theology (features that Barth wants to resist following his break with

52. Ibid., 63.
53. See Bowie, *Introduction to German Philosophy*, 31.
54. Pinkard, *German Philosophy*, 49.
55. Kant, *Critique of Practical Reason*, 18; 26.
56. Ibid., 28. See also Kant, *Groundwork of the Metaphysics of Morals*, 34.
57. See Jenson, "Karl Barth," 22–23.
58. Ibid., 24.

liberalism) are the reduction of the scope of the term "God" to a necessary postulate for "understanding the world as world,"[59] the exclusion of speech about the graceful God from conversations about the world,[60] and the turn to the rational capacities of the human subject as the basic site of interest for investigations into the shape of reality. In short, speech about the living God becomes increasingly untenable after Kant, and theologians are called to justify their place within the modern scientific university. This sets the context for the emergence of liberal theology, which "sought to take onboard the challenges of the Enlightenment and modernity, and so to transform the content of the Christian religion," by mediating "between faith and reason, [and] theology and science," emphasizing the Enlightenment principle of the "individual's right to autonomy in all areas of life," especially with respect to "the importance of individual religious experience."[61]

The very different projects of Schleiermacher, Strauss, Ritschl, Troeltsch, Harnack, Herrmann, and Rade, share in common the attempt to accommodate Christianity to the modern principles of *Wissenschaft* and autonomy. The threefold loci of historicism, religious experience and reason form the core of liberal theological attentions, and it would not be inappropriate to describe Schleiermacher, the father of modern theology, as standing at the head of liberalism's entire post-Kantian history.[62] It was in the liberal school that Barth was educated during his time in university at Marburg. In addition to working on the production of the journal *Die Christliche Welt*, which disseminated a Ritschlian historical criticism, Barth was particularly influenced by Wilhelm Herrmann, in whom he found a scholar capable of mediating between Kant and Schleiermacher.[63] Herrmann accepted the basic epistemological commitments of Kant, but sought to overcome the Kantian reduction of God and faith to postulates of reason by emphasizing a personal relation to Christ.[64] Under Herrmann Barth found himself committed to the "modern school" in which "Christianity was interpreted on the one hand as a historical phenomenon to be subjected to critical examination, and on the other hand as a matter of inner experience."[65]

---

59. Jüngel, *God as the Mystery of the World*, 30.
60. Ibid., 131.
61. Axt-Piscalar, "Liberal Theology in Germany," 470.
62. See Barth, *Protestant Theology*, 412–13.
63. Webster, *Barth*, 3; see also, Busch, *Karl Barth*, 45.
64. Dorrien, *The Barthian Revolt*, 19.
65. Busch, *Karl Barth*, 46.

The Barthian Revolution

With the outbreak of the Great War, and the declaration of support for Kaiser Wilhelm by most of the liberal theologians,[66] Barth found the liberals he had hitherto largely followed "to be hopelessly compromised by their submission to the ideology of war,"[67] and he now came to distrust the ethics and dogmatics of his early education. In Barth's opinion the failure of liberalism was the construction of theology around the affirmation of God's historical immanence, which reduced God to a given factor of human culture and experience, and thus relieved theology of the need to refer to God's gracious, intervening activity.[68] The problem with the affirmation of immanence was its undermining of God's "sheer originality."[69] Barth was thus forced to develop "a new conception of the speaking of God which was better calculated to protect the sovereign freedom of the divine Subject in the process of revelation."[70] Barth's new starting-point in theology would refer theologians to the sovereign Word of the self-revealing divine subject over against the "transient" words of the religious subject,[71] and would seek, in the first instance, to uphold the radical autonomy, transcendence and power of God in place of that of the hitherto disproportionately venerated religious believer. Thereby Barth both sought to overcome some of the problems created for theology by Kant and post-Kantian philosophy, and also to remain faithful to the critical gains and basic conceptual foundations of Kant's works. But first and foremost, Barth sought to remain faithful to Scripture in the face of a tradition that he had found exegetically vacuous. His time in the pulpit at Safenwil taught Barth the need to find a theological way "more rigorously and attentively biblical, more objectively tied to the biblical text and less linked to human subjectivity, more peculiarly theological and more particularly Christian."[72]

As Jenson rightly says, "*The Epistle to the Romans* was the step between two stages of Barth's life and thinking. It also made the break between the nineteenth and twentieth theological centuries."[73] The second edition of

---

66. See Parker, *Karl Barth*, 16.

67. Webster, *Barth*, 4. See Barth, "Evangelical Theology in the Nineteenth Century," 12–13.

68. Webster, *Barth*, 25.

69. Ibid., 25.

70. McCormack, *Karl Barth's Critically Realistic Dialectical Theology*, 107.

71. *Romans* II, 341.

72. Willimon, introduction to *The Early Preaching of Karl* Barth, x.

73. Jenson, "Karl Barth," 26.

Barth's commentary on *Romans* launched Barth to fame,[74] and in this early text the concept of freedom functions prominently. Here, Barth's theology of divine freedom attempts to protect the identity of God against idolatry by safeguarding the assumption that "God is God,"[75] and, *contra* the liberal tradition, cannot be adequately described on the basis of subjectivistic religious speculation. Busch has convincingly argued that the equation "God is God" is not "self-evident because it implies the critical thesis that our speaking of God does not automatically speak of *God*."[76] Liberal theology had gone about the theological task with various forms of the assumption that human reason or experience constituted a legitimate starting point for speech about God; but by speaking "of God simply by speaking of mankind in a loud voice" these theologies had ended up articulating a no-God.[77] Barth's claim in *Romans* II that "God is God" is deliberately tautological;[78] it defines precisely nothing about God, suggesting thereby that God is disclosed by Godself alone, and that God has the power and the freedom to determine and to communicate Godself.

We see here that Barth's early references to God's freedom function within the wider concern to propose a legitimate basis for theological epistemology. As McCormack states, the fundamental question Barth addresses himself to in *Romans* II is "how can God make Himself known to human beings without ceasing—at any point in the process of Self-communication—to be the *Subject* of revelation?"[79] At this point Barth's commitment to the Kantian object-subject paradigm becomes essential in understanding the description of God's freedom.[80] For Barth, as for Kant, "knowledge is only possible where there is 'intuitable' empirical data. If God is to be known by humans, God must somehow make Himself to be "objective" to the human knower; He must place Himself within the range of "objects" which can be intuited by human beings."[81] In Kantian epistemology there is no pure, immediate intuition. Hence, if knowledge of God functions in the same way that human subjects cognize other phenomena, the concept

---

74. Ibid., 22.

75. *Romans* II, 11.

76. Busch, "God Is God," 104.

77. Barth, "The Word of God and the Task of the Ministry," 196. See also, *Romans* II, 50–51.

78. Busch, "God Is God," 107.

79. McCormack, *Karl Barth's Critically Realistic Dialectical Theology*, 207.

80. "Barth's theological epistemology in *Romans* II stands everywhere in the long shadow cast by Immanuel Kant . . . [Barth] took for granted the validity of Kant's epistemology set forth in the First Critique" (ibid., 245).

81. Ibid., 207.

of God is exposed to the fallibility and manipulation of human subjectivity, since knowledge of objects requires the application of a spontaneously derived concept of human thinking. If God were known like any other object, knowledge of Him would be dependent upon "some previous superior knowledge,"[82] and this would be to say that knowledge of God is dependent upon the prowess of human subjectivity.[83] As McCormack notes, Barth therefore asks himself "how could God become an 'object' of human intuition without making Himself subject to the control (the disposition, the management) of the human knowing apparatus?"[84] In light of liberalism's failures, as Bonhoeffer indicates, the task of post-liberal theology was to determine adequately "the relationship between 'the being of God' and the mental act which grasps that being. In other words, the meaning of 'the being of God in revelation' must be interpreted theologically, including how it is known, how faith as act, and revelation as being, are related to one another."[85]

In the *Romans* commentaries Barth seeks to redefine the relation between revelatory objectivity and human subjectivity by establishing the priority of divine subjectivity in the order of knowing. God's act precedes all talk of God's being in speech about revelation and the order of human knowing. As Barth would later put it in 1929,

> Theology thus has God as its object [*Objekt*], but only to the extent that . . . theology has God as its subject [*Subjekt*]. That is, theology has God as its object only to the extent that it strives to have absolutely no other origin than the communication which God actually gives of himself.[86]

Here, God is not an object in the world like any other to be cognitively processed by the human subject. Knowledge of God arises not by means of the human subject's active application of the rules of the understanding to sense data, nor in continuity with religious experience, but only on the basis of God's miraculous, self-giving activity. God breaks into the world "from above,"[87] crossing the infinite qualitative "abyss which separates men from

---

82. *Romans* II, 82.

83. "At this point Barth is at one with his Kantian heritage in its refusal to treat God as if he were just another phenomenon within the world of human experience" (Hart, "Revelation," 42).

84. McCormack, *Karl Barth's Critically Realistic Dialectical Theology*, 207.

85. Bonhoeffer, *Act and Being*, 27–28.

86. Barth, "Fate and Idea in Theology," 27 = "Schicksal und Idee in der Theologie," 56.

87. This is a favorite image of Barth, particularly in the first edition of *Romans*. See

God," thereby, paradoxically and dialectically, revealing the eternal permanency of that chasm;[88] revelation, by its "shocking" truth stands in "judgement" over against all fallible efforts of the human subject, who, in trying to name "God" the "No-God of unbelief," is greeted by God's "No."[89] Barth speaks of God's revelation and salvation as a *Krisis*, which occasions the embarrassment of all human knowledge, and identifies the radical otherness of the Kingdom of God from the world.[90] God's activity in God's otherness at all points controls speech about God's identity. This is a dynamic, act-based theological epistemology, which transfers subjective primacy from humanity to God.

Moreover, if God in God's self-revealing subjectivity is to be spoken of as an object for religious cognition, it is as an object which remains hidden by means of God's self-veiling activity. Precisely in the moment that God objectifies Godself for human cognition, God remains ungraspable; the *Deus Revelatus* is the *Deus Absconditus*.[91] As McCormack says,

> Barth's favourite way of describing [God's retention of sovereignty in the act of revelation] in *Romans* II—drawing upon the term employed in Kant's epistemology—is to say, the Unintuitable (*das Unanschauliche*, God) must become intuitable; but in such a way that no change in the Unintuitable is involved. So, in order that God remain distinct from the medium of revelation, He *veils* Himself in the medium. He hides Himself and remains hidden in the medium of revelation.[92]

This dialectically hidden and revealed divine subject cannot be comprehended or consumed by the human act of faith, but as pure, mysterious act, is dialectically elusive and self-giving.[93]

Barth's new theology climaxes in the leitmotif "God is free,"[94] and Barth elevates the concept of freedom to a position of thematic centrality by using it as the title for the seventh chapter of *Romans* II, which is a critique of religion.[95] The freedom of God in *Romans* II is the transcendence, power

Gorringe, *Karl Barth against Hegemony*, 39–40, and Jehle, *Ever Against the Stream*, 38.

88. *Romans* II, 332.
89. Ibid., 42–43.
90. See, for example, ibid., 40–41, 91, 363.
91. Ibid., 422.
92. McCormack, *Karl Barth's Critically Realistic Dialectical Theology*, 249. See also, *Romans* II, 77, "God is known as the Unknown."
93. *Romans* II, 98.
94. Ibid., 92.
95. See also Barth's critique of religion in the Tambach lecture of 1919: Karl Barth,

and priority of the divine subject. Notice the strong resemblance here to Kant's understanding of human freedom as the self-legislative authority of one who is not pushed around or controlled by external forces. God is the supreme subject whose self-determined identity radically transcends conformity with the world of objects.

Kant's understanding of human freedom as moral autonomy also underwrites Barth's early conception of human freedom, though it does so negatively. Barth seeks to reverse Kant's theory of human freedom, first by applying a quasi-Kantian idea of human freedom to God, and then by describing human flourishing as precisely the opposite of the Kantian ethical model. "What the Enlightenment thus thought of as human freedom is what Christianity means by 'sin.' . . . The would-be autonomous subject, hostile to everything by which his or her intentions or judgement might be relativised, is precisely the person 'curved in on self' of the Reformation's hamartiology."[96] For Barth we are not simply the authors of our own freedom, agents called to usurp nature and to define the conditions of our own reality; rather, our reality is defined by and determined in the graceful revelation of God which calls us to new modes of being and becoming, and which sets us free from sin through the transformation of human nature. In critical recollection of the ethics of Kant, Barth theologically reverses the vision for human freedom as independence from external pressures, claiming that the free human is "oppressed on all sides by God and wholly dissolved by Him."[97]

Human freedom is now defined by Pauline motifs such as obedience to grace, the possession of humans by the grace of God, being made free from slavery to sin, and liberty for relationship with God.[98] Adapting Kant's categorical imperative, Barth describes freedom as "the categorical imperative of grace and of the existential belonging-to-God."[99] That is, for Barth we are not called to act as though we will our own maxims to be universally valid moral laws, but as confronted by the truth, unknown prior to our seizure by revelation, that there is no other possibility for genuine human being than obedience to and relationship with the sovereign lord revealed in Christ. It is not we who govern whom we may freely be, but Christ.

As Busch points out, by placing the possibility of human freedom in God, Barth is able to affirm the radicality of grace's call to new life; since

"The Christian's Place in Society," 272–327.

96. Jenson, "Karl Barth," 23.
97. *Romans* II, 503.
98. See ibid., 213, 216, 220, 234, 237, 246, 269.
99. Ibid., 220.

God is revealed in God's freedom, and not on the basis of any prior human knowledge or capacity, God's revelation has the distinct character of newness.[100] Grace interrupts, disturbs and transforms the life of the believer, bringing the individual to a radical new freedom in God.

Barth and the Being-Act Tradition

Before we move to Barth's theology of freedom as it develops in the first volume of the *Church Dogmatics*, it will be beneficial to locate the so-called "dialectical" theology of the younger Barth within the being-act tradition. The relation of being and act, object and subject in Barth's early theology forms the framework within which Barth's ideas about the freedom of God and the freedom of humanity will develop throughout his career. In an important lecture of 1929, "Fate and Idea in Theology," Barth considers the way in which his "new starting-point" for theological epistemology relates to the philosophical projects of realism (fate) and idealism (idea). Here, as Sykes indicates, "Barth presents himself, in philosophical terms, as a critical realist, that is to say one who primarily is concerned with actuality and occurrence, but who acknowledges the necessity of attending to the conditions and limitations of human knowing."[101]

Discussing the benefits and dangers of realism and idealism for theology, Barth insists that theology must, to an extent, be realist in dimension since its basic claim "God is" "is a realist utterance not easily dispensed with if theology is not to fall into mystical silence the first time it ventures to speak."[102] But the problem with realist theologies is that they treat God as a given reality in the sense that that reality can be grasped, empirically known, verified; they pursue an inductive logic, starting with the objective world, and reasoning up towards God.[103] The danger of realism for theology is "its simple confidence that via certain precise conceptual formulations

---

100. See Busch, "God is God," 112–13.

101. Sykes, introduction to *The Way of Theology in Karl Barth*, 12. See also, McCormack, *Karl Barth's Critically Realistic Dialectical Theology*, 129–30.

102. Barth, "Fate and Idea in Theology," 35. See also, Diller, "Karl Barth and the Relationship Between Philosophy and Theology," 11.

103. Barth's new starting point proposed an *Erkenntnisweg von oben nach unten*, a "way of knowledge from above to below" (Diller, "Karl Barth and the Relationship Between Philosophy and Theology," 2). Diller explains that for Barth the "possibility of theological knowing was a valid assumption, not on the basis of a foregoing confidence in human noetic capacity, but only as *nachdenken* (reflection, lit. thinking after) on an already given reality" (ibid., 2). See also, Macken, who claims that after Barth's break with liberalism "Every theological statement must be derived 'from above,' from the Word of God" (Macken, *The Autonomy Theme in the Church Dogmatics*, 24).

God can be found in a subjective-objective givenness, and that therefore the *similtudo Dei* must also occur in the knower and known."[104]

Barth therefore calls for the application of idealism's "chastening criticism" to the basic realistic claim "God is." The strength of idealism is that "it worries about the realist's naïve confidence"[105] by questioning the givenness of objects, and by asking about the noetic possibilities of the one processing an object. In asking this question idealism "discovers something not given over against the given subject and object. It discovers itself as a criterion that must at least be taken into account."[106] Barth approves of idealism's awareness that the self posits itself and is not given, and that reference to any object must also include the awareness that the self plays a role in the formation of knowledge.[107] This upholds the freedom of God over against all attempts of the human thinker to play a part in or determine the terms of God's self-revelation. "Isn't the idealist principle of differentiating the non-given from the given justified by our need to understand revelation as *God's* revelation in contrast to whatever else might somehow be revealed?"[108] The critical value of idealism for theology is that by "stressing God's non-objectivity it reminds us that all human thinking about God is inadequate. It protects theology's object from being confused with other objects . . . Theology needs this antidote and this modesty."[109] The danger of pure idealism for theology, however, lies in reason's discovery of "itself as original and superior to mere being."[110] For Barth, "to equate reason with God (*ratio sive Deus*) is just as intolerable as to equate nature with God (*natura sive Deus*). Faith believes in neither."[111] Faith "can only rest on God having spoken, not on our having said something to ourselves."[112] In the attempt to protect the freedom of God against the manipulative hegemonies of all human ideologies, Barth can be seen as fashioning modern discourses on realism and idealism into a unique, theological "critical realism."

But does Barth's critical realism of the 1920s strike an appropriate balance between being and act, that is, between the ontological reality of God and the subjectivity of God's activity, and between God's objective being in

---

104. Barth, "Fate and Idea in Theology," 38.
105. Ibid., 43.
106. Ibid., 43.
107. See also, Pinkard, *German Philosophy*, 34.
108. Barth, "Fate and Idea in Theology," 45.
109. Ibid., 47.
110. Ibid., 43.
111. Ibid., 50.
112. Ibid., 51.

the world and the human act of faith? And what are the results of Barth's variations on the being-act theme for his accounts of divine and human freedom? Bonhoeffer wrote that "all of theology, in its teaching concerning knowledge of God, of human beings, and of sin and grace, crucially depends on whether it begins with the concept of act or being."[113] And he insisted that theology must not be based solely on a concept of act, or of being—what he calls the "purely transcendental or the purely ontological starting points."[114] Barth's "Fate and Idea" amply demonstrates that he perceived the importance of establishing a theology of revelation on the basis of a healthy mediation between being and act, object and subject. Yet Bonhoeffer questions whether Barth has fulfilled this obligation. He suspects that Barth is unable to escape his Kantian presuppositions, and that he therefore one-sidedly favors act over being, and subject over object.[115] "Revelation" he finds, "is interpreted purely in terms of act,"[116] and hence Bonhoeffer suggests that Kant's "transcendentalism is lurking here."[117] Barth's methodological prioritization of divine subjectivity and activity over the objectivity and being of God was, as we have seen, designed to protect the freedom of God. "God remains always the Lord, always subject, so that whoever claims to have God as an object no longer has *God*; God is always the God who 'comes' and never the God who 'is there.'"[118] But for Bonhoeffer, this one-sidedness distorts the theological account of freedom, by rendering God solely free *from* humanity, and not free *for* them.[119] If God's freedom is the utter transcendence of God secured by means of the radical non-objectivity of God's being in "pure act,"[120] then God becomes an abstract and alien

---

113. Bonhoeffer, *Act and Being*, 29–30.

114. Ibid., 31.

115. Hegel critiqued Kant on precisely this point. As Adams shows, Hegel thinks "Kant is to be applauded for insisting that philosophy must be an account of the relation of subject to object" but he "interprets Kant's transcendental idealism as one which opposes subject to object, and which resolves this opposition on the side of the subject." Kant's "combination" of the objective and subjective in judgment "is firmly on the side of the subjective, rather than reflecting a genuine relation between subject and object" (Adams, *Eclipse of Grace*, 22).

116. Bonhoeffer, *Act and Being*, 83.

117. Ibid., 83.

118. Ibid., 85.

119. For Bonhoeffer, as Reuter notes, Barth's Kantian precedence of act over being leaves him with "a merely formal understanding of the freedom of God, an understanding which—heavily favoring the side of the concept—places the living God of the Bible again into the role of the absolute subject" (Reuter, afterword to Bonhoeffer, *Act and Being*, 170).

120. Bonhoeffer, *Act and Being*, 87.

other, incapable of really loving humanity, because God will not risk Godself by becoming trapped in the world. "Thus the problem of transcendental philosophy . . . presents itself anew. God recedes into the non-objective, into what is beyond our disposition."[121] Precisely in his attempt to overcome the Kantian tradition's devaluation of God as an abstract and superior other, Barth perpetuates, to some extent, the modern "unspeakability" and "unthinkability" of God (to use Jüngel's terminology).[122] For Bonhoeffer the divine self-limitation in Christ does not risk God's freedom, but is exactly what is meant by it:

> In revelation it is not so much a question of the freedom of God—eternally remaining within the divine self, aseity—on the other side of revelation, as it is of God's coming out of God's own self in revelation. It is a matter of God's *given* Word, the covenant in which God is bound by God's own action. It is a question of the freedom of God, which finds its strongest evidence precisely in that God freely chose to be bound to historical human beings and to be placed at the disposal of human beings. God is free not from human beings but for them. Christ is the word of God's freedom. God *is* present, that is, not in eternal nonobjectivity but . . . "haveable," graspable in the Word within the church. Here the formal understanding of God's freedom is countered by a substantial one.[123]

And if Barth has limited the divine freedom to a purely formal understanding of God in God's transcendence, then he also devalues human freedom within the Church, Bonhoeffer suggests. Barth's God is "bound to nothing, not even the 'existing,' 'historical' Word."[124] But this means that "God's freedom and the act of faith are essentially supratemporal."[125] There is no space for the historicity of the divine life, or the humanity of Christ's divinity in Barth's early theology, and this introduces both a sense of opposition or competition between God and the world, and a strong devaluation of the created order. The axiom "Finitum non capax infiniti"[126] results in a somewhat non-participatory theology of divine and human freedom.

---

121. Ibid., 85.
122. See Jüngel, *God as the Mystery of the World*, 14.
123. Bonhoeffer, *Act and Being*, 90–91.
124. Ibid., 82.
125. Ibid., 84.
126. *Romans* II, 212.

As Sherman notes, however, "Bonhoeffer was aiming at a moving target,"[127] since by the time Bonhoeffer completed his *Habilitationsschrift* in 1930, Barth had already begun to rectify the mistakes identified by Bonhoeffer by tying being more firmly to act, object to subject, and by shifting "from his earlier exclusive emphasis on God's transcendence . . . [and] an abstract notion of God's freedom . . . to a radical stress on God's immanence."[128] As we shall see, however, Barth was unable, in *Church Dogmatics* volume I, to carry through these changes with the conviction that he later achieved, and his doctrine of revelation could only anticipate in an incomplete fashion the gains of his radically actualistic theological ontology developed after 1936, and fully realized in II/2.

Barth's Theology of Freedom in *Church Dogmatics* I

Barth's Emerging Actualism: God's Sovereign Relationality

Barth's Anselm book represents a key transition in his theological development since he later claimed that it was in this text that he realized decisively that theology must start "exclusively and conclusively with the doctrine of Jesus Christ—of Jesus Christ as the living Word of God spoken to us men."[129] Describing God's Word as speech-event forms the core of I/1, and the attempt here is to indicate how theological investigation is a possibility for the Church only where God is described with both ontic and noetic reference to God's self-mediating activity as Word. Barth's method may be described by the key term *nachdenken* (literally "thinking after"): "The *reality* of the Word of God as event precedes and grounds the *possibility* of the knowledge of it. 'Knowledge here means fundamentally acknowledgement [*An-erkenntnis*]. Thinking means thinking-after [*Nach-denken*] . . . '"[130] Barth's emphasis on thinking after the Word indicates his desire to emphasize the non-objectivity of divine truth, so as to insist that knowledge of

---

127. Sherman, "Act and Being," 105.

128. Ibid., 105.

129. Barth, *How I Changed My Mind*, 43. (See also, Barth, *Anselm*, 11) McCormack denies that the *Anselm* book was "a kind of watershed in Barth's development" (McCormack, *Karl Barth's Critically Realistic Dialectical Theology*, 422). The *Anselm* book, for McCormack, invokes a methodology that had already begun to emerge in *Die christliche Dogmatik* and in the *Göttingen Dogmatics*. Regardless of the precise nature of Barth's formation, the *Anselm* text serves our purposes by summarizing the nature of Barth's development in anticipation of the *Church Dogmatics*.

130. McCormack, *Karl Barth's Critically Realistic Dialectical Theology*, 425, citing Barth, *Die christliche Dogmatik*, 136.

God occurs in and through the event of God's living self-attestation, and not because God is a static entity generally available for human examination:

> God's Word means that God speaks. This implies... its personal quality. God's Word is not a thing [*Ding*] to be described nor a term to be defined. It is neither a matter nor an idea. It is not "a truth," not even the very highest truth. It is *the* truth as it is God's speaking person, *Dei loquentis persona*. It is not an objective reality [*Objektives*]. It is *the* objective reality [das *Objektive*], in that it is also subjective, *the* subjective [das *Subjektive*] that is God.[131]

God is free as "speaking person." It is this notion that foreshadows the participative gains of Barth's mature works, since the description of God's Word as "speech-event" strives simultaneously to protect the sovereignty and relationality of God by indicating that knowledge of God occurs only as the living event of divine-human encounter. God's Word is not generally available in the world of objects to be cognized and consumed by human subjects; nor is knowledge of God entirely unattainable as Kant had maintained. Rather, knowledge of God occurs as and when the Word encounters human subjects in a concrete "address."[132] As Williams says, "The freedom of the Word is God's capacity to speak not 'publicly' or 'generally,' in a single form (*Gestalt*) which is then once and for all accessible to all men without mediation, but in hiddenness which requires his own free decision in every particular instance to become manifest."[133]

The identity of Word and act is key to understanding the personal nature of the freedom of God in God's speech-act, and therefore to overcoming some of the abstractions of the earlier works. To expound God's Word in terms of act is to point to the truth of God's ontic reality as that of a dynamic, relational identity. "God's Word is itself act."[134] The Word of God is not to be understood as a certain kind of information or truth about God that will be communicated by a separate act of God, or by any human act. God's freedom to give Godself in the act of God's speech is sufficient for all knowledge of God, and indeed is fully revealing of God, because the act of God's speech and the form of God's Word is identical with the being and content of God's Word. "When God speaks, there is no point in looking about for a related act... The Word of God does not need to be supplemented by an act.

---

131. I/1, 136 = *KD* I/1, 141.
132. I/1, 41; 136–37.
133. Williams, "Barth on the Triune God," 151.
134. I/1, 147. See also, Torrance, *Persons in Communion*, 31ff.

The Word of God is itself the act of God."[135] The truth of God's being, then, is unveiled because God is identical with the event of God's speaking to humanity. "God's Word is identical with God Himself."[136] God *is* an eventful, communicative truth; God wills to be known, and God *is* in the event of God's being made known. Hence, Barth insists that

> The Word of God is first understood as decision [*Entscheidung*] or it is not understood at all. We might also say quite simply: as divine act [*Tat*] ... [A]s act and event [the Word] is free, as free as God Himself, for indeed God Himself is in the act [*in der Tat Gott selber ist*]. God is the Lord. There is no one and nothing above Him and no one and nothing beside Him, either on the right hand or the left, to condition Him or to be in a nexus with Him. God is *a se* ... But God's aseity is not empty freedom. In God all potentiality is included in His actuality and therefore all freedom in His decision. Decision means choice, exercised freedom. We understand the Word of God very badly in isolation from the unconditional freedom in which it is spoken, but we also understand it very badly if we regard it as a mere possibility rather than freedom exercised, a decision made, a choice taking place.[137]

Here, then, we see that Barth retains the notion of God's freedom as radical non-manipulability and self-determination. God's being and God's being made known are controlled solely by the power of God. "Godhead," Barth says, "means in the Bible freedom, ontic and noetic autonomy."[138] But ontic and noetic autonomy, in I/1, is not intended to indicate the abstract autonomy of a supreme lord breaking forth into the world in spite of God's transcendence. God is not conceived as a transcendent alien existing in an unapproachable and abstract freedom, but exists in the form of a decision for concrete encounter with that which is distinct from God. Hence, the freedom of God consists in the fact that God is ontologically involved with the event of God's self-giving, and is therefore the one who freely decides to relate Godself, to enact God's story with and for another. The personal nature of God's Word as speech-event, the fact that God speaks Godself in the world towards God's creatures, implies "what one might call the purposive character of the Word of God. This might also be called its relatedness or pertinence, its character as address ... we do [not] know God's Word as an

---

135. I/1, 143.
136. Ibid., 304.
137. Ibid., 157 = *KD* I/1, 162.
138. I/1, 307.

entity that exists or could exist merely in and for itself. We know it only as a Word that is directed to us and applies to us."[139]

One sees, then, that Barth is trying to modify his notion of the freedom of God in personalistic and actualistic terms, whilst also retaining a sense of the non-manipulability of God. He is trying to unite the form and content of revelation, the objectivity and subjectivity of God's identity, and the being of God with the activity of God, such that God is described ontologically as relational and self-mediating, whilst also being the sovereign author of God's being and God's being made known—the subject who remains radically non-objective even in the event of God's self-objectification, even in the event of God's "taking form."[140] Torrance therefore finds that "Just as there can be no dichotomy between God's Word and Act, neither can, nor rather must, God's Work and Essence be conceived as being of two different kinds."[141] God is as God does. If we wish to answer the question "Who is God in His revelation?" we must "answer at once the two other questions: What is He doing? and: What does He effect?"[142] Thus Jüngel describes Barth's doctrine of the Word not only as the revelation of God's being, but as God's *being-revealed*: "*Gottes Offenbar-Sein.*"[143]

God's Revelatory Being-in-Act as a Trinitarian Affair

Barth chooses to open his *Dogmatics* with the doctrine of the trinity in order to refuse any *a priori* notions of the existence of "God" which would then determine the way we speak of the triune God revealed in Scripture. If theology has its object only insofar as it has God as its subject, it must first listen to the threefold activity of God in God's three modes of being (*Seinsweisen*),[144] and then allow the concrete event of God's being-in-speech to answer the "Who" question of God.[145] It is as Father, Son and Holy Spirit that God is revealer, revelation and revealedness, and it is as the triune economy that God reveals God's triune life *in se*. For the Barth of I/1 the speech-event of God *ad extra* is God's self-interpretation, a perfect analogical

---

139. Ibid., 139.

140. Ibid., 316. "The distinction between form and content cannot be applied to the biblical concept of revelation" (ibid., 306).

141. Torrance, *Persons in Communion*, 32. See Jüngel, *God's Being Is in Becoming*, 27.

142. I/1, 297.

143. Jüngel, *Gottes Sein ist im Werden*, 13.

144. I/1, 333 = *KD* I/1, 352.

145. Torrance, *Persons in Communion*, 72–73. See I/1, 300ff.

repetition corresponding exactly to God's being in and for Godself.[146] God interprets Godself as the one who is free to be Godself in whatever manner God wills, but in this freedom the triune God reveals Godself to be wholly God for us, precisely in and through the event of God's being-in-speech. If the form of God's revelation is that of gracious address, then the content of the revelation is a gracious speaker, one whose threefold lordship is that of a divine I who speaks *"for the sake of* the recipient thou."[147]

There is here a unification of God's essence (objectivity) and God's work (subjectivity) [*Wesen und Wirken Gottes sind ja nicht zweierlei sondern eins*],[148] and this forms the new terms on which Barth can speak of God's freedom, marrying the sovereignty and relationality of God. God's relationality *ad extra* is grounded in God's freedom *in se*; that is, the triune economy has its "basis and prototype in His own essence, in His being as God. As Father, Son and Spirit, God is, so to speak, ours in advance."[149] The key phrase "ours in advance" indicates that to the depths of God's being, God is ordered for relations, and in revealing Godself to another, God remains supremely faithful to Godself. "God is precisely the One He is in showing and giving Himself."[150] By uniting the act of God with God's being, the subjectivity of God's self-interpretative being *ad extra* with God's essential identity *in se*, Barth retains the transcendence of God aimed at in texts such as *Romans II*, whilst also indicating, in response to criticisms such as Bonhoeffer's, that God is supremely faithful to Godself by being God for us. God is said to interpret Godself by re-iterating Godself for a second time in history.[151] Hence there is a kind of grammatical correspondence between God's being in and for Godself and God's being for us. The free God is also the God of the history of Jesus Christ. As Jüngel explains, "That God corresponds to himself is a statement of relation. The statement means that God's being is a relationally structured being."[152] It is because the triune being of God *in se* is the "pure event" of God's threefold "*repetitio aeternitatis in aeternitate*"[153] that we can say that God is ours in advance, because this is to say God is the event of the three-fold occurrence of self-giving love. "Because God's

---

146. I/1, 311. Jüngel, *God's Being Is in Becoming*, 36.
147. Torrance, *Persons in Communion*, 81.
148. I/1, 371 = *KD* I/1, 391.
149. I/1, 383.
150. Ibid., 382.
151. Ibid., 316.
152. Jüngel, *God's Being Is in Becoming*, 37.
153. Ibid., 39; see also, I/1, 366.

being as threehood is self-giving (love), this being may not be conceived as something abstract."[154]

Critical Engagement with the Early Barth on Freedom

It is clear that Barth has made significant progress in reclaiming what Jüngel describes as "responsible speech about God's being" (*Verantwortliche Rede vom Sein Gottes*)[155] in response to the post-Kantian theological tradition, and Barth has obviously attempted to reflect on God's freedom to be our God with an appropriate balance between being and act, and object and subject. And yet, despite Barth's efforts, the object-subject problem is not satisfactorily resolved in *Church Dogmatics* I, and damage is unwittingly done to the conception of the divine-human relationship, and therefore to the freedom of God and humanity to exist in a participative, covenantal relationship. In later volumes of the *Dogmatics*, as we shall see, Barth will need to redress the somewhat narrowly conceived epistemic concerns that continue to shape his theological interests in *Church Dogmatics* I.

The Ambiguous Relation of God's Being to God's Act

I have demonstrated that Barth wishes to describe the triune objectivity of God in terms of God's historical subjectivity or activity, which is said to correspond perfectly to the former as a repetition and interpretation of God's relational being in and for Godself. But he is keen to avoid introducing any notion of the necessity of humanity to God; God can in no sense be thought of as being compelled to create. Since God's freedom is conceived as radical independence, Barth refuses that the existence of humanity is essential to God's being. Hence, whilst the immanent and economic trinity must not be separated, neither can they be simply identified. Since God's economy corresponds to God's essence as interpretation, it reveals the "capacity" of God in Godself to reveal Godself,[156] the kind of structures in place in God's being as threefold love that allow God to be one disposed towards another, but in no way ontologically conditions God as one whose revelation is integral to God's identity. For although God "in fact" reveals Godself for the sake of

---

154. Jüngel, *God's Being Is in Becoming*, 41.

155. This is the German subtitle of Jüngel's *Gottes Sein ist im Werden*, which is rendered differently in the ET.

156. Jüngel, *God's Being Is in Becoming*, 47.

another, this fact makes no difference to God's being, and might just as well "not be."¹⁵⁷

> In the inter-trinitarian life of God the eternal generation of the Son or Logos is, of course, the expression of God's love, of His will not to be alone. But it does not follow from this that God could not be God without speaking to us. We undoubtedly understand God's love for man . . . only when we understand it as free and unmerited love not resting on any need. God would be no less God if He had created no world and no man . . . God is not at all lonely even without the world and us . . . And so one cannot say that our existence as that of the recipients of God's Word is constitutive for the concept of the Word. It could be no less what it is even without us.¹⁵⁸

Barth wishes to stress the non-necessity of creation to God in order to secure this as the basis for the sheer grace of God's decision in favor of a creation that exists completely without necessity. Moreover, we can only speak of the relation between God and humanity *a posteriori* in light of its concrete historical occurrence, and not because *a priori* we might discern in our conceptions of God's being the necessity to create the world. "The coming of God's Word to man is the act of divine freedom and choice. It does not have to come to him. It comes according to God's good-pleasure."¹⁵⁹ What is more, the sharp distinction between the immanent and economic trinity is supposed to uphold the dialectic of veiling and unveiling. When God gives Godself, it is always the free giving of God which is radically nonobjective. God in God's self-giving does not give Godself away, so to speak. Hence, whilst the economy of God perfectly corresponds to or interprets God's being in itself, it does so in a veiled form. God remains a mystery even in God's self-unveiling.¹⁶⁰ So the secularity of the Word is a "paradox." "First the Word of God meets us in a form that is to be distinguished from its content, and secondly the form as such is an enigma, a concealing of the Word of God."¹⁶¹ This is because

> The place where God's Word is revealed is objectively and subjectively the cosmos in which sin reigns. The form of God's Word, then, is in fact the form of the cosmos which stands in contradiction to God. It has as little ability to reveal God to us

---

157. I/1, 139.
158. Ibid., 139–40.
159. Ibid., 206.
160. Ibid., 165.
161. Ibid., 166.

as we have to see God in it. If God's Word is revealed in it, it is revealed "through it," of course, but in such a way that this "through it" means "in spite of it."[162]

Here Barth is resisting any notion of the *analogia entis* or the *vestigium trinitatis*, in continuation of his debate with Roman Catholic theologian Erich Przywara.[163] If a correspondence exists between God's eternal being *in se* and God's being *ad extra*, the nature of this correspondence is known only to Godself. Having insisted that the form and content of revelation are inseparable—such that God is known only in and through the event of God's being *qua* relational speech-act—Barth now also maintains that "Erasure of the distinction and indeed of the antithesis of form and content we cannot achieve. The coincidence of the two is clear to God but is not discernable to us."[164] It is here that tensions arise in Barth's early conception of the divine reality.

Barth means simultaneously to protect the autonomy of God and the relationality of God by saying that in the divine life *ad extra* God assumes a form which is radically unlike Godself, such that God can reveal who God is without ever collapsing the infinite qualitative distinction between God and humanity.[165] God has "the freedom to be unlike Himself . . . the freedom of God to differentiate Himself from Himself . . . in such a way that He is not tied to His secret eternity and eternal secrecy but can and will and does in fact take temporal form as well."[166] Barth is wrestling with two theological poles which cannot, at this stage, be brought into satisfactory harmony: i) the freedom of God in God's relationality to speak Godself in and through creation, and ii) the freedom of God in God's lordship to remain eternally transcendent from that reality which is distinct from God.[167]

The Word as A-Historical

At this point in his theology, Barth one-sidedly favors the distinction of God from the world over against God's being in the world, leading to something

---

162. Ibid., 166.
163. See Dorrien, *The Barthian Revolt*, 95–96; See also, I/1, 41; 168–69; 333ff.
164. I/1, 175.
165. Williams, "Barth on the Triune God," 153.
166. I/1, 320.
167. Gogarten criticized Barth on this front, suggesting that he is unable to mediate between divine objectivity and subjectivity, and is therefore unable to make sense of the distinction between God's being in and for Godself and God's being for humanity (see I/1, 170–71).

of a devaluation of the historical, and a sense of dualism or competition between God's being *in se* and the world. "History and the *world* as such, are wholly foreign to God: he can act through, but not in, the historical *qua* historical."[168] On this basis Williams notes

> the awkwardness of a scheme which so divorces the substance of revelation from its historical form, in making the latter's relation to the former basically external. Revelation demands, we are told, historical predicates, yet there is nothing *in* these predicates which in any sense makes them "appropriate" to their content. Despite Barth's vehement disavowals (*CD* I/1, 168–74), it is hard not to conclude that this does indeed make the revealing Word's secularity and historicity "accidental" to its nature.[169]

It would seem that Barth has failed to overcome the object-subject, being-act dichotomy that marked his earlier works, since although he is keenly aware of the importance of uniting the two sets of terms, he strongly prefers a concept of divine freedom as absolute sovereignty, for which he sees the non-objectivity of the Word as an essential feature. "While [Barth] continues to stress the inseparability of form and content in revelation" by affirming that God's being *in se* is the act of fellowship which subsequently overflows in a historical event of perfect revelatory correspondence and self-interpretation, in reality he "allows no possibility at all of any *unity* between them. The power of God and freedom of God can make form and content one in effect or operation; but there is nothing here . . . to suggest that, even *ex parte Dei*, any more internal or substantial union can ever be envisaged."[170]

In a similar vein, Wingren complains of the earlier Barth that the Word can "assume" flesh in order to speak across the God-human chasm, but cannot "become" flesh, as John 1:14 insists, in order to banish the very notion of any fundamental God-human binary or opposition.[171] Jesus is "God's own

---

168. Williams, "Barth on the Triune God," 153. Jones agrees with Williams's criticisms, suggesting that in §15 "what God does, in and as Christ, has no bearing on who God eternally is; Barth's early concern for God's immutability and self-sufficient ontological priority requires a clear-cut dissociation of God's eternal being qua Son and God's concrete incarnational existence qua Son" (Jones, *The Humanity of Christ*, 65).

169. Williams, "Barth on the Triune God," 153.

170. Ibid.

171. See Wingren, *Theology in Conflict*, 30–31. In support of Wingren's observation, the phrase, "Without ceasing to be the Word, he ceased to be only the Word" (I/2, 149), suggests that the identity of the Word can assume a manner other than itself, but does not "have" flesh, *incarnandus*, at the core of His identity.

alter ego [*Doppelgänger*],"[172] but is not the truth of God's freedom and power *qua* Jesus. At this point in his career, then, Barth does not share Lutheran suspicions about the *extra Calvinisticum*, the firm doctrinal separation of the *logos asarkos* from the *logos ensarkos*.[173] According to Barth's early, Reformed commitments,

> God is present *mit und unter*, with and under, the contingent and historical, but he cannot be said to be *in* it, identified with it in the way Luther envisages. For the Lutheran, what is involved in the revelation of God in suffering and darkness is a real communication of God; the worldly circumstances of Cross and dereliction *themselves* say something about God. They are not simply a concealing exterior vehicle.[174]

At this point several critical questions arise about the propriety of Barth's trinitarian theology of freedom, its function within a rather narrowly epistemological setting, the role of the humanity of Christ, and subsequently the notion of human freedom operative in *Church Dogmatics* I. Consequently, the reader remains unconvinced that Barth's theology of freedom achieves its aim: the liberation of theology from the errors of liberal Protestantism. These issues revolve around Barth's acceptance of an agenda set for theology by the liberal tradition after Kant, namely, the idea that the task of theology is, in the first place, to explain the possibility of theological knowledge.

As Laats identifies,

> The Trinity explains the reality and possibility of the knowledge of God. This is its main function. Of course Barth does not reduce this doctrine to that function. But nevertheless the shape of the doctrine of the Trinity is determined by theological epistemology.[175]

---

172. I/1, 316 = *KD*, 333. See also, Jones, *The Humanity of Christ*, 64, and Williams, "Barth on the Triune God," 160.

173. For Jones, the early Barth simply takes for granted the validity of the ontological separation of the *logos asarkos* and the *logos ensarkos*. Barth briefly reminds the reader that "The Word is what He is even before and apart from His being flesh. Even as incarnate He derives His being to all eternity from the Father and from Himself, and not from the flesh" (I/2, 136). "Barth simply does not ask whether God wills to complicate, ontologically, God's being in light of the Son's assumption of humanity. And one gets the distinct impression that, at this point, Barth would not want to dwell on such a question, lest the 'infinite qualitative distinction' appear to be compromised" (Jones, *The Humanity of Christ*, 41).

174. Williams, "Barth on the Triune God," 154–55.

175. Laats, *Doctrines of the Trinity in Eastern and Western Theologies*, 38.

If this is the case, then Barth may be guilty of an internal inconsistency, whereby he allows the identity of the trinity (or at least the parameters within which we interpret the doctrine of the trinity) to be determined in advance of the event of revelation on the basis of a preconceived notion of what it means for God to be free.[176] In the reaction against liberalism Barth wishes to insist that the revealing God remains absolutely independent of creation, even in the event of speaking to creation. Barth seeks to avoid risking the sovereignty of God's lordship with respect to any betrayal of a fixed relation between God and the world, and he allows this to shape the way he speaks of God's triune self-interpretation. As we have seen, however, it is precisely this concern that leads to a sense of disjunction between God's identity *in se* and *ad extra*, which in turn perpetuates a notion of dualism between God and the world. Barth presupposes that human subjectivity, and the humanity of God's subjectivity, might be said to infringe upon the freedom of the radically autonomous God, and he thus contrives to speak of the triune grace of God as utterly transcendent from the natural realm. This is an epistemological model in which the opposition of grace to nature conditions all that is said about the freedom of the triune God. But does this not mean that Barth has allowed his own theological agenda to compromise his insistence that theology is *nachdenken*? His "entire conviction that we recognise the methodological and epistemological significance of divine freedom must, to be consistent, repose on an *a posteriori* expression not only of the *facticity* but also of the *nature* of divine 'freedom'—of the meaning which the concept acquires when used of God."[177] For Williams, "Barth's account of revelation is by no means as neutral as it purports to be. A powerful ideological motive—the need to assert the infallibility and irresistibility of God's self-communication—underlies all that is said about the revealing event."[178]

With Wingren, this study argues that where "God's love could become a threat to his majesty and freedom,"[179] the conception of freedom in play requires drastic revision.[180] God's power to take a distinct reality to Godself

176. See Torrance, *Persons in Communion*, 48.
177. Ibid., 50.
178. Williams, "Barth on the Triune God," 158.
179. Wingren, *Theology in Conflict*, 119.
180. Moltmann has expressed similar concerns: "What concept of liberty is Barth applying to God here? Is this concept of absolute freedom of choice not a threat to God's truth and goodness?" In response to Barth's claims that God could have remained God even without us, Moltmann says "The reasoning 'God could,' or 'God could have,' is inappropriate. It does not lead to an understanding of God's freedom. God's freedom can never contradict the truth which God himself is" (Moltmann, *The Trinity and the*

in and through the history of Jesus Christ ought not to be seen as a result of God's seemingly arbitrary freedom to create or not to create according to the pre-determined, purely formal concept of freedom as divine possibility, but as being itself fundamental to the nature of the freedom of God to be our God and no other. Does the biblical testimony not suggest that the events of God's secular history themselves say something about God's identity? If this is so, freedom must not be conceived as the freedom of God either to give or to withhold knowledge of God, but as the radicality of God's power as lord to have lordship even over God's own being, and therefore to allow humanity a share in the story of God's eternal identity.

Moreover, if Barth's primary interest in *Church Dogmatics* I is indeed to protect the freedom of God in the event of revelation by insisting that the triune God at all points controls the possibility of theological knowledge, then the question arises as to whether Barth has effectively proposed a genuinely "new starting-point" for theology. It was seen above that in the wake of what some take to be Kant's object-subject binary, liberalism was forced to explain the possibility of Christian speech about God. The central theological question became the possibility of knowledge of God. But for Wingren the theological task is not to articulate how we can know God, but to describe the nature of humanity's relationship with God, and the way in which God wages war on sin, liberating humanity from its self-incurred separation from God. Rowan Williams says of Wingren's critique that "It is a situation not without its ludicrous aspect to find Barth being attacked for anthropocentrism," but Barth leaves us with "a system in which human knowledge, not the activity of God, is central."[181] For Wingren it is of little significance that Barth refused natural theology for a doctrine of divine revelation that sought to protect the non-objectivity of God's truth; once one has assumed the validity of an errant premise, the nature of the response is of superficial importance. "Placing the question of knowledge in the centre is in itself a pregnant theological thesis, no matter whether it is solved by the help of natural theology or by the exclusive concept of revelation."[182] Barth says no to natural theology, but he says yes to the underlying question that liberal versions of natural theology were conceived to answer: how do we know God? And the acceptance of this premise indicates that Barth has also accepted the epistemologically derived God-world disjunction that he sought to repair. God (object) and the world (subjects) are separated by an epistemological gulf, and theology is called to account for the bridg-

---

Kingdom of God, 53).

181. Williams, "Barth on the Triune God," 172–73.

182. Wingren, *Theology in Conflict*, 42.

ing of the divide, but in such a way that God remains free from ideological manipulation. Questions concerning the interrelation of divine and human agency fall from the fore, because of Barth's one-sided concern with the possibility of theological knowledge, and his inability at this point to ground epistemology in the historicity of God's being-in-becoming.

This results in something of a devaluation of the biblical accounts of human liberation, since freedom here must mean (rather reductively) the acquisition of knowledge (where knowledge is defined in somewhat narrowly conceptual and dogmatic terms). Hence in *Church Dogmatics* I/2, in conjunction with the epistemologically derived notion of divine freedom, the question of human freedom regards the legitimate means by which humanity is invited to share in the knowledge of God, which, aside from the grace of God, remains inaccessible.[183] It does not primarily entail the liberation from sin for flourishing in reconciled relations with the God of the covenant. Barth's theology of human freedom is not, therefore, particularly participative at this stage. This is perhaps because Barth's abiding object-subject, being-act separation results in the failure to integrate the Word's humanity with the Word's eternal identity, such that the pattern of the relation between God and humanity must remain fixed in a one-directional linearity ("God—the Word—the hearing of the Word").[184] God may speak to humanity in the form of a human Word, but there is nothing in God's own assumption of the flesh that allows for the participation of humanity in the Son's address *qua* Jesus to the Father, or therefore for their being drawn into the very life of God. Hence, human flourishing must remain the freedom to

---

183. Barth discusses human freedom in I/2 as the freedom granted to humanity by God to receive knowledge of God. §16 describes "The Freedom of Man for God" as a gift of "The Outpouring of the Holy Spirit," and §21 discusses "Freedom in the Church." Barth claims here that the reality of the event of the outpouring of the Holy Spirit manifests in our "freedom to be the children of God and to know and love and praise Him in His revelation" (I/2, 203). Barth's main interest is in describing the possibility of human faith in such a way that the Church is given noetic responsibility (ibid., 662) without forgetting the "freedom of grace" upon which all human knowledge of God depends: "God Himself and God alone turns man into a recipient of His revelation" (ibid., 210). The freedom of humanity for God gifted by the Spirit consists in being "led by God to a certain conviction" (ibid., 232). It is largely a matter of "acknowledgement" and "affirmation" of what is objectively true in Jesus Christ (ibid., 239). Hence to be free means to make use of one's subjective "spontaneous activity" under the guidance of the Spirit (ibid., 715); it is that active and obedient assent by the human creature to allow God to determine all knowledge of Godself through Scripture, proclamation and the power of the Spirit to reveal Jesus Christ. "This readiness and willingness to make one's own the responsibility for understanding of the Word of God is freedom under the Word" (ibid., 696).

184. Williams, "Barth on the Triune God," 180–81. See also, Wingren, *Theology in Conflict*, 32.

receive God's Word, the freedom to acquire knowledge of God, but cannot be the freedom given when we are drawn up in the counter-movement of Christ's human address to the Father on our behalf.[185]

According to Wingren, Barth's reduction of the story of human liberation to a narrative about theological epistemology thereby jeopardizes the heart of the biblical narrative in line with the rest of the post-Kantian liberal tradition. In Barth, as with his liberal teachers, God's redemption of humanity from its sinful conflict with evil is erroneously replaced with the "liberal" assumption that "The predicament is ignorance."[186] But for Wingren "it is exactly this framework which is questionable. 'Revelation' stands in the place where 'justification,' or 'forgiveness of sins,' i.e. the gospel in the essential meaning of the word, ought to stand."[187] Wingren makes an interesting point, even if his description of Barth tends to be somewhat reductive. If Barth is to do justice to the biblical account of divine reality and human flourishing as mediated in the covenantal identity of Jesus Christ, then the rather restrictive epistemological concerns that frame everything the early Barth says will need to undergo significant change in the later volumes of the *Church Dogmatics*. Since, as Ford suggests, "Barth draws his main conclusions from stories the crucial test of his theology is whether his interpretation and assessment of those stories is convincing."[188] If his portrayal of the biblical narrative is to be persuasive, he will be required to transcend the ideological boundaries of a modern conceptual tradition for which epistemological questions, and not soteriological ones, are of primary urgency.

Finally, if Barth's first volume of the *Dogmatics* itself appears to be trapped in the thought-world of neo-Protestantism, then so too, it may be argued, is the very definition of freedom central to it. Rendtorff suggests that Barth attempts to counter the Enlightenment's opposition of classical Christian belief in God to the relativizing principle of complete, independent agential self-determination, by himself applying to the modern autonomy theme, and using it to safeguard not the authority of the human subject, but of the divine. Far from escaping the Enlightenment tradition, with its strict definition of freedom as absolute self-determination, Barth unveils "a new Enlightenment," theologically conceived, simply by replacing the freedom of the human agent with that of the divine agent.[189] The liberals

---

185. See also, Torrance, *Persons in Communion*, 104ff.
186. Williams, "Barth on the Triune God," 173.
187. Wingren, *Theology in Conflict*, 28–29.
188. Ford, *Barth and God's Story*, 13.
189. Rendtorff, "Radikale Autonomie Gottes," 164.

had tried to marry Christian faith with modernity's burgeoning optimism in the capabilities of the autonomous, rational subjectivity of the human individual. In so doing it had, for Barth, failed to rescue Christianity from the anthropocentrism of modernity. But Barth does not himself penetrate beneath the modern interest in freedom as self-determining autonomy at this stage; he simply diverts the autonomy theme towards a different subject. Rendtorff, like Wingren, therefore concludes that Barth, accepting the validity of a modern conceptual vocabulary, remains a liberal in disguise, for he considers that the task of theology is to accommodate Christianity to the modern, post-Kantian notion of freedom as radical autonomy.[190]

Furthermore, for Rendtorff, Barth's application to an Enlightenment notion of freedom as radical autonomy reveals his epistemological favor for Kantian criticism, whereby the freedom of God is designed to remind liberal contemporaries of the object-subject distinction, and therefore of the inability of human subjects to speak adequately of God. God's freedom is thus conceived in advance, and within a Kantian framework. "The epistemological problems that had been the daily bread of Barth's Neokantian theological schooling under Wilhelm Herrmann were turned in a deft dialectical reversal into evidence for the impossibility of speaking about God apart from Revelation."[191]

Conclusion

In summary, it is helpful to recall Jüngel's appeal against the modern obsession with autonomy as naked independence and agential sovereignty, which was ultimately forced to conceive of God as an abstract other, the final reason for things, and the personification of Kant's transcendental freedom. On such an account, God is perceived to be so completely free from creation, in and for Godself, that the truth of God's being is alienated from the world. Once God in God's freedom is placed in abstract superiority over against the world, there can be no space within the infinite for the participation of the finite, and no authentic place for the participation of the infinite in the finite.[192] The early Barth, perceiving the living reality of the graceful, speaking, personal God as witnessed to in Scripture and by the Church, sought to refuse all such "concepts tending in this direction, even that of a supreme being, an *ens perfectissimum* or an unconditioned . . . As general concepts they suppress the essential point that the Word of God is a reality only in

---

190. Ibid., 164.
191. Macken, *The Autonomy Theme*, 126.
192. Jüngel, *God as the Mystery of the World*, 103.

its own decision."[193] Barth pursued a critical realism which attempted to do justice to the being-act, object-subject pattern in various forms, ultimately trying to integrate God's being with God's act. It was this movement towards an actualistic and Christological theological method and ontology that would provide the platform for key developments in Barth's later works, particularly with reference to his accounts of divine and human freedom. Nevertheless, a persistent ambiguity in Barth's relation of divine being and divine act manifested in a failure to integrate satisfactorily God's immanent objectivity (the being-in-act of the triune Godhead) with the account of God's historical subjectivity (God's being-in-act *pro nobis*). The extent to which God's being really is in God's historical act, for the younger Barth, is questionable, as is the extent to which God's being in and for itself can bear the historical predicates of God's revealing activity. While Barth's *Church Dogmatics* I anticipates future advances, at this stage his work cannot be said to have evaded, with complete success, the aprioristic tendency to conceive the free God as the unthinkably superior God.

---

193. I/1, 159.

2

"BEING-IN-BECOMING"

The Development of Barth's Actualistic Theology of Freedom

The taking up of humanity into the event of the knowledge of God is grounded in the taking up of humanity into the event of the being of God.

—Eberhard Jüngel[1]

Introduction

The purpose of Chapter 2 is to trace the development of Barth's theology of freedom after *Church Dogmatics* I towards the establishment of a fully realized actualistic ontology in II/2, paving the way for the investigation of IV/3 in the second part of the book. Given the criticisms of Barth raised in Chapter 1, it is necessary to explore how he attempts to shift away from the dualistic tendencies in his earlier works, and to examine the extent to which a sense of divine-human competition or opposition persists in the mature texts (those from 1936 onwards, after the publication of I/2 and hearing an

---

1. Jüngel, *God's Being Is in Becoming*, 75.

important lecture on election given by Pierre Maury). Since the predominant concern so far has been to trace Barth's theological epistemology in the doctrine of revelation, I now investigate how his dogmatic transition to divine ontology in *Church Dogmatics* II furthers his reflections on the relation between divine being and human knowing. In light of the charge, levelled at the earlier Barth in Chapter 1, that God's history in the world is accidental to the eternal divine identity, "we must ask about the *ground* of humanity's being taken up into the event of God's being."[2] For the mature Barth, does God simply express God's being to humanity in revelation, or is there a deeper ontological significance to God's eventful presence in the created order suggesting that the relationship between God and humanity—and therefore the event of humanity's knowledge of God—is integral to God's very being? While from II/1 Barth began to establish the theological conditions for an identification of God's eternal self-determination in and through the history of Jesus Christ, it was not until II/2 and the doctrine of election that he explicitly resolved on the "actualistism" that would provide the methodological foundation for his later doctrinal endeavors.

In Part B of this book I shall argue that Barth's account of Jesus Christ's mediatorship in IV/3 engenders the integration of the ontological and epistemological categories, which itself facilitates Barth's fullest expression of divine-human unity. What are the developments in Barth's theology that foreshadow that anti-dualistic and participative Christology of freedom? Chapter 2 addresses this question, suggesting that Barth gradually moves towards an ontology in which God's vision for the divine-human covenant is part of the eternal event of divine self-determination, thereby investing humanity with an ontic integrity that reaches to the very depths of God's sovereignty. The freedom of God's eventful being and the flourishing of humanity are deeply entwined from at least II/2 onwards. Exploring this integration of the divine and human agencies, Chapter 2 falls into two sections. In the first I assess how Barth sought to move beyond dualistic tensions between God and the world in his doctrine of God. In the second part of the chapter, I tour Barth's theological ethics as it develops in light of the Christocentric actualism of the doctrine of election, addressing his account of human freedom in detail for the first time.

---

2. Ibid., 76.

"Being-in-Becoming":
Towards an Actualistic Ontology
in *Church Dogmatics* II/1

The God Who Loves in Freedom

Church Dogmatics II/1 picks up where the first volume left off, with the problem of the knowledge of God. This part-volume, however, addresses the question not from the realm of subjectivity and epistemology, but from the perspective of objectivity and ontology. In volume I Barth had insisted upon the non-objectivity of God so as to remind the reader that God is not an object in the world like any other, and II/1 opens by re-affirming this principle.[3] For Barth, similar to the Kantian tradition, "We have all other objects [*Gegenstände*] as they are determined by the pre-arranged disposition and pre-arranged mode of our existence."[4] Since the supremely distinct ontic reality of God bears no continuities with being in general, Barth expressly forbids the *analogia entis*.[5] If we are to talk of God's being it will be in very different terms to the ordinary language of being. And yet clearly if we are to hold that human persons are the subjects of the knowledge of God, God must be described in some sense as the object of that knowledge.[6] Barth must speak of God as an object of human knowledge in such a way that makes clear the objective "readiness" God has in and for Godself for human subjects, and must indicate that it is the unique ontic structures of God's living reality that conditions all theological knowledge, and not the epistemic capacities of human subjects. Barth is asking what it is about God's "essence" that means God is "so constituted that He can be known by us."[7]

He responds by discussing the objectivity of God in terms of pure event or act:

> We are dealing with the being of God: but with regard to the being of God, the word "event" [*Ereignis*] or "act" [*Akt*] is *final*, and cannot be surpassed or compromised. To its very deepest depths, God's Godhead consists in the fact that it is an event— and not any event, not events in general, but the event of His action, in which we have a share in God's revelation.[8]

---

3. II/1, 15; 21. See also, Jüngel, *God's Being Is in Becoming*, 55–56.
4. II/1, 21 = *KD* II/1, 22.
5. See II/1, 81ff. for Barth's rejection of the *analogia entis*.
6. Jüngel, *God's Being Is in Becoming*, 55.
7. II/1, 65. See also Gunton, *The Barth Lectures*, 140.
8. II/1, 263 = *KD* II/1, 294.

On one level, to name Barth's theology "actualistic" is to acknowledge that "act and event are his central ontological categories."[9] Below, I shall argue with McCormack that Barth's actualism takes on a radical Christocentric determination in II/2. But the decision to identify Jesus as both elected man and electing God is foreshadowed in the ontology of II/1, which drives the categories of act and knowledge deeper into the structures of divine being than had been expressed in Barth's earlier works. As Colwell notes, Barth modifies the claim of volume I that "we may speak of the being of God exclusively with reference to His self-revelation" with the ontological resolution that "we may speak of God in this way because God is truly who He actually is in the event of His Word; He is not another in Himself than He is in His works."[10] For Barth we may assert the objective possibility or capacity of God for revelation only on the basis of the identification of God's ontic actuality as the one who "is" identical with God's revelatory relationality, since it is a basic principle of his theology that "Where the actuality exists there is also the corresponding possibility."[11] To borrow from Jüngel, this "being-as-object is his being-revealed."[12] If God were not ontologically identical with the activity which grounds the event of revelation, we would know nothing of God's reality, since God's being would then become a static metaphysical substance lurking behind revelation. If God's revelation is not only manifestation, but more definitely *self*-manifestation, then we are to identify the objectivity of God with the divine subjectivity. And it is just this supreme ontic eventfulness that differentiates God from other objects:

> The fact that God's being is event, the event of God's act, necessarily . . . means that it is His own conscious, willed and executed decision . . . No other being *is* absolutely in its *act* [*Kein anderes Sein* ist *schlechterdings in seiner Tat*]. No other being is absolutely its own, conscious, willed and executed *decision* [*Entscheidung*].[13]

On the basis of Barth's identification of God's being with the event or decision to relate to a reality distinct from Godself, we may follow Jüngel and others who have described God's being as a "being-in-becoming." God is, objectively, for the human subject only as God's being is the event of becoming related to another in a living encounter. God's becoming for humanity in the event of revelation is "a becoming in which God truly is

---

9. Gorringe, *Karl Barth against Hegemony*, 233.
10. Colwell, *Actuality and Provisionality*, 184.
11. II/1, 5. See also, Jüngel, *God's Being Is in Becoming*, 63.
12. Jüngel, *God's Being Is in Becoming*, 57.
13. II/1, 271 rev. = *KD* II/1, 304.

who he is; a becoming which, though a free becoming on God's part, cannot ultimately be excluded from a description of the Being of God."[14] In defense of the integration of being and act, of objectivity and subjectivity in his theological ontology, Barth asks

> How could He be our Creator, Reconciler and Redeemer, how could He be the living Lord, if it were not so, and if His *being for us* [*sein Sein für uns*] were ever to be separated from His *act* [*Akt*], so that a direction of man to God's being could exist in something other than his being directed by God's act? Man's being directed is his direction to . . . the actual [*das aktuelle*] being of God.[15]

This makes it possible, on the basis of 1 John 4:8, 16, for Barth to identify God's being with "love." Love is not just something that God does; God loves insofar as God is, ontologically, the enactment or becoming of love. As Creator, Reconciler, and Redeemer, God *becomes* the love for humanity which God had already *decided* to be in the depths of God's inner being.[16] This suggests God's freedom is not an abstract indeterminacy in which God is eternally free to be and to choose between an infinite range of possibilities.

Yet Barth insists that God is not to be passed wholly into God's works, as if the phrases "being-in-becoming" and "God becomes" are univocal. God is not to be identified *simpliciter* with the event of God's becoming an object for human knowledge, as this would be to collapse theology into a crude absolute idealism or process ontology, and thus to reduce God to God's historical immanence (i.e. precisely what Barth fought to resist from *Romans* II to *Church Dogmatics* I).[17]

For the Barth of II/1, God's being as love is an event of divine freedom, which means it is not inevitable, and is grounded in God's ontological priority over and freedom from all other realities. If God exists as the event of God's love for humanity, this must be because God makes the free, self-determined decision in and for Godself to do so, without compulsion or necessity. God's relationality is not an *a priori* necessity of God's being but is "grounded in His own self-determination to so exist."[18] For this reason, in addition to thinking of God's being in terms of the decision for and the actualization of relations with humanity, Barth also wants to think of God's being in independence from humanity:

14. Torrance, "The Trinity," 86.
15. II/1, 22 rev. = *KD* II/1, 22–23.
16. II/1, 275.
17. See also, Torrance, "The Trinity," 86.
18. Colwell, *Actuality and Provisionality*, 192.

> God's freedom in relation to all that is not God signifies that He is distinct from everything, that He is self-sufficient and independent in relation to it . . . God confronts all that is in supreme and utter independence, i.e., He would be no less and no different even if they all did not exist or existed differently . . . If they [viz. humanity] belong to Him and He to them, this dual relationship does not spring from any need of His eternal being . . . He does not enter with them into a higher synthesis.[19]

Here, then, we see the second locus of Barth's divine ontology in II/1. Whilst he wants to identify God's objectivity (essence) with God's activity (existence), he also wants to distinguish God's being in and for Godself from God's being for us, so as to maintain the "infinite distance" of God from everything else.[20] Barth's intention here is not to renege on his emerging actualism, but to qualify it by suggesting that God's being in decision is an objectivity proper to the free God. "Freedom" he says "is, of course, more than the absence of limits, restrictions, or conditions . . . [F]reedom in its positive and proper qualities means to be grounded in one's own being, to be determined and moved by oneself."[21] So whilst Barth at this stage distinguishes being and historical becoming, he does not wish to divorce the two, as if God could be thought of as a naked substance located arbitrarily above and beyond God's works, as in classical metaphysics. God is not a prisoner of God's own freedom: God is "free also with regard to His own freedom, free not to surrender Himself to it, but to use it and to give Himself communion and to practise this faithfulness in it, in this way being really free, free in Himself."[22]

Barth is striving to say simultaneously that God is, to the depths of God's Godhead, the God who loves humanity, but that God is so freely, i.e. God is free to condition God's own being in favor of humanity, and is not required or compelled externally to do so. He wants to say both that God is absolutely relational, and that God is absolutely unique. He wishes to suggest that the "becoming in which God's being is cannot mean either an augmentation or a diminution of God's being."[23] The editors of the ET of the *Church Dogmatics* observantly located the interpretative key to wrestling with Barth in II/1 when they wrote in the preface, "Barth is concerned

---

19. II/1, 311.

20. Ibid., 311.

21. Ibid., 301.

22. Ibid., 303. See also, Busch, *The Great Passion*, 114; Colwell, *Actuality and Provisionality*, 220.

23. Jüngel, *God's Being Is in Becoming*, xxv.

to correct the scholastic and philosophical separation between the being of God and His actions and attributes, but he is equally careful to avoid the other error which thinks of God's being only in terms of His ways and works, as if it were exhausted in them or passed wholly into them."[24] He is trying to mediate between the "absorption of the doctrine of God into a general ontology or metaphysics of first principles" in pre-critical orthodoxy, and the liberal "hostility towards so-called metaphysical discussion of the being of God."[25] In other words, he endeavors to produce a doctrine of God for the twentieth century that is critically realistic, balancing the relation between objectivity and subjectivity, and being and act, in a way that had eluded his Protestant forebears. But does this "di-polar"[26] theological ontology convince, or is Barth caught between two irreconcilable modes of thinking about the divine reality in relation to human knowing? As we shall see, it is this ongoing tussle between realism and idealism (what Bonhoeffer described as the ontological and transcendental starting points for theology) that lead, on the one hand, to some of the most profound theological contributions of Barth's work, and, on the other hand, to some of the most intractable conflicts within his texts.

Divine Di-polarity: The "Double-Structure" of God's Being, and the Persistence of Participative Tensions in *Church Dogmatics* II/1

Barth proceeds by identifying what Jüngel calls the "double structure"[27] of God's objectivity, parsed through the grammar of event or act. The "primary objectivity" of God is the knowledge of God's identity that God has in and for Godself as Father, Son, and Holy Spirit.[28] Outside of the history of revelation God knows who God is immediately, without need of a form of mediation by which God might come to know the fullness of God's being. God knows Godself as the relationality of the triune communion, and is

24. II/1, viii.

25. Webster, *Barth*, 83–84.

26. To describe Barth's ontology as di-polar is to suggest that Barth is pulled between the statements of God's utter ontic distinction from the world, and God's self-grounded and self-actualized relation to the world. It is to point to the dialectics of being and becoming; being and acting; divine-human distinction and divine-human unity; God's being *in se* and God's being *ad extra*; divine freedom and divine love; as well as divine absoluteness and divine relatedness. See also, Gunton, *Becoming and Being*, 137ff; Colwell, *Actuality and Provisionality*, 217ff.; Jenson, *God after God*, 151.

27. Jüngel, *God's Being Is in Becoming*, 83.

28. II/1, 16; See also, Bromiley, *Introduction to the Theology of Karl Barth*, 58; see also, Jüngel, *God's Being Is in Becoming*, 62.

objectively the immediacy of triune self-loving. God's primary objectivity is therefore

> *self-related* being. As being it is relationally structured . . . [T]he modes of God's being which are differentiated from each other are related to each other in such a way that each mode of God's being *becomes* what it *is* only *with* the two other modes of being.[29]

In God's primary objectivity God is that triune eventfulness which is the "readiness"[30] for humanity before the existence of creation, because as *perichoretic* movement the trinity is the eternal prototype of divine other-relatedness *ad extra*.[31]

God's "secondary objectivity" is "the objectivity which [God] has for us too in His revelation, in which He gives Himself to be known by us as He knows Himself."[32] Secondary objectivity is the form of God's being that God has under the veil of mediation in created reality.[33] The secondary objectivity of God is distinguished from the primary mode "not by a lesser degree of truth, but by its particular form suitable for us, the creature."[34] The distinction between the primary and secondary objectivity of God's triune relationality is designed to maintain that God is objectively in and for Godself the one who *can* become mediated in creaturely reality for the sake of the other, and yet who does not require this form of mediation in and for Godself in order to be God. It seeks to uphold the love and freedom of God in a triune communion. The relation between the two forms of God's triune objectivity are to be interpreted by means of the *analogia relationis*, according to which God's being *in se* is dialectically hidden and revealed.[35] For although God "is" absolutely in the event of God's triune revelation, and therefore reveals the fullness of God's being *ad intra* in the form of God's being *ad extra*, yet God "is" in this event in a hidden form, under the veil of a creaturely objectivity which is foreign to God.[36] God's being *pro nobis* is simultaneously absolutely who God is, and absolutely distinct from who God is. For Molnar we must not attempt to explain this mystery, but must

---

29. Jüngel, *God's Being Is in Becoming*, 77.

30. II/1, §26.1.

31. See also, Gunton, *Becoming and Being*, 131, 167.

32. II/1, 16.

33. Ibid., 16. See also, Bromiley, *Introduction to the Theology of Karl Barth*, 58; and Jüngel, *God's Being Is in Becoming*, 62.

34. II/1, 16.

35. See also, Jüngel, *God's Being Is in Becoming*, 37ff. and 82–83.

36. II/1, 16ff.

accept that it simply "is."³⁷ The paradoxical simultaneity of the complete sufficiency of God's being in and for Godself *without* humanity, and the graceful decision of God only to exist *with* humanity, just "is." It is a fact which is revealed but not explained.³⁸

However, at this point Barth is on the verge of sliding into deep theological ambiguity, and multiple interpretative possibilities open up. Although Barth wants to say that the relation of the trinity *in se* and *ad extra* remains a mystery, even as it is revealed in the *analogia relationis*, he actually begins to say rather a lot more than he had perhaps initially intended. And this is because in II/1 Barth is in transit, shifting from the sharp distinction between the immanent and economic trinity of volume I, towards the much deeper ontological integration of the two as expounded in II/2. As Jones says, Barth is moving between the "ontological reservation" of I/1 in which "God exists as a self-sufficient Subject before, beyond and unrelated to God's self-presentation" and "the contention, dominant from *Church Dogmatics* II onwards, that God wills eternally to be 'with us'; that, more specifically, God orients and determines Godself, *ab initio* and eternally, in terms of a concrete companionship with humankind effected in Jesus Christ."³⁹ So whilst Bromiley says "we cannot speak [of God's primary objectivity] and need not try to do so,"⁴⁰ in fact this is exactly what Barth begins to do from II/1 onwards.

Questions over how to interpret Barth's ontology arise over the possibility of taking the eventfulness or activity of God's primary and secondary objectivity as a single activity.⁴¹ Barth refers to God as *actus purus et singularis*,⁴² and McCormack explains that "to speak of God as *actus purus et singularis* is to say that God has his being in the singularity of an event in history in which God simply *is* the mode of his self-revelation in time."⁴³

---

37. Molnar, *Divine Freedom and the Doctrine of the Immanent Trinity*, 246.
38. See Dempsey, Introduction to *Trinity and Election in Contemporary Theology*, 7
39. Jones, *The Humanity of Christ*, 64–65.
40. Bromiley, *Introduction to the Theology of Karl Barth*, 58.
41. Molnar expressly refuses such an interpretation, suggesting it is unwarranted in the texts. "God's triune existence and his act of self-determination to be God-for-us are *two distinct acts* on the part of the triune God and cannot be conflated" (Molnar, "Can the Electing God Be God Without Us?," 202). See also ibid., 215, where Molnar finds evidence for the double act of God's being in Barth's statement that "There is, for example, the distinction between His willing of Himself and His willing of the possibility and reality of His creation as distinct from Himself" (II/1, 590).
42. II/1, 264.
43. McCormack, "Election and the Trinity," 217–18.

Barth continues: God's being "in His revelation and in eternity is a specific act" (n.b. not two related acts), and God's self-revelation

> does not add a second and extrinsic truth to the first intrinsic truth of His intimate, hidden essence, but . . . is the name and criterion (i.e. the disclosure and description) of His innermost hidden essence . . . The fact that we cannot go behind His livingness for a definition of His being means in fact that we cannot go behind this name of His, because in the very revelation of His name there occurs the act which is His being to all eternity [*die Tat geschieht, die auch sein Sein ist in alle Ewigkeit*].[44]

It would seem that Barth shifts from a position in which the divine economy is ontologically subsequent to the immanent trinity (as God's self-interpretative *Doppelgänger*), and hence a "free" divine decision (in the sense of "non-inevitable"), to a position in which the eventfulness of the triune Godhead is itself the decision in favor of Jesus Christ and therefore the decision *pro nobis*, behind which stands no divine existence or essence; here the freedom of God is delineated as the fact that God alone gives Godself this being, and is therefore sovereign, in control, absolutely self-determined in the eventfulness of God's being as a being-in-becoming. In addition to having two ways of thinking about the immanent-economic relation, Barth also therefore has numerous slightly different ways of conceiving divine freedom. And the transition between one and the other is not clean; Barth's use of the word freedom seems to oscillate between multiple definitions.[45] The implications of this confusion in Barth's divine ontology for a theological anthropology of freedom are major, since the question is whether human flourishing is itself integral to God's eternal self-determination, or whether it is merely a gift which bears no ultimate ontological significance to God's being in and for Godself.

There is not space here to trace the ambiguities of Barth's conception of divine freedom in II/1 in further detail. It must suffice simply to note that despite certain passages in this text where Barth seems to uphold a sharp distinction between the immanent and economic trinity, he seems

---

44. II/1, 272–73 = *KD* II/1, 306–07.

45. So argues Hendry, "The Freedom of God in the Theology of Karl Barth," 229–44. For Hendry, Barth often unwittingly conflates the notions of freedom as i) "gratuity" (ibid., 233); ii) "option, or choice between alternatives" (ibid., 233); iii) "self-determination" (ibid., 234); iv) "initiative" (ibid., 234); v) "energy," by which is meant the eventful, dynamic activity of God's ontic constitution (ibid., 235). "Barth does not observe these distinctions in the meaning of freedom" (236), and the "possibilities of equivocation in the concept" (ibid., 244) often leave the reader puzzled as to the precise nature of Barth's divine ontology.

increasingly ready to relax the disjunction between God's being *in se* and God's being *ad extra* in order to prevent any notion of a metaphysical gap opening up between the two, which would imply an isolated essence of God above and behind God's historical existence. Jones rightly says that Barth "only gestures towards his revolutionary doctrine of election in *Church Dogmatics* II/1. Although II/1 can and should be read as preparatory for the radical moves of II/2, Barth probably had not committed fully to the future trajectory of his thought when writing this part volume."[46] Nonetheless, as McCormack has convincingly argued, "Already in *CD* II/1, intimations of the coming [Christocentric] change are present. The explanation lies in the fact that Barth had begun to rethink the doctrine of election as a consequence of hearing a lecture on the subject by Pierre Maury [in 1936]."[47]

The Doctrine of Election: Beyond Dualism

Trinity, Election, and Divine Freedom: Framing a Debate

So far I have shown that Barth's theological ontology fluctuates somewhat ambiguously between a dialectic of being and becoming: on the one hand Barth says that God's essence is identical with the act in which God's being is in becoming, thus affirming the relationality of God; and on the other hand Barth refuses the claim that God becomes, as if God were ontologically dependent upon or compelled by a reality distinct from Godself for God's sovereign self-determination. In an influential and controversial essay on Barth's doctrine of election, Bruce McCormack framed his interpretation of II/2 by posing the question we have been considering hitherto:

> Does [Barth] merely wish to say that the activity of God the Reconciler is the perfect expression of the divine essence (so that essence precedes act as the ground of the latter)? Or, is he suggesting that the activity of God the Reconciler is in some sense ... constitutive of the divine essence (so that what God is essentially is itself constituted by an eternal act of Self-determination

---

46. Jones, *The Humanity of Christ*, 68. Incidentally, the weakness of Jüngel's trinitarian paraphrase is the failure to indicate, as Jones and others have done more recently, the gradual emergence of Barth's actualism throughout the *Church Dogmatics*. Jüngel therefore does not do justice to the tensions latent in Barth's thought, tending to smooth them over with his own constructive reading.

47. McCormack, "Election and the Trinity," 213-14. See also, II/2, 154-55. Barth did not publish II/1 until 1939, so Maury's influence already began to shape Barth's thinking in II/1 in anticipation of II/2.

for becoming incarnate in time—in which case eternal divine action would ground divine essence)?[48]

Both readings, McCormack notes, would affirm Barth's interest in protecting the sovereignty of God's freedom from external manipulation, since both include the ontological priority of God over creation; both, that is, maintain the distinction between the *logos asarkos* and the *logos ensarkos* thereby insisting that prior to all other realities, God has ontological satisfaction in and for Godself. The question is, though, does Barth modify his earlier Reformed trinitarianism by radically integrating the immanent and economic trinity through the identification of the *logos asarkos* with the *logos incarnandus* (the Word who is going to become incarnate)? According to this position God's being *qua* second person of the trinity is already determined by the will to become Jesus Christ *ad extra*, even before the creation of time and humanity.

This is the central point of contention in the contemporary trinity-election debate, which asks "[i]s the Trinity complete in itself from all eternity and apart from God's determination to become incarnate in Jesus Christ, or is it constituted by the eternal decision of election?"[49] Does Barth move beyond the dualisms of his di-polar doctrine of God, which it has been suggested imply the kind of metaphysical gap between God's essence and God's love for humanity prevalent in the metaphysical traditions in theology and philosophy prior to liberalism? Or does he remain resolute, in critical response to the liberal tradition, that any deep unification of the immanent and economic trinity would betray an unwarranted ontological necessity of humanity to God?

Once again, multiple interpretative possibilities open up here, because Barth seems ambiguously to fluctuate between the two poles of the doctrine of God. So in II/2 Barth can imply i) a clear integration of the immanent and economic trinity:

> we maintain of God that in Himself, in the primal and basic decision in which He wills to be and actually is God, in the mystery of what takes place from and to all eternity within Himself, within His triune being, God is none other than the One who in His Son or Word elects Himself, and in and with Himself elects His people.[50]

---

48. McCormack, "Grace and Being," 96–97.
49. Dempsey, introduction to *Trinity and Election in Contemporary Theology*, 1.
50. II/2, 76.

Or ii) a clear distinction of the being of God *in se* and the being of God *ad extra*: "Once made [the decision of God to relate to humanity] belongs definitively to God Himself, not in His being in and for Himself, but in His being within this relationship."[51]

Trinity, Election, and Divine Freedom: Bruce McCormack

For McCormack, in II/2 Barth moves away from the notion that the divine economy is the perfect analogical expression of the immanent trinity *ad extra* towards the highly original claim that God's triune activity *in se* is itself an act of divine self-determination in which God decides only to exist as the God of humanity. Hence God's being-in-act *ad extra* is the spatio-temporal actualization of God's eternal being as decision *in se*.[52] This transition occurs on the basis of Barth's claim that Jesus Christ is both the object and subject of election, both elect human being and electing God.[53] To name Jesus the subject of election is to suggest that Jesus Christ is not only elect by God as the object of the Son's becoming in time and space, but is in fact the electing subject identical with the second person of the immanent trinity. For McCormack this entails a massive revision of seventeenth-century Reformed theology, which held that the determination of God to become incarnate occurred only on the basis of a prior decision by the triune God.[54] In other words, the being of the trinity preceded the decision of God to become incarnate in Jesus Christ, such that whilst Christ was the object of election, only the trinity *in se*, *qua* abstracted from the history of Jesus Christ, could be described as the subject of election. According to McCormack, Barth names Jesus the subject of election because he became increasingly wary of the metaphysical gap that had opened up between an abstract *logos asarkos* and the decision of God to become the God of humanity; a

---

51. Ibid., 6.

52. By contrast with I/1, then, Barth begins radically to apply "Rahner's rule": the thesis that "The 'economic' Trinity is the 'immanent' Trinity and the 'immanent' Trinity is the 'economic' Trinity" (Rahner, *The Trinity*, 22). McCormack states this explicitly: "the immanent Trinity and the economic Trinity will be identical in content" (McCormack, "Karl Barth's Historicized Christology, 218; see also, Jones, *The Humanity of Christ*, 63). Jüngel, whose own thought was heavily influenced by the increasingly radical elements of Barth's trinitarian scheme, finds that Rahner's rule "should be given unqualified agreement" (Jüngel, *God as the Mystery of the World*, 369–70). Molnar strongly rejects the legitimacy of this thesis, and denies that Barth ever adhered to it, as we shall see below (Molnar, *Divine Freedom and the Doctrine of the Immanent Trinity*, 261–62).

53. II/2, 102; see also, McCormack, "Grace and Being," 93.

54. McCormack, "Grace and Being," 94.

gap which would imply that Jesus Christ's existence is accidental to God's eternal identity.[55] Since Barth's efforts from II/1 onwards to integrate the act of God with God's being were designed to rule out speculation about God's identity, and to permit theological conceptuality solely on the basis of the revelatory fact that God is as God does, he now takes this latter claim to new depths: God *is*, in and for Godself, the one who wills to become the human Jesus Christ. This is not a decision that takes place in posteriority to God's eternal triune identity, but in its depths. "If now Barth wishes to speak of Jesus Christ (and not an abstractly conceived *Logos asarkos*) as the *Subject* of election, he must deny to the Logos a mode or state of being above and prior to the decision to be incarnate in time."[56] Hence the *logos asarkos* is unified with the *logos ensarkos* from all eternity in the triune Godhead as the *logos incarnandus* (the Word of God without flesh is always the Word who wills to become enfleshed). Thus, when the Word becomes incarnate, God is not only revealing Godself in a perfect subjective manifestation of God's prior triune being, but is actualizing in space and time the being that God elected to give Godself from all eternity. Hence the freedom of God to be this God means God is *pro nobis in se* and not merely *ad extra*.

Barth's identification of the *logos asarkos* with the *logos incarnandus* indicates a concern he begins to share with the Lutheran tradition over the Nestorian tendencies of the Reformed *extra Calvinisticum*.[57] Barth became uneasy with a notion of God's essence which could be thought in abstraction from what God the Son achieves in the assumption of flesh *ad extra*; to hold the immanent being of the Son in absolute distinction from the economic work of Christ would be to deny that the life of Jesus has any eternal significance for God, or any true revelatory value for humanity, thereby rendering the incarnation accidental to God's identity. He therefore sought to avoid

> fatal speculation about the being and work of the *logos asarkos*, or a God whom we think we can know elsewhere, and whose divine being we can define from elsewhere than in and from the contemplation of His presence and activity as the Word made flesh.[58]

---

55. For McCormack, God's elective decision in favor of Jesus Christ is not "mere role play; it is a decision with ontological significance" (McCormack, "Karl Barth's Historicized Christology," 216. See also, Jones, *The Humanity of Christ*, 65–66). Here we see Barth taking steps to overcome the complaints lodged against him, explicated in Chapter 1, of the accidence of Jesus Christ's history to the identity of God's triune life.

56. McCormack, "Grace and Being," 94–95.

57. Ibid., 95; see also, Jones, *The Humanity of Christ*, 96.

58. IV/1, 181.

"Being-in-Becoming" 69

Barth articulates his rejection of the *extra Calvinisticum* in "The Way of the Son of God into the Far Country"[59] with a Christological clarification of the doctrine of election. Here he explicitly denies that the incarnation is subsequent or alien to God's second mode of being *in se*, and therefore insists upon a doctrine of immutability in which it is maintained that God is the saving God of humanity from all eternity, to the depths of God's triune being.[60]

In this relation of the second person of the trinity to the man Jesus, McCormack identifies Barth's desire, from the doctrine of election onwards, to collapse the eternal processions (by which the being of God is constituted) and eternal missions (by which God sets Godself into relationship with humanity) into a single eternal event.[61] God's eternal being-in-act *is* the triune setting of Godself in relation to humanity. McCormack suggests that Barth's trinitarian formula has changed significantly since I/1 which identified the three modes of God's being (*Seinsweisen*) with the one-directional, linear subjectivity of God by which knowledge of God becomes possible.[62] Barth no longer thinks of the economic trinity as the mere *Doppelgänger* of the immanent trinity whose sole significance is to give creation knowledge of God. The relation between God's inner being and human existence is not defined in such stark epistemic terms, but takes on deeper ontic and soteriological consequence. "What has changed is that Barth no longer derives his doctrine of the Trinity from the *logic* of revelation (i.e. from the structure of the address of God to the believer) but from the *history* of Jesus Christ, the God-human who exists in the unity of humiliation and exaltation."[63] For this reason the obedience of Jesus Christ is itself related to "an obedience of the one true God Himself in His proper being"[64] and is not "a mere appearance of God."[65] God's being in and for Godself as commanding Father, obedient Son and unifying Spirit is the self-determined communion of the Godhead in which God is already ours in anticipation of the covenant that God wills eternally to establish and fulfill. God "is in and for the world what He is in and for Himself"[66] not simply as a revelatory repetition or re-iteration,

---

59. Ibid., §59.1
60. Ibid., 184ff., esp. 193.
61. McCormack, "Election and the Trinity," 214.
62. Ibid., 214–15.
63. Ibid., 215.
64. IV/1, 200.
65. Ibid., 201.
66. Ibid., 204.

but as the temporal actualization of what God willed to become before the foundation of the world in the obedience of the Son.

> In the work of the reconciliation of the world with God the inward divine relationship between the One who rules and commands in majesty and the One who obeys in humility is identical with the very different relationship between God and one of His creatures, a man. God goes into the far country for this to happen. He becomes what He had not previously been ... But as in His action as Creator, He does not do it apart from its basis in His own being, in His own inner life. He does not do it without any correspondence to, but as the strangely logical final continuation of, the history in which He is God.[67]

The place of Jesus in this soteriologically re-defined trinitarian doctrine is not simply to be the bearer of a revelatory message about God's hidden being, but is one with far deeper ontological significance.[68] Jesus Christ reveals to the extent that He demonstrates and actualizes what God wills to become *qua* second person of the trinity from all eternity: Jesus Christ is the "primal decision of God, and as such the authentic revelation of it."[69] To identify the history of the incarnation as the "strangely logical final continuation" of God's triune being is, for Jones, to present "an ontological narrative that describes God's free self-constitution as the incarnate Son."[70] In this narrative, the beginning, middle and end are eternally simultaneous, where "God's pre-temporal intention to convey Godself in human history," God's temporal unification of Godself *qua* Son with the human Jesus, and Christ's post-temporal "'session' at the right hand of God the Father" are mutually implicated in an act of graceful divine self-determination. "Indeed, the end ... becomes the beginning."[71] This ontological narrative makes the historicity of Christ's life proper to God's self-identification in a way that the earlier theology was unable to achieve, and it therefore affirms the divinity of Christ where the revelatory trinitarian model risked jeopardizing this, and where the early theology unwittingly posited a dualism between the human and divine lives. The soteriological history of Christ's journey towards Calvary becomes the spatio-temporal actualization of the Son's eternal obedience to

---

67. Ibid., 205.

68. See II/2, 157.

69. Ibid., 91. The election of humanity to relations with God in Jesus Christ is "proper to the will of God in virtue of the decision made between Father and Son from all eternity" (ibid., 90).

70. Jones, *The Humanity of Christ*, 93.

71. Ibid., 93–94.

the Father in a manner that binds up human being into the event of God's own self-determination:[72] "obediently, the Son lives and dies in a way that actualizes God's decision to exist in loving fellowship with humankind."[73]

The ontological, narrative correspondence of the passionate history of Christ and the eternal history of the Son allows Barth to deny the thought of a naked, absolute divine sovereignty which results from the sharp distinction of the immanent and economic trinity: "There is no such thing as Godhead in itself."[74] The triune Godhead is, to the depths of its eternal identity, that decision, that act of command, obedience and fellowship, by which "from all eternity, in an act of unconditional self-determination" God ordains Godself the bearer of the divine-human name Jesus Christ:[75]

> In Jesus Christ He has chosen man from all eternity as His own ... In Him He has bound Himself to us, before He bound us to Himself, and before we bound ourselves to Him ... In Him, the everlasting Son, He has recognised us as His servants from and to all eternity ... Jesus Christ Himself is the divine pre-decision, made in God's eternal decree and at the heart of time.[76]

And for McCormack this equates to the controversial proposition that election must logically precede trinity.[77] This is not an ontological or chronological claim.[78] The distinction between substance or essence and event can exist only for those who suffer the discontinuities of time, but since God's pre-temporal, supra-temporal and post-temporal eternity embraces temporal distinctions without itself enduring temporal disjunctions,[79] God's being and God's act cannot be thought in abstraction from each other. God *is* act. As Jenson explains,

---

72. Jones, "Obedience, Trinity, and Election," 148.
73. Ibid., 149. See also, Jüngel, *God's Being Is in Becoming*, 98–103.
74. II/2, 115.
75. Ibid., 100.
76. Ibid., 736–37.
77. McCormack, "Grace and Being," 101–2.
78. Ibid., 101.
79. See II/1, 609ff. Barth wants simultaneously to differentiate God's eternal, immutable and sovereign being from finite, creaturely existence, whilst also refusing the notion of God's life simply as an abstract "negation of time *simpliciter*" (ibid., 613). He therefore describes God's being as the complete and perfect possession of unending life (ibid., 610), which includes the drama of history within itself as the simultaneity of past, present and future. This allows Barth to retain the ontological priority of God's being over creation, whilst also saying that "eternity is planned around ... Jesus" (Jüngel, *God's Being Is in Becoming*, 96. See also, Ford, *Barth and God's Story*, 141).

> The difference between an event and a substance is given by the discontinuity of time. What we mean by a substance . . . is the something that we posit to provide continuity of a series of successive and so temporally separated events. *As* distinct from what I do, "I" am a "something we know not what" that bridges the temporal discontinuities of the various things I do. But precisely the absence of such discontinuities is what distinguishes God from us—and therefore the dichotomy between an event and its agent or sufferer does not apply to God.[80]

Human decision-making implies a temporal structure, and a discontinuity between being and act that does not apply to the eternally active being of God. Human being involves deliberation between various alternative possibilities prior to action; the deliberation native to human being is "an attempt to think through the consequences of available alternatives before acting. The 'before' in this statement reflects the fact that human decision-making is temporally structured."[81] Since, however, God does not suffer the discontinuities of time, God's being is identical with God's act.

> God's freedom does not consist . . . in a choice between alternatives . . . It requires "time" for deliberation in order to be meaningful. God's freedom, by contrast, is a freedom *for* time. It is not a freedom which presupposes time. God's freedom is finally the freedom to exist—or not to exist. The opposite of the determination to be God in the covenant of grace is not a determination to be God in some other way; it is rather the absence of such a determination, which would mean choosing not to exist.[82]

For this reason there can be no "before" or "after" when thinking of election and trinity.[83] To speak, as McCormack does, of a "logical" precedence of election over trinity is to indicate that for the purposes of human thought we must order the relation of act and being.[84] To name the logical

---

80. Jenson, *God after God*, 126.

81. McCormack, "Election and Trinity," 222.

82. Ibid., 223. Busch makes the same point: "God did not originally exist in a state of (indecisive) rest, in order then to make this choice later! God's being is in this act, and in this act God 'is' (II/1, 260)" (Busch, *The Great Passion*, 114). On this basis we are ruling out the possibility of defining divine freedom as the choice between alternatives (identified by Hendry, "The Freedom of God in the Theology of Karl Barth," 233). God does not need to deliberate what kind of God to become. God simply is what God wills to be; there is no uncertainty in God, no eternal wavering between various possibilities. God's power is Christologically and trinitarianally definite, not eternally indeterminate.

83. McCormack, "Grace and Being," 101.

84. Ibid., 101.

precedence of election over trinity is simply to say that God's triune life *in se* is a freely self-determined essence in perfect continuity with God's will.[85] God's being as Father, Son and Holy Spirit is, from and to all eternity, constituted by or simultaneous with God's triune desire to exist in covenantal fellowship with humanity, in and through the sounding of the name Jesus Christ.

This reading of the doctrine of election, promulgated chiefly by McCormack, has the advantage of overcoming, to a large extent, the ontological reserve and consequent sense of divine-human opposition that haunted the earlier works. It does so by uniting the objectivity and subjectivity of God in the eternal subjectivity of Christ's election, and it fulfils Bonhoeffer's desire—identified in Chapter 1—that divine freedom be defined not in terms of God's "eternally remaining within the divine self, aseity," but as the free decision of God *in se* "to be bound to historical human beings and to be placed at the disposal of human beings. God is free not from human beings but for them. Christ is the word of God's freedom. God *is* present, that is, not in an eternal nonobjectivity but . . . 'haveable', graspable in the Word within the Church."[86]

Trinity, Election, and Divine Freedom: Paul Molnar and George Hunsinger

It is precisely this concept of divine freedom and McCormack's interpretation of the doctrine of election that commentators such as Molnar and Hunsinger have argued forcefully against. For Molnar, McCormack's position is neither theologically tenable nor textually warranted.[87] Molnar contends

---

85. Nimmo explains that this logical ordering indicates that "the eternal act of election as an act of self-determination is primal and there is no triunity behind or without it" (Nimmo, "Barth and the Election-Trinity Debate," 173).

86. Bonhoeffer, *Act and Being*, 90–91.

87. Indeed, there is—at least ostensibly—ample evidence even in Barth's later texts to support Molnar's position, and McCormack is forced to accept that "even after his mature doctrine of election was in place, he continued to make statements which created the space for an independent doctrine of the Trinity; a triune being of God which was seen as independent of the covenant of grace" (McCormack, "Grace and Being," 102). For instance, Barth says "In Himself and as such [God] is not *Deus pro nobis*, either ontologically or epistemologically" (IV/1, 52; see also, Molnar, *Divine Freedom and the Doctrine of the Immanent Trinity*, 62). McCormack, it should be noted, has countered Molnar and Hunsinger by questioning the textual basis for Molnar's strict separation of the *logos asarkos* and *logos incarnandus*, stating that the latter has made no attempt to explain the key claim of II/2 that Jesus Christ (not the *logos asarkos*) is the "subject" of election, and not merely its object (McCormack, "Seek God Where He

that Barth quite rightly upheld a "clear and sharp distinction" between the immanent and economic trinity throughout the *Church Dogmatics*.[88] The immanent-economic distinction serves to protect God's freedom to be God without humanity, and therefore God's freedom from external conditioning.[89] Molnar insists that if God's eternal essence in and for itself were defined by the act of election, then God would be ontologically dependent upon a reality external to Godself "in precisely the Hegelian way that he recognises is so mistaken in this regard."[90] McCormack's thesis "binds the being of God to the world in a way that Barth would never have allowed."[91] For Molnar, whilst God becomes related to humanity *ad extra*, God's being *in se* as Father, Son and Holy Spirit is in no way determined by this relation, but is eternally self-sufficient.[92] God's free decision to relate to humanity is graceful precisely because God did not have to elect and create another in order to be God, but chose to do so purely for the sake of humanity.[93] This other-relatedness is a possibility because of whom God is in and for Godself, but it is not ontologically determinative of God's being *in se*. God's triune life *ad extra* is an over-flowing of God's relationality *in se*, and not *vice versa*. Hence Molnar upholds the interpretation of God's economy as a perfect self-interpretative correspondence to God's immanent being, but refuses to attribute any deeper ontological relation between the two, lest he sacrifice Barth's basic commitment to God's sovereign freedom as ontic independence. In fact, for Molnar there is a clear ontological and logical priority of God's immanent triune Godhead over God's decision for and actualization of the economic presence.[94] It is the ontic freedom of God to be God without us, in and for Godself, against which we must view the positive

---

May Be Found," 62).

88. Molnar, *Divine Freedom and the Doctrine of the Immanent Trinity*, 64; see also, Molnar, "The Trinity, Election, and God's Ontological Freedom," 295.

89. Molnar, "Can the Electing God be God Without Us?," 214.

90. Molnar, *Divine Freedom and the Doctrine of the Immanent Trinity*, 64.

91. Dempsey, introduction to *Trinity and Election in Contemporary Theology*, 8.

92. Molnar refuses to "run the risk of reducing God's eternal being as triune to a function of his decisions to act *ad extra* and his subsequent actions *ad extra* . . . [which] would in reality make God a prisoner of his electing to be God-for-us" (Molnar, "Can the Electing God be God Without Us?," 211).

93. See Molnar, "Can the Electing God be God without Us?," 203; Molnar, "The Trinity, Election, and God's Ontological Freedom," 297–99; Molnar, *Divine Freedom and the Doctrine of the Immanent Trinity*, 63.

94. Molnar, "The Trinity, Election, and God's Ontological Freedom," 305. So argues Hunsinger, "Election and the Trinity," 181. God's decision to become *logos incarnandus* is the first of God's ways and works *ad extra* and is not itself constitutive of God's second mode of being *in se*.

freedom of God's choice *ad extra* not to be God without us after all.[95] God's freedom *from* humanity is the ground of God's free choice *for* humanity; a choice which is ontologically unnecessary for God and precisely as such a *loving* choice. God is not bound by an eternal need for humanity.[96]

Whilst there is ample evidence in Barth's texts to support what Nimmo has usefully labelled the "strong" (McCormack) and "weak" (Molnar and Hunsinger) interpretations of Barth on the trinity and election,[97] it is the contention of this study that it is a "strong" reading of Barth in line with McCormack that is generative for a contemporary theology of divine and human freedom. Given the lack of consistency in Barth's mature writing, which we have seen fluctuates between multiple conceptions of freedom and multiple ontological poles, it must be acknowledged that "the full implications of his more radical work only penetrate his constructive work in an inconsistent and fragmentary way."[98] Nevertheless, "certain crucial moments" in Barth's theology advocate a "strong" reading,[99] representing a deliberate effort on Barth's part to overcome the sense of divine-human opposition prevalent in the earlier works, and to integrate being and act, and object and subject in a more thoroughgoing manner than had been possible on the basis of his heavily "critical," neo-Kantian theological epistemology. Barth's early ambivalence towards divine being, and the strong separation of divine primary objectivity from the event of human knowing, had resulted in a sense of the accidence of Christ's human history to the divine identity, and therefore of the arbitrariness of God's attitude towards humanity. The advantage of the "strong" reading is that it accounts for Barth's Christocentric attempts, after II/2, to redress the object-subject balance in light of the earlier one-sided favor of the subjective category, and the consequent commitment to "the abstract metaphysical subject of Chalcedon."[100] In short, this reading suggests that Barth comes increasingly to realize the importance of affirming the ontological depth of God's love for humanity, as well as the ontic significance of God's subjective actualization of the divine identity in the covenantal history elected by God from all eternity.[101] This

---

95. Molnar, "Can the Electing God be God Without Us?," 220–21.

96. Ibid., 220–21.

97. These descriptors do not refer to the theological adequacy of each argument, but merely serve to indicate the "relative perceived 'radicality' of the respective readings" (Nimmo, "Barth and the Election-Trinity Debate," 163).

98. Ibid., 177.

99. Ibid., 172.

100. McCormack, "Karl Barth's Historicized Christology," 206; see also, Jones, *The Humanity of Christ*, 65–66.

101. As McCormack has said, Barth spent a long theological apprenticeship

reading refuses a dualism between God's prevenient, self-constituted activity *in se* and God's spatio-temporal becoming *ad extra*.

A "strong" reading also refuses certain dualistic tendencies that arise on the "weak" reading when God's eternal being-in-act is described in terms of "two distinct acts."[102] Molnar rejects what he sees as McCormack's identification of eternity with election, saying that "while God's self-determination to be for us is a decision made by God 'from all eternity,' as Barth says, that does not mean there is nothing more to God's eternity than that decision."[103] If, however, eternity is a predicate of God's immutable being, and if God's immutable freedom to love humanity is secured in terms of God's pure duration which is the simultaneity of beginning, succession and end, it is difficult to see what Barth might intend to describe by the eternity of God's self-determination other than that there is no point in God's triune life above or behind God's self-determination as the God of humanity. Even if one accepts that the mystery of God's eternal being admits a dialectical simultaneity of God's eternal being apart from humanity and God's eternal being for humanity,[104] one cannot help feeling that this would rather divorce ontologically God's triune being from the history of Jesus Christ, and therefore human history from God's history (dualistic dangers Barth surely would not have wished to admit). If it is "eternally necessary that the Son be *asarkos*, but eternally contingent that he also be *ensarkos*"[105] then it must be said that God is eternally ambivalent towards the history of Christ; the incarnation is a matter of supreme divine insignificance. Once made this decision stands; but it matters not one iota to God's identity whether or not the decision is made in the first place.

Moreover, to posit eternity as the dialectical existence of God's being without us and God's being for us is to make nonsense of Barth's theological intentions when he united God's being and God's act. That move was made to refuse metaphysical speculation about God's being, and to refuse the abstractness of an infinitely transcendent being of God *in se*.[106] It was precisely Barth's increased endeavors to integrate being and act, objectivity and subjectivity, that were designed to overcome the metaphysical traditions in philosophy and theology, which had rendered knowledge of God

---

working towards this radically revised (and often inconsistently expressed) theological ontology. McCormack, "Karl Barth's Historicized Christology," 206; McCormack, "Election and the Trinity," 213.

102. Molnar, "Can the Electing God be God Without Us?," 202.

103. Molnar, "The Trinity, Election, and God's Ontological Freedom," 301.

104. Hunsinger, "Election and the Trinity," 194–95.

105. Ibid., 191.

106. See McCormack, "Election and the Trinity," 210.

impossible, and which therefore encouraged the erroneous reaction of the liberal theologians, who reduced God's being to God's historical immanence. Barth's theological ontology makes sense only when it is read as the attempt to unite the being of God *in se* with the historical actualization of God's love for humanity *ad extra*. Where Molnar and Hunsinger (and occasionally Barth himself) continue to speak of God's triune being "prior" to the eternal decision of God to relate to humanity, it seems to me that they slip into the kind of dualistic speculation that Barth wished increasingly to refuse. Such speculation attempts to think the primary objectivity of God in abstraction from the historical subjectivity of God by which alone it may be thought; but as McCormack questions, "how can [anyone] *know* that God is triune in and for himself, independent of his eternal will to be revealed?"[107]

If, as has been argued here, Barth does wish to integrate God's eternally free self-determination *in se* and God's desire for fellowship with humanity *ad extra*, does he not admit the necessity of creation to God in a manner that his theology of divine freedom had hitherto assiduously attempted to avoid?[108] I suggest not. While a distinction between the *logos asarkos* and *logos ensarkos* is necessary (for clearly God's being precedes creation, and obviously the *logos* did not come to earth already in possession of a body and soul: the historical person of Jesus began to be in a particular space and time),[109] yet Barth wants to affirm the *logos asarkos* only in the sense of a *logos incarnandus*. Barth wishes to show that God's triune pre-eminence is the sole ontic ground for all realities, including God's own. God is not subject to the control or influence of any other being, but exists only in the manner freely determined by Godself. Yet God is not other than the one who decides to determine Godself in the event of God's temporal becoming (and this decision does not require some sort of temporal annex within God's eternity in which God may deliberate). God does not need to exist as another than the God of humanity before God's pre-temporal decision to elect humanity in Jesus Christ in order to be free. For such an argument conflates a negative concept of freedom ("that which might have been otherwise") with a positive account ("that which freely determines itself in this manner").[110]

---

107. McCormack, "Grace and Being," 102.

108. So argue exponents of the "weak" interpretation against those of the "strong" reading. See, Molnar, *Divine Freedom and the Doctrine of the Immanent Trinity*, 64; Molnar, "Can the Electing God be God Without Us?," 220–21; Molnar, "The Trinity, Election, and God's Ontological Freedom," 297ff.; Hunsinger, "Election and the Trinity," 192f; van Driel, "Karl Barth on the Eternal Existence of Jesus Christ," 54.

109. McCormack, "Grace and Being," 96.

110. Barth seems to reject this conflation, when he says that the incarnation "takes place in the freedom of God, but in the inner necessity of the freedom of God and not

Molnar sees the former as the appropriate ground of the latter;[111] but once one has articulated the positive claim that God alone has the eternal power to determine all reality, including God's own, there is little need to fear the necessity of creation to God. Creation is necessary to God only insofar as God freely determines, in the power identical with God's being-in-act, to be this God, the God of Jesus Christ and no other.[112] No loss of control is permitted here: "Who has the initiative in this relationship? Who has the precedence? Who decides? Who rules? God, always God."[113] As Nimmo articulates, such a view of the elective power of God suggests that "God is Lord to such an extent that God is Lord over the very being and essence of God."[114] There is no space above and beyond the trinity where God deliberates whether or not to become the God of Jesus Christ. Jones quite rightly asks, therefore, "why presume that God being ontologically "pure"—that is, God being a being who never takes leave of his pre-temporal state—forms a necessary correlate to God's ontological priority?"[115]

Given the Christocentric election of humanity to eternal participation in the self-determined, covenantal being of God it now becomes possible to turn for the first time to Barth's understanding of *human* freedom, which is grounded in God's radically deep freedom for humanity.

Human Freedom as Being-in-Becoming: Flourishing in Christ

The Significance of the Doctrine of Election

Barth's theological ethics flows naturally from his doctrine of election, since the election of Jesus Christ is both an election of God to God's own freedom, and the election of humanity to its secondary and derivative freedom.[116] For

---

in the play of a sovereign *liberum arbitrium*. There is no possibility of something quite different happening" (IV/1, 195).

111. Molnar denies Hector's claim that he has confused "God's freedom with an abstract account of freedom as absolute independence" (Hector, "God's Triunity and Self-Determination," 257).

112. See, Nimmo, "Barth and the Election-Trinity Debate," 179.

113. II/2, 177.

114. Nimmo, *Being in Action*, 8. For Jones, Molnar actually risks "*inhibiting* God's freedom" by refusing to accept that God has the freedom and the power to condition Godself eternally as triune Godhead by means of "a particular action in the creaturely sphere" (Jones, *The Humanity of Christ*, 69).

115. Jones, *The Humanity of Christ*, 92.

116. Nimmo observes that Barth's ethical methodology underwent a fundamental

Barth, Christian ethics belongs not only to the doctrines of creation and reconciliation, but primarily to the doctrine of God, because it is God's free *self*-determination in Jesus Christ for covenantal fellowship with creation that also determines humanity as those who are, from all eternity, elected to responsibility before God.[117] Humans are elected "subjects" in the encounter with God which is ordained at the primal depths of God's triune eventfulness.[118] This election grounds Barth's entire anthropology of freedom, since "outside the encounter between God and humanity it is not theologically meaningful to speak of humanity at all."[119] What is more, since the election of this eternally-willed, covenantal determination occurs not in general, but concretely in Christ, it is theologically untenable to speak of humanity in abstraction from Christ.[120] We can neither understand true divinity nor true humanity other than as they are actualized in relation to one another in and through Jesus Christ.[121]

The ontological significance of God's Christological being-in-becoming for human subjects should not be underestimated; the event of God's being made known to human subjects is the event in which God takes humanity into God's own being. For Jüngel revelation therefore characterizes a profound "intensification" of being:

> The correspondence between person (mind) [*als intellectus*] and reality [*Wirklichkeit*], which occurs in all true knowledge, means, in the case of knowledge *of God*, a gain to being which at the level of practice makes *more possible* in the actuality of the

---

revision in 1936 with the decision to "recast his doctrine of election Christocentrically," since, by contrast with the *Ethics* of Münster and Bonn (1928–1931) (See Barth, *Ethics*), Barth now grounded his understanding of human flourishing and the ordering of creation by God both ontically and noetically in Christology. (Nimmo, "The Orders of Creation in the Theological Ethics of Karl Barth," 24–35 (esp. 32–33).

117. We are responsible to God only because God "makes Himself originally responsible for [humanity]" (II/2, 509). See Nimmo, *Being in Action*, 11; Gunton, *The Barth Lectures*, 125; Webster, *Barth*, 154; Webster, *Barth's Ethics of Reconciliation*, 62; Macken, *The Autonomy Theme*, 56.

118. See Macken, *The Autonomy Theme*, 43.

119. Webster, *Barth's Ethics of Reconciliation*, 69. Indeed, this primary encounter between God and humanity forms the basis of human inter-subjectivity in a wider sense, since for Barth we are beings in encounter: "There is no 'pure subject' apart from encounter . . . Human essence is, then, mutual determination in freedom" (Gorringe, *Karl Barth against Hegemony*, 200).

120. Macken, *The Autonomy Theme*, 43.

121. Jüngel, *Karl Barth*, 129–30.

world than that actuality is capable of granting to itself. If God's being is in becoming, then for us, too, more is possible.[122]

In other words, God's being-in-becoming actualizes the event of our becoming the subjects of God, which itself entails our correspondence with the depths of elected reality. And this correspondence of knowledge and being is brought about with an immeasurable intensity, since the reality being made known is the ontological unity of God and humanity which existed before the foundation of the universe. The freedom of the human subject is therefore the supreme liberty given by God through attraction into the knowledge of God, which is ultimately knowledge of the covenant, of eternal divine-human encounter.

Placing an account of human freedom under the ontological rubric of divine election critically resists capitulation to an anthropocentric Enlightenment model by transferring the center of human dignity away from the unbridled choice of the absolute human subject, and locating it in the eternally determinative, graceful choice of God (*Erwählung, Gottes Gnadenwahl*). Hence human freedom is autonomy only to the extent that "it is a *given* one, shaped and . . . determined by God."[123] Corresponding to God's free choice is a free human choice consisting in the fact that "for his part, man can and actually does elect God."[124] The responsibility given to human subjects "is certainly freedom of choice. But as freedom given by God, as freedom in action, it is the freedom of a right choice . . . What does the free man choose? He chooses himself to fulfil this responsibility."[125]

Command and Obedience

The truly free human choice, then, is not spontaneous self-authorization, but obedient response to a command.[126] As Webster notes, "taken at face value the term 'command' seems in danger of grounding human action in a purely heteronomous divine will."[127] How is it that Barth thinks an anthropology of freedom can arise through the explication of a *command*, that which seems to rob humanity precisely of its freedom? The reason,

---

122. Jüngel, *God's Being Is in Becoming*, 139 = *Gottes Sein ist im Werden*, 138.

123. Gunton, "Barth, the Trinity, and Human Freedom," 320.

124. II/2, 177. See also, Nimmo, *Being in Action*, 113.

125. III/2, 197.

126. Barth therefore places his ethics in the doctrine of God under the title "The Command of God" (II/2, chap. VIII).

127. Webster, *Barth*, 155.

once again, lies in the centrality of the divine-human encounter to Barth's theological ontology. Barth sought deliberately to resist what he saw as the spiritual vacuity of a concept of freedom without the concrete limitations of a divinely determined "moral space."[128] The moral space defined by Barth is "an account of what the good *is*, rather than is *chosen* or *desired* to be."[129] Within this space, God encounters humanity at the deepest depths of reality, and sets their existence in relation to God's desire for fellowship, a desire which forms the boundary and Archimedean point of human purpose. Barth contends we ought to "divest ourselves of the idea that limitation implies something derogatory, or even a curse or affliction. When the reference is to the limitation which comes from God, limitation is not a negation but the most positive affirmation . . . God limits [the creature] to be His creature and thus gives it its specific and genuine reality."[130] Without this encounter between the divine "I" and human "Thou"[131] the human subject lacks the moral space from which it derives its integrity. Barth refers here to the Titanism of Fichte's absolute idealism, against which he throws his own theological anthropology into relief.[132] According to Barth, it is because Fichte lacks a divine subject that he collapses the limitations by which humans are liberated, championing the infinite self-projection of the boundless Ego, and finding in return that the self has become a prisoner of its own subjectivity.[133] Fichte's "true man" is "inconsolably poor" just "at the point which constitutes his remarkable wealth. He has no limits."[134] This human subject "is self-enclosed, self-sufficient, confined to its own resources."[135] So it is that Barth finds that the post-Kantian rhetoric of absolute free will and

---

128. Here Webster follows the language employed by Charles Taylor in *Sources of the Self*, 3–4. Barth sees as pernicious the tendency in the modern Western moral tradition to view the flourishing agent as the one who transcends nature through spirit in the realm of "deliberative consciousness or spontaneous action" (Webster, *Barth's Ethics of Reconciliation*, 215). The result of that tradition, as Taylor has observed, was to dispossess ethical agents of a "moral ontology" or "moral space" against which our moral judgments might be interpreted (Taylor, *Sources of the Self*, 3).

129. Webster, *Barth's Ethics of Reconciliation*, 216; 227.

130. III/4, 567.

131. Ibid., 567.

132. See III/2, 96–109. See also, Macken, *The Autonomy Theme*, 47–50; Gorringe, *Karl Barth against Hegemony*, 198.

133. III/2, 108–9; see also, Macken, *The Autonomy Theme*, 50.

134. III/2, 103.

135. Ibid., 104. Bonhoeffer had a similar critique of Fichte in *Act and Being*, 39; 44: "The boundlessness of the claim of thinking turns into its exact opposite. Thinking languishes in itself; precisely where it is free from the transcendent, from reality, there it is imprisoned in itself."

absolute self-determination "has nothing to do with permission, freedom and joy. It is in his free will that [the human subject] is tricked and tricks himself out of all this."[136] Employing one of his favorite images, Barth reminds us that the free human is not like "Hercules at the cross-roads":[137]

> we cannot understand the ethical question as the question of human existence as if it were posed in a vacuum . . . as if it were not first posed by the grace of God—and not only posed but already answered by the grace of God . . . We cannot act as if we had to ask and decide for ourselves what the good is and how we can achieve it; as if we were free to make this or that answer as the one that appears to us to be right.[138]

All this is to say that the command of God is not autocratic hegemony by an abstract and transcendent power, but rather has the character of "permission—the granting of a very definite freedom."[139] And it is this characterization of command and obedience that concretely resists the viability of casuistry for Barth.[140] We are constituted as ethical subjects not as those in possession of an abstract list of rules to be followed, but as those bound up in an address and summons by the living Word of God.[141] Scripture forms a narrative witnessing to the obedience of its central characters to God's Word. Because this narrative is alive in and through the contemporaneous life of Christ and the Spirit, we are implicated in the moral universe of its stories, called to be disciples of the living Christ.[142] Casuistry destroys human freedom by depicting the command of God as a universal rule, as opposed to a living encounter between the loving God and the freely obedient human subject.[143]

For this reason, Barth depicts the command of God as simultaneously Gospel and Law.[144] The good news, delivered by the Word, that God wills for us to be God's creatures, and that in Christ God accepts us in spite of all our

---

136. II/2, 594. See also, Nimmo, *Being in Action*, 116

137. II/2, 517. See also, Barth, "The Gift of Freedom," 73; IV/2, 494; IV/3, 449; 665; IV/4, 204.

138. II/2, 518.

139. Ibid., 585.

140. Gorringe, *Karl Barth against Hegemony*, 209; See Biggar, *The Hastening that Waits*, 12; 40–45 for a critical engagement with Barth's refusal of casuistry.

141. III/2, 150; Gorringe, *Karl Barth against Hegemony*, 199.

142. Werpehowski, "Narrative and Ethics in Barth," 342.

143. III/4, 13.

144. II/2, 511. See also, Nimmo, *Being in Action*, 22–23; Busch, *The Great Passion*, 158.

creaturely sinfulness, comes with a definite instruction to obey a specific Law: "it is a command which requires us to be what the gospel declares that we are."[145] And since God became human in Jesus Christ, it is there that real humanity is revealed. It is in Christ's becoming that humanity becomes most fully itself. Hence, all we have to do in order to obey the Law is to accept our own election, justification, and sanctification in Christ.[146]

Human Freedom and the Question of Determinism

At this point it is worth pausing to parse Barth's ostensibly awkward placement of human autonomy under the rubric of divine determination, and to consider whether his refusal to construe human freedom as contra-causal freedom is fundamentally incoherent in light of his affirmation that self-determination is basic to humanity.[147] Since Barth himself was not concerned with constructing a systematic response to the problem of determinism or clarifying his work philosophically, careful reconstruction is needed to assess his positions. Given that Barth deliberately resists any Pelagian or Enlightenment attempt to authenticate the language of praise and blame by identifying human freedom with uninhibited choice or absolute autonomy,[148] one might ask whether he risks expunging any genuine sense of human agency and, with it, any meaningful speech about ethical responsibility.

Two related potential anxieties about the loss, in Barth's work, of the human's freedom to have done otherwise require attention. The first is Barth's apparent unconcern with the philosophical question of causal determinism and its implications for human free will: this is the view that, given the laws of nature, every event can be described as the necessary causal outcome of the preceding state of the universe, such that from the beginning of time and space all occurrences are inevitable. If this is true for every event, then it is also true for human actions, and hence no human action could have been otherwise. The second is the theological question of whether God's eternity precludes, rather than grounds, human freedom by requiring all historical events to corroborate the divine foreknowledge.

Since Barth himself admits that we must be ready to concede that the fact of human self-determination and absolute divine lordship is

---

145. Webster, *Barth*, 155–56.
146. II/2, 588.
147. III/3, 188–89; see Webster, "Freedom in Limitation," 100–102.
148. Gunton, "Barth, the Trinity, and Human Freedom," 320.

a deep mystery,[149] and that "necessity and contingence" are "universal antinomies,"[150] commentators might be forgiven for reaching the conclusion that he is either unable, or uninterested in trying, to resolve the dichotomy. But on closer inspection it emerges that Barth clearly signals how his entire theological project is a re-conceptualization of the covenant in actualistic terms which is designed to subvert those intellectual traditions which erroneously construed human freedom as a metaphysical capacity to be secured theoretically over against divine agency.

Barth's tacit response to the apparent loss of human freedom entailed by the possibilities of causal determinism and theological determinism involves an insistence that freedom is non-theorizable in abstraction from its occurrence.[151] He thinks it deeply mistaken to gloss self-determination as naked indeterminateness, and then to discover deductively either that God and humanity are thereby mutually jeopardized, or that metaphysical speculation about the nature of causality would rupture meaningful speech about human agency. By contrast, he insists that we ought to re-train our theological habits of thought to appreciate a properly Christian account of divine and human freedom by increasing our attention to the "factual relationship" between God and humanity. All attempts to define the divine and human natures *a priori* and in abstraction from the history of the covenant, before commencing in speculation about how these two seemingly irreconcilable identities might be rendered compatible are bound to fail.[152] Barth therefore attempts to resolve the apparent incoherence between human self-determination and divine determinism *descriptively* rather than *theoretically*, and in theological rather than metaphysical terms.[153]

This descriptive approach to metaphysical questions emerges from the methodology of the *Church Dogmatics*, which, according to Hans Frei, refuses to correlate theology to other intellectual disciplines.[154] Theology, first and foremost, is Christian self-description. It makes no apology for the foundational belief in the truth of God and the testimony of Scripture to God's living, revelatory presence in human history, and therefore consists in service to a Church whose accountability is to God for its discourse about God.[155] What is more, as the critical self-description and self-examination

149. III/3, 191.
150. Ibid., 187.
151. Webster, "Freedom in Limitation," 102.
152. Ibid., 103; see III/3 189.
153. Webster, "Freedom in Limitation," 101–2.
154. Frei, *Types of Christian Theology*, 39.
155. Ibid., 39.

of the Christian community, theology is not obliged to respond to questions posed by philosophy either as a "conceptual system referring to 'reality'" or "as a set of formal, universal rules or criteria for what may count as coherent and true in Christian discourse as in every other kind of conceptual practice."[156] Consequently, Barth insists that the theologian is under no obligation to offer a formal philosophical response to causal determinism, or the problem of materialism entailed by it, because such conceptions play absolutely no part in biblical thinking whatsoever.[157] Barth accepts, as a matter of faith and as a prolegomenon to theological discourse, that the biblical testimony to human acting and creaturely occurrence is primary and need not be absorbed into any external philosophical conceptuality. Since the Bible embraces and affirms human contingency and agency as a basic feature of the actual, historical encounter between God and humans—revealed primarily in the Gospel's portrayal of Jesus Christ as a genuine human agent in full possession of the simple autonomy of the creature[158]—Barth sees no need to enter into an apologetic response to any traditions in philosophy and science that would portray human choice and responsibility as illusory.[159]

Given Barth's theological method, and since the Christian doctrine of providence is a matter of faith, grounded on the Word of God as revealed through Scripture, the orders of cosmic occurrence cannot be viewed as a matter of general hypothesis, or available to systematic construction through speculative inference about historical and natural processes.[160] Once the Christian has accepted in faith that everything which may happen in the history of created being has to do with God, it is impossible to go above or behind that faith and imagine or observe the causal realm from a neutral philosophical or scientific standpoint.[161] "A free and secular

---

156. Ibid., 40.

157. See, for example, III/3, 123–24; III/2, 383.

158. See Nimmo, "Karl Barth and the *concursus Dei*," 59.

159. Indeed, Barth was relatively unconcerned with any atheistic claims regarding the impossibility of speaking of God or of the human as a creature of God because atheism is merely a "rash variant" of religion in which human beings "blurt out" what religion tends to conceal; namely, that when approached on the basis of human efforts in abstraction from revelation it is quite impossible to speak meaningfully of God. Atheism and general philosophy merely serve to prove the insufficiency of natural theology. See Krötke, "The humanity of the human person in Karl Barth's anthropology," 161; and *ChrL*, 128ff.

160. III/3, 16–17.

161. Ibid., 18–21. As Tanner observes, when Barth discusses creation and providence he is not discussing nature in contrast to grace, (Tanner, "Creation and Providence," 113); to attempt to offer a general metaphysical defense against causal determinism before securing the freedom of the creature would be, in Barth's view,

creaturely occurrence, standing in a neutral relation to [God's covenantal presence and action] is quite inconceivable in the context of biblical thought and perception."[162] All human conceptions of one's place in history and of the nature of the cosmic process itself—whether theological, political, social, moral or metaphysical—are limited by the fact that to have faith in providence is to believe in *God's* providence grounded in Jesus Christ and not in the course of time and space as documented in any human system.[163] The epistemic humility Barth calls for with regard to all fallible theories about the orders of the cosmos is therefore a function of his sustained attack on natural theology which, with the same stroke, precludes both abstract philosophical speculation about a cosmos conceived without God as its author and object, and any Christian instinct to synonymize one's own notions about God's operation in history with God's actual historical involvement.[164] It is for this theological reason—rather than any willful ignorance of or obstinate disinterest in pressing philosophical questions—that Barth does not seriously entertain the need to engage systematically with the question of causal determinism.

Yet Barth does not wish to eliminate philosophical enterprises or technical metaphysical vocabulary from theology altogether.[165] While theology is not beholden to the criteria and questions proposed by secular philosophy, it may nevertheless be instructive to the Christian theologian to make use of them instrumentally in clarifying the Church's own discourse. And Barth does in fact throw his Christian doctrine of providence into relief by disambiguating it from the theologically errant presuppositions involved in metaphysical speculation about causal determinism and libertarianism.

For a start, Barth has no interest in rejecting the thesis of causal determinism only to safeguard its antitheses: the ideas of contra-causal human autonomy or indeterminism. To state that we are absolutely unequivocally the authors of our own decisions would be to fantasize about an autonomy in which God leaves us entirely to our own devices, and with an infinite range of possibilities open to us in any given moment. This would not be autonomy and contingency, but godlessness: an abstract aloofness from the

---

to commit to the theological fallacy that it is possible first to view nature and grace in sharp distinction from one another, and then to resolve the emergent opposition between the two concepts on the side of grace, presumably with some reference to a mythical agent mysteriously capable of transcending the natural realm.

162. III/3, 41; see also Tanner, "Creation and Providence," 112.

163. III/3, 21.

164. Ibid., 21–26; see also Tanner, "Creation and Providence," 111–12; Nimmo, "Karl Barth and the *concursus Dei*," 59.

165. Frei, *Types of Christian Theology*, 41.

moral space created by God which grounds and shapes authentic agency.[166] Equally, the idea of chance or capriciousness is as theologically illegitimate as any mechanistic notion of determinism, since God does not allow the fulfilment of the covenant to be one random possibility among others. The Christian conception of autonomy is therefore modified in light of the givenness of creation and the fact that godlessness is an ontological impossibility for the creature in light of the self-election of God to the covenant as the internal basis of creation.[167] Even the freedom of the creature is a gift of God, so that although we are not a "puppet or tool or dead matter," the genuine autonomy, contingency, and intentionality which God affords us is a gift that is congruent with the divinely determined *telos* of God's Kingdom.[168]

However, it is also the case that the idea of causal determinism, which entails the conclusion that no event could have been otherwise, is antithetical to the notion of genuine creaturely self-determination revealed in Jesus Christ and affirmed by the biblical witness. It is a presupposition of causal determinism that all human actions can be sufficiently explained in terms of physical events. Barth certainly wants to avoid any defense of human free will that depends on the "abstract dualism" of the Greek and—lamentably—Christian intellectual traditions. Such dualism drives a wedge between two supposedly qualitatively opposed "substances" of the body and soul, and then names the unity of these a "mystery."[169] But at the same time he warns against "monistic materialism" which eliminates all talk of the soul and seeks to equate human agency with the body and its functions. A proper understanding of the human being, he maintains, will view the body and soul not as alien substances, nor as merely identical, but as forming a unity in distinction. "For if [a human] is really seen as body, he is seen also as soul, that is, as the subject which gives life to his material body, to the spatio-temporal system of relations which physiology describes, thus distinguishing it as an organic body from a purely material body."[170]

---

166. This is one of the reasons that Barth rejects the existentialist libertarianism of Heidegger and Sartre, which view the agent as emerging out of and (at least in Sartre's view) mastering nothingness, their existence preceding any notion of essence. The groundlessness that secures the freedom of the creature to choose is precisely the site of their impoverishment and condemnation, since their self-election over against "nothing" robs them of the simplicity of gratefully becoming what they already are in Christ. See III/3, 334–49. On Barth's opposition to freedom as transcendence see Krötke, "The Humanity of the Human Person in Karl Barth's Anthropology," 160.

167. See III/3, 91.

168. Ibid., 92–93. See also III/3, 155.

169. III/2, 380.

170. Ibid., 383. See Krötke, "The Humanity of the Human Person in Karl Barth's Anthropology," 170.

Barth does not himself draw out the implications of his view of the interconnection of body and soul for a conception of human freedom, but they are worth exploring. If Barth is to protect an account of genuine creaturely contingency and self-determination then it cannot be the case that the actions of human beings could sufficiently be described as causally inevitable physical states. There must be a sense in which during the course of history leading up to an event I could have done otherwise. We may infer from Barth's view of the soul as the irreducibly subjective or organic aspect of one's intentional states, that such freedom is possible because I am not simply a passive collection of material states and functions, responding mechanically and arbitrarily to physical stimuli in accordance with the laws of nature, but an agent who possesses—as Rowan Williams has put it—"the capacity to picture myself, to question myself, and so to explore and modify my intentions."[171] Viewing the agent as an ensouled body and an embodied soul in this way allows Barth to avoid the abstract dualistic conception of an illusive will which is free because it is wholly transcendent of the causal nexus, while also protecting against the somewhat fatuous notion that the deliberation entailed in genuinely contingent agency could ever adequately be explained in the reductive physicalist terms proposed by the determinist.[172] Barth might well accept, as Williams does, that "at the exact moment of

---

171. Williams, "Triumph of the will," 43.

172. It is beyond the scope of this book to offer an investigation into Christian attitudes to the body, soul, and human agency. One suspects that a twenty-first century theology of freedom might well require a more sustained engagement with and renewal of natural theology than Barth was himself willing to offer, given the prevalence of physicalism in contemporary popularist debates about faith and science, and in light of the ease with which untenable reductive views of causality and agency are assumed in secularist attacks on religion. (On this, see Rowan Williams's 2008 lecture, "Faith and Science."). One avenue of approach in developing a Christian response to physicalism and determinism might consist in teasing out—in a way that Barth did not—how talk of an ensouled, organic body, and of an embodied soul, is indicative of the irreducible freedom, creativity and agency that human beings possess as *linguistic* beings. In his chapter "Can We Say What We Like? Language, Determinism and Freedom," (in Williams, *The Edge of Words*, 35–65) Williams explores the complex interactions of humans with their environments in terms of a linguistic agency that simply will not yield either to dualistic or physicalist explanation. Williams painstakingly explicates the position that human language is non-reducible to physical states or explicable in mechanistic causal terms. Hence no explanation of agency is satisfactory if it renders the way I represent the world to myself in language as nothing more than an arbitrary collection of sounds considered *qua* mere causally inevitable physical processes (a portrayal of language that is in fact self-defeating for determinists, in Williams's view (Williams, *The Edge of Words* 36); or if it sees language simply as an index of what there is in the world. Language, in short, indicates that we not only register the world and respond to its stimuli, but that we consciously engage with and shape our environment through non-deterministic patterns of reflection.

my deciding something, those intentions have been settled or determined; but that is only trivially true," since such determinations are the contingent results of myriad complex objective causal factors and subjective processes of discernment. In short, to be an ensouled body or a genuine subject is to affirm the basic principle that one may "shape one's own life in the light of complex circumstances."[173]

As well as rejecting the determinist's materialism as sufficient to explain human decisions, Barth critiques the ease with which determinists assume the sufficiency of the laws of nature to explain all historical and natural processes. The thesis of causal determinism, if it is to explain all occurrences within the causal nexus as the inevitable outcome of the preceding state of the nexus, and thereby to prove all human action mechanistic and arbitrary, must maintain that we could—at least in principle—identify the laws or law of nature by virtue of which any given occurrence could be described as necessary. But Barth is deeply suspicious of this claim.

Even if we could know the laws of nature with such confidence that we could condense them into a single mathematical equation (of the sort Laplace envisaged) to explain the whole causal framework "as a process predetermined by law," we would at most be able to describe "the order and form imposed by this law."[174] But Barth points out that being able to describe how events seem to conform to laws of nature is a very different prospect from explaining why these events should occur at all. "No law, not even that which is absolutely valid and therefore absolutely effective in that sense, has the power to cause even the most trivial of creaturely events actually to take place."[175] Even if we could calculate that any given event should take place in the order and form foreseen by such an all-encompassing law of nature, it would not be sufficient to explain *that* the event should actually

---

173. Williams, "Triumph of the Will," 43. It is worth noting, with Krötke, that for Barth the subjectivity proper to each person as an ensouled body afforded by God is not founded or abolished by actual religiosity or a-religiosity (Krötke, "The Humanity of the Human Person in Karl Barth's Anthropology," 170). And this ought to qualify our interpretations of those passages in Barth's works when he affirms that despite our genuine autonomy there is really only one choice we can freely make: the choice for God (see for example Godsey, *Karl Barth's Table Talk*, 37). By this, Barth clearly does not mean that God mechanistically causes some individual subjects to live fully as themselves by receiving and ratifying God's Word in their own private experience, and some not to. Rather, Barth means that while all creatures inhabit a genuine subjectivity, our choices—whether for God or not—are *all* relativized by the ultimate ontological impossibility of sin.

174. III/3, 125.

175. Ibid.

take place in the first place, or where and when it should occur.[176] It seems that what Barth has in his sights here is the notion that the causal nexus could be sufficiently explained in terms of the laws which govern it, as if the supreme mechanistic reductionism popularized in the idea of determinism would furnish us with a complete account of reality.[177] If causal determinism presupposes the principle of sufficient reason—the idea that there can be no brute or unexplainable facts—then it will have to contend with the apparent problem that whilst it might be able to explain any given event as causally necessary in accordance with the universal laws of nature, it cannot explain why any given state of affairs should come about in the first place, or why indeed the causal realm conforms to this particular set of laws. This seems to violate the very principle of sufficient reason on which it rests, and it might give us legitimate pause to reconsider the epistemic confidence with which we assume everything in the universe is sufficiently explicable in causal terms.

Yet this observation alone is not capable of dismantling determinism since although the determinist might not be able to explain why the causal nexus unfolds mechanistically and inevitably in the way it does, that would not change the *fact* that it does so; and such a fact could be maintained so long as we could establish that the laws of nature are absolute. But given the limitations of human knowledge about the cosmos Barth questions whether we have any legitimate epistemological reason to presume that they are. He reminds us that it is "we ourselves who discover and guarantee" the laws of nature, and that given they emerge from our own experiences and in virtue of the coherence they have within our own systems of knowledge, no "measure of noetic certainty or clarity can give to laws known to us . . . the character of ontic laws."[178] In other words, what reason do we have to suppose that the way we take things to be is the way things are in reality? The case for determinism is epistemologically irresponsible because it presupposes that

> the individual laws of creaturely activity can be known with an absolute certainty which excludes all doubts and exceptions,

---

176. Ibid., 125.

177. Rowan Williams is helpful again here in crystalizing a Christian perspective on mechanical reductionism. In "Faith and Science," he identifies the problem for reductionist materialists of having, in the course of offering a complete theory of natural and historical processes, to decide "what's the most basic form of explanation and whether you think that the most basic form of explanation is the only *real* form of explanation." Since different scientific discourses do not themselves appear to admit of neat assimilation, there is little reason to suppose that even given a comprehensive knowledge of the laws of nature could furnish us with a complete account of the causal totality.

178. III/3, 127.

and with such clarity that we can responsibly describe [the laws] as in their own sphere at least the formal foreordination of a particular event. But in fact we are going much too far if we seriously suppose that there is any such knowledge. What we know as [the laws] of creaturely activity are noetic assertions for whose ontic content we have no guarantee which can justify us in raising them to such a height.[179]

In sum, Barth does not believe that the Christian really ought to be anxious about causal determinism because both the thesis and its intellectual presuppositions are antithetical to the biblical account of creaturely reality that informs the doctrine of providence. By contrast, the risks posed to the authenticity of creaturely agency by theological determinism—the view that if God knows everything that will happen, including who will be saved and rejected, then every human action is necessary and arbitrary—have been far more damaging in Christian history, and Barth expends significant theological energy in redressing much impoverished theological thinking about the relation of an eternal God to the historical nexus.

Barth's response to the question of theological determinism is of a piece with his subversion of questions about causal determinism, in that he refuses to define the divine subject *a priori* and a-historically, and views most problems associated with theological determinism as stemming from this error.[180] In contrast to "the older Protestant theology" of both the Lutheran and Reformed traditions, Barth completely rejects the alien superiority of the "abstract and absolutely omniscient, omnipotent and omnioperative" God of classical theism who would annihilate human contingency.[181] The foreknowledge and predestination of history determined by a God so conceived would indeed make human freedom unthinkable; but for Barth, God's omnipotence, providence and eternity is revealed trinitarianally and grounded in the history of the incarnation and Pentecost.[182] Tanner reminds us that "predestination . . . is not a particular instance of some general way that God is with the world as a whole."[183] God's power and lordship consists in God's self-election to the covenant—the freedom to be absolutely what

---

179. Ibid., 126.

180. See Ibid., 139–43. Barth complains with surprise that even Calvin failed to explain the doctrine of providence Christologically.

181. Ibid., 31. See Webster, "Freedom in Limitation," 105.

182. See III/1, 65, where Barth forbids the abstract conception of God the creator as "present always and never, everywhere and nowhere" or of an "inaudible and unutterable Logos" since "the Word through whom the world is created is a historical actuality revealed in Jesus Christ." See also, Webster, "Freedom in Limitation," 106.

183. Tanner, "Creation and Providence," 121.

God is without any threat of external determination—not in the abstract power for power's sake to have every moment of history wrapped up in advance of its actual occurrence, so to speak. Consequently, as Webster puts it, "God is 'omnipotent in the freedom of His creatures,' rather than omnipotent in competition with, or opposition to, that freedom."[184] The foreknowledge and foreordination of God consist in the fact that while allowing the creature her own freedom for self-determination, God knows that there is nothing that can or will prevent God from being the graceful God of the covenant who decides trinitarianally, and in an act of sheer super-abundant love, not to be a God without genuine historical predicates.

But if this is true, Barth's understanding of the relation of time to eternity needs some unpacking, since it will be necessary to show that the foreknowledge of God cannot be thought in separation from the historical determination of the divine life in a genuine history. Accounts of God's foreknowledge which obliterate the authenticity of historical contingency do so because—in attempting to secure the aseity of God within a kind of timeless anteriority to creation—they are guilty of unduly prioritizing God's pre-temporality at the expense of God's embrace of creaturely time within the divine supra- and post-temporal eternity.[185] That is, the eternity of a God whose foreknowledge would necessitate human actions as automatic corroborations of what God already knows does so because it has been construed in a linear, static and mechanistic relation to time.[186] But in the doctrine of God Barth had already warned that Christian doctrine had to

---

184. Webster, "Freedom in Limitation," 105. See II/1, 598. See also McDowell, *Hope in Barth's Eschatology*, 138; and Nimmo, *Being in Action*, 125.

185. For Barth on God's eternity as pre-, supra-, and post-temporality see II/1 619–40. See especially 631–32 where Barth, seeking to reclaim the doctrines of predestination and providence from their misapplication in much Protestant thought, observes that "the Reformers showed an interest not free from dangerous one-sidedness in . . . eternity as pre-temporality." While they, like Augustine, did so in order to secure the sheer gracefulness of God's love and to resist synergism, their one-sided identification of God's lordship with God's eternal pre-temporality amounted to an inaccurate theological calibration of the triune Godhead which obscured the temporality of God's eternal self-determination in and through the history of Jesus Christ, and which therefore viewed God's eternity as a quality God possesses or as a space God occupies (see ibid., 638–39).

186. Krötke insists that while it "is meaningless to speak of God if in His eternity He is not understood as the God who precedes the human and acts freely" it is equally meaningless to think of this precedence in separation from the history of Christ through which God wills the free correspondence of humans to God and the covenant (Krötke, "The Humanity of the Human Person in Karl Barth's Anthropology," 164).

liberate the concept of divine eternity from its "Babylonian captivity" to a construal of the mere opposition of time.[187]

As Tom Greggs has observed, Barth's doctrine of eternity constitutes a *"ressourcement"* of Boethius's Plotinian understanding of eternity as the "simultaneous and perfect possession of unending life [*Aeternitas est interminabilis vitae tota simul et perfecta possessio*]"[188] which recovers a genuine order of temporality within eternity and protects the coherence of God's immutable sovereignty with the integrity of a distinct creaturely order. Greggs subtly places Barth in conversation with the Augustinian and Thomist trajectories in Christian intellectual history, and demonstrates that both Augustine and Aquinas had erred in their understanding of God's eternity as a consequence of their appropriation of classical philosophy. On the one hand, Augustine had endorsed Plato's vision of eternity as timelessness in order to protect the immutability of the Godhead. Since time is related to movement, and since there can be no movement before the creation of bodies, God's eternal reality (as ontologically distinct from creation) must be the antithesis of time.[189] By contrast, Aquinas translated the Boethian idea of simultaneity into a timeless present as a consequence of his application of an Aristotelian account of number and movement. Nervous about the fleeting nature of time in relation to the absence of succession in God's eternity, Aquinas imported the Augustinian concern for the immutability of God into his own thought by conceiving the simultaneity of God's possession of all time effectively as a form of timelessness.[190] Thomas's Aristotelian conception of number and motion function to secure the aseity of an uncaused causer and unmoved mover by utilizing the principles of simplicity and non-movement as a foundation for specifying the nature of eternity.[191]

So on Greggs's view Augustine and Aquinas were both guilty of making the same mistake, via slightly different metaphysical routes. Neither could accommodate a genuine sense of temporality within God's eternal life, and as such it is difficult not to view creaturely time as in some sense already having been concluded in advance of its occurrence. It therefore becomes evident as to why a good deal of the subsequent Christian tradition failed to conceive of God's eternal foreordination in a manner that did not annihilate genuine creaturely contingency, or that set grace in stark opposition to nature.

187. II/1, 611. See Greggs, "The Order and Movement of Eternity," 2.
188. Greggs, "The Order and Movement of Eternity," 2.
189. Ibid., 3.
190. Ibid., 4–5. See Thomas Aquinas, *Summa Theologiae*, 137.
191. See Greggs, "The Order and Movement of Eternity," 9; 11.

Barth, however, attempts to circumvent this opposition by offering an "*enhypostatic* temporality within the divine eternal life."[192] For Barth, while the doctrine of election in no way serves to make God a creature in time by passing God wholly into God's acts, its Christocentric calibration allows the Godhead to take time into God's eternity by means of the "*Logos incarnandus* who is present in the willing of time, with the progression of time and after time."[193] On this view, while the omniscient God clearly knows what will happen in advance of its occurrence, God does so only in the sense that such foreknowledge is perfectly simultaneous with God's accompaniment and eschatological resolution of time through Christ and the Spirit. God's eternal "now" as "the total simultaneous and complete present of His life"[194] may be thought of as both "*stare and fluere*—but not *fluere* in the instability of creaturely times—and *fluere and stare*—but without the inability to become that belongs to all creaturely *stare*."[195] Such a view of eternity attempts to resist the notion that God is a static monad for whom time is an irrelevant posteriority, while preserving the aseity and lordship of a God whose ontological distinction from all creatures, including time itself, is maintained in the simultaneous and perfect possession (not annihilation) of beginning, middle and end.[196]

The consequence of Barth's view of the eternity of God is that a temporal space for human self-determination is preserved even while it is subject to determination by God.[197] This apparent paradox is perhaps clarified when we understand that for Barth God's omnicausality (*Allwirksamkeit*) cannot be equated with the divine sole causality (*Alleinwirksamkeit*) of a monadic tyrant.[198] God has lordship over every event without directly or mechanically causing their occurrence. To be sure, this is not to equate Barth's position with those attempts he so deplores in Lutheranism to avoid the fatalism involved in the Calvinist doctrine of predestination by saying that God foresees the choices creatures make and then awaits the accomplishment of these choices, exercising God's power only to facilitate the execution of particular human decisions.[199] Such a view would uphold the moral respon-

---

192. Ibid., 2.
193. Ibid., 18.
194. II/1, 611.
195. Greggs, "The Order and Movement of Eternity," 9.
196. II/1, 608. See Greggs, "The Order and Movement of Eternity," 7.
197. See I/I, 201.
198. Nimmo, *Being in Action*, 128. See II/2, 586; IV/4 22 = *KD* IV/4, 25; see also *KD* IV/4, 180.
199. III/3, 120.

"Being-in-Becoming"   95

sibility of the creature at the expense of making God a "strangely passive spectator and assistant of the creature."[200] Yet, on the other hand, God's control of history does not mean substituting it for God's own activity, which would amount to suspending and destroying it.[201] Instead, God "controls its independent activity as such. He uses it for His own ends. And in so doing He does not encroach too much upon it. He does not do violence to the character and dignity which it has as the reality which is distinct from Him."[202]

Barth does not offer a technical defense of the idea that God is lord over every action without directly causing it, again because the Bible does not offer any metaphysical resolution of the antinomies of necessity and contingence, law and freedom, or the lordship of God and the autonomy of the creature.[203] But he does draw attention to the manner in which we ought to distinguish between God's causality and our ordinary observation of causality in creation through general experience and the natural sciences. Firstly, the scientific concept of causality in which the effect follows the cause automatically cannot be applied to God's operation within the natural order because this would be to view God's activity in mechanical terms which are wholly inadequate to describe the divine causality.[204] Secondly, since God and humans are not mere things or objects, but living subjects, it would be quite inappropriate to imagine the causal relationship between them in the same way that we imagine the causality between two objects.[205] Thirdly, since God and humans are absolutely ontologically distinct it would be foolish to attempt to reconcile the distinction between the lordship of God and the self-determination of the creature with reference to a unifying master-concept of causality.[206] Finally, from all this the impossibility of offering a philosophical "total scheme of things" to explain the factual relationship between the eternal determination of God and the contingency of history should be quite apparent.[207] In the final resort, the only evidence the Church need trust to prove the simultaneous facts of God's causal control over history and the authenticity of creaturely history is that in Jesus Christ

---

200. Ibid., 120.
201. Ibid., 165.
202. Ibid., 165. See also ibid., 188–89.
203. Ibid., 187–89. See Nimmo, *Being in Action*, 129.
204. III/3, 101.
205. Ibid., 101–2.
206. Ibid., 102–3.
207. Ibid., 104.

God willed to become and actually became a genuine creature, thereby establishing a real covenant with two real partners.[208]

That creatures are given a limited freedom and autonomy to serve the covenant through submission to the authority of God does not entail a contradiction because, as we have seen, self-determination is not unequivocal self-authorship, but acknowledgement and awakening "at a specific point in a specific context."[209] Put in non-Barthian terms we could say the intentionality or subjectivity of human acknowledgement secures the authenticity of the creature's response to the Spirit's call and guidance in a way that is simply not explicable in reductive, externalistic, and mechanical terms. One's speaking to oneself is the site of the human's choice about the covenant; one's desires, fallibilities, education, hopes, and fears are authentic experiences which inform genuinely personal decisions—including ones about faith. But for the Church, these authentic creaturely moments can never be viewed in abstraction from God's eternal decision not to be God without us, and therefore not to let any human make a final or absolutely free decision about the covenant's status.

Below, I shall return to the question of how the Spirit calls individuals and communities to serve the covenant, and why some seem not to respond to the universal election of humanity (Chapter 5). In the interim, it is helpful to reiterate that the Barthian response to theological determinism is that it makes the mistake of neglecting the Christological and pneumatological revelation of God's eternity and lordship, in place of which it forces an opposition between an abstract first cause and a natural order whose predicates have nothing whatsoever to do with God's foreknowledge, predestination or eschatological determination for covenant. Barth therefore insists that we ought to redress those Christian habits of thinking about "God," "will of God," "work of God," which arise out of "godless" notions of causality.[210]

---

208. Ibid., 105–6.

209. I/1, 207. See Webster, "Freedom in Limitation," 109.

210. III/3, 117–18. Before leaving the conversation about theological determinism, it is worth mentioning Jesse Couenhoven's reconstruction of Barth's position on freedom and determinism ("Karl Barth's Conception(s) of Human and Divine Freedom(s)," 239–55) which seems to ignore Barth's warning to the church not to force theological concepts to satisfy generally deduced philosophical conditions. Couenhoven claims that although most scholars take Barth to be an "incompatibilist" about divine freedom (ibid., 243), once we understand Barth's "compatibilist" conception of human freedom (ibid., 246–51) an alternative "compatibilist" reading of Barth's understanding of divine freedom opens up (ibid., 251–54). Couenhoven's attempts to square Barth's theology with a general philosophical discussion that defines the conditions for freedom in advance of exegesis and theology has the unfortunate effects i) of forcing Barth's Christocentric understanding of the divine and human freedoms to conform with the very traditions he was trying to subvert because of their theological inadequacy, and

Christocentric Being-in-Becoming: Justification and Sanctification

The simultaneity of Gospel and Law, and of liberty and determination, discloses the key to Barth's view of human freedom: the being-in-becoming of Jesus Christ, which is the being-in-becoming of all humanity. The summons to freedom issued by God to the human subject is both declared and fulfilled in the history of Jesus Christ.[211] "Because it is the history in which the covenant between God and humanity is fulfilled from both sides, Jesus's history is the true essence of created being."[212] The sinfulness in which humanity persists is therefore a denial of the true being to which it has been elected in Christ,[213] but this refusal "to allow God's Son to speak for us,"[214] the desire for "Godlessness," is ultimately an "ontological impossibility."[215] As Gorringe notes, "to call sin an impossibility is not to deny its existence but to recognise it as a radical attack on the foundation of what it means to be human."[216] God does not allow the sinfulness of humanity to interrupt the covenantal fellowship desired by God from all eternity, but actualizes and fulfils the relationship between God and humanity in the coming of

---

consequently ii) of misinterpreting Barth's theology of freedom. Couenhoven insists that Barth's compatibilism precludes the view of freedom as a choice between alternatives: neither God's actions nor ours could have been otherwise. Freedom simply means the identification and affirmation of one's desires with one's actions. It is difficult to see how this does not i) divest Barth's God of the graceful decision to be the God of Jesus Christ and no other; ii) strip humans of authentic contingency (since we can only "ratify" what God has directly caused to happen for us (ibid., 249–50); and iii) by extension, dispossess Jesus Christ of the genuine historicity that is foundational for both the identity of God and humanity. Despite acknowledging that for Barth human freedom cannot be considered mechanistically in relation to God's grace (ibid., 249), that is precisely what ends up happening on Couenhoven's reading. His main error seems to consist in abstracting a conception of the divine *concursus* from a nuanced account of God's eternal relation to time, which would resist the need to draw an opposition between God's foreknowledge and foreordination, on the one hand, and created history on the other. And by eradicating the disanalogy between the divine and human freedoms, he also seems to fall into the trap Barth warned against of treating freedom and causality as master-concepts and then trying to force God and humanity to fit into a total theory of everything. The fact that Couenhoven sees it as a happy corollary of his reading that Barth can be brought into line with the very traditions on election that he sought so radically to re-interpret and re-invent perhaps signals the oddity of his interpretation (ibid., 255).

211. III/2, 147–48. See also, Webster, *Barth's Ethics of Reconciliation*, 68.
212. Webster, *Barth's Ethics of Reconciliation*, 85.
213. II/2, 761.
214. Ibid.
215. III/2, 136.
216. Gorringe, *Karl Barth against Hegemony*, 199.

Christ. If we are to become most fully ourselves, therefore, we have only to give thanks for and obediently to participate in the humanity of Christ:

> we are what we are, not in our own name or person, but in the name and person of Jesus Christ. The existence of the new man in us, which is so hidden when we try to observe and investigate and confirm it in ourselves; our existence in eternal membership in God's Son; our being in Jesus Christ . . . are real because they are the predicates of Jesus Christ . . .[217]

As Jüngel observes, the becoming of Christ is the becoming of all humans because the faithfulness of the man Jesus to the Father corresponds to and actualizes in time the eternal faithfulness of the Son, through which humanity is elected to relations with God in the beginning.[218] The vicarious obedience of Christ to the divine covenantal command consists in the justification and sanctification of humanity, by which we are "awakened to our own truest being" both ontically and noetically, because "God has made Himself our peacemaker and the giver and gift of our salvation. By it we are made free for Him."[219] As the simultaneous subordination and humiliation of God (IV/1), and super-ordination and exaltation of humanity (IV/2), Christ actualizes the fellowship proper to God and humanity which, in our finitude and sinfulness, we can neither initiate nor maintain. He is our "Representative and Substitute" before God, the One whose perfect humanity cannot be completed or augmented, but must simply be followed in faith and with gratitude.[220] One sees, then, that Barth's soteriology of freedom signals his commitment to the doctrine of justification by faith alone (*iustitia aliena* and *sola fide*):[221] it is Christ's history which "is our true history, in an incomparably more direct and intimate way than anything which might present itself as our history in our own subjective experience."[222] We have to "participate in this drama" solely through the humility of faith, by which we acknowledge "that that which is said of the prodigal son is said of me."[223]

---

217. II/2, 761.

218. Jüngel, *God's Being Is in Becoming*, 103. See also, Jones, *The Humanity of Christ*, 132–33.

219. IV/1, 14.

220. Ibid., 230. Christ is "for us" as our "Judge, the judged and the judgement" restoring us to right relations with God the Father, in whose eyes we find favor through the obedience of the Son (ibid., 256).

221. Nimmo, *Being in Action*, 162–63; Macken, *The Autonomy Theme*, 58–59.

222. IV/1, 547. The deliberate contrast with Bultmann is apparent here.

223. Ibid.

"Being-in-Becoming"

To acknowledge that Christ's becoming is the vicarious justification of all humans before God is not, however, to deny the importance of human activity, or of the particular agential becoming in which each individual corresponds to the universal human becoming in Christ. Christ does not render human agency superfluous, but issues a supreme summons to authentic agency by encountering us with the command to conform ourselves to Him: the human subject "is confronted with the command of God in the ethical event . . . This man [viz. the ethical agent] is the other participant in this event. He is wholly secondary and subordinate to the first; indeed, it is only by the first that he is what he is."[224] And yet, because Christ *has* pardoned and represented the ethical agent, she is free to participate in the event of His holiness. Hence, to justification in Christ corresponds the doctrine of sanctification, according to which Barth says humanity is exalted in Christ, and summoned to active affirmation and mobilization of our true humanity.[225]

> In line with Barth's actualistic ontology, the Christological and pneumatological determination of the ethical agent in the covenant of grace directs her to *actualise* her freedom: her freedom in Jesus Christ is a freedom to which she is chosen and called, a freedom which only exists in her exercise, in her correct use of it. The freedom of the ethical agent is the freedom of a being in action.[226]

As with the doctrine of justification, so the human activity in sanctification is consummated supremely by Christ, and not by ourselves.[227] Christ vicariously makes the appropriate human response to God"s covenantal declaration "I will be your God," obeying God's commandment "Ye shall be my people."[228] By making this unique and kingly response on our behalf, Jesus Christ becomes the "exaltation of our essence." For

> Jesus is the man in whose human being and thinking and willing and speaking and acting there takes place the grateful affirmation of the grace of God addressed to the human race and the whole created cosmos—an affirmation which we all owe but

---

224. III/4, 26.
225. Ibid., 474.
226. Nimmo, *Being in Action*, 114.
227. IV/2, 499.
228. Ibid.

none of us makes. He is the man who . . . does not break but keeps the covenant . . .²²⁹

Through Christ's exaltation of human nature, willed in eternity and actualized in time, humanity is given a share in the very being of God, since God's being is the eventful decision for covenantal relations, and to be exalted is to be "placed at God's side, not in identity, but in true fellowship with Him."²³⁰ McCormack is keen to stress that participation does not mean synergism, and exaltation does not mean identification with God.²³¹ Firstly it is Christ's sovereign humanity that exalts humanity before God, and therefore it is Christ alone who consummates our place in the eternal will of God. Secondly, Barth refuses to identify *simpliciter* the divine and human natures in Christ; the divinity and humanity of Christ are different in character, one being wholly giving, the other wholly receiving.²³² Hence what Christ achieves as the exalted human is always the grateful reception of a gift from God, and human essence thereby remains definitely human; exaltation is not deification. "Barth concludes that although the divine humiliation means that 'God became man', it is not the case that the exaltation of the human means that 'He [Jesus] became God.'"²³³ Our exaltation in God does not mean that we become God, it simply entails the permission to exist as those willed to exist as the eternal partners of God. Hence, with these Reformed caveats in place, Barth does affirm that by the sanctifying life of Christ "There is no moment of the human essence which is untouched or excluded from its existence in and with that of the Son of God and, thereby, from the union with and participation in this divine essence."²³⁴

Prayerful Responsibility

Since the being-in-becoming of the God-man Jesus does not obliterate the integrity of the human individual, but rather awakens her to participation in her true covenantal being in Christ, it is possible for Barth to affirm God's preservation of a genuinely autonomous (though never independent) agential reality in the doctrine of the *concursus Dei*.²³⁵ According to the *concursus*,

---

229. Ibid., 30.
230. Ibid., 6.
231. McCormack, "Participation in God, Yes, Deification, No," 347–74.
232. IV/2, 72.
233. McCormack, "Participation in God, Yes, Deification, No," 354.
234. IV/2, 64.
235. III/3, 94ff.

God accompanies, preserves and rules human existence, calling humanity to participate in the true covenantal humanity of Christ, whilst allowing the human agent an authentically "free, contingent and autonomous" activity.[236] Providence is God's sovereign gift and guidance of a created realm in which humanity is given an authentic space for covenantal service.[237] Within this agential moral space the "true man [is] characterised by action, by good action, as the true God is also characterised by action, by good action."[238] To live an active life is to be "caught up in responsibility before God. This responsibility implies man's acknowledgement that God his Creator is in the right in all that He does."[239] In everything that we do we are called to the freedom proper to human essence through acknowledgement, obedience, and gratitude. It is the freedom for this active service that constitutes us as authentically human, because it is here that we become like Christ, namely, those whom God willed for obedient fellowship from the depths of eternity.

It is therefore surprising, although theologically quite appropriate, that Barth commences his actualistic ethics of freedom by reflecting on "The Holy Day," the Sabbath, the day of rest.[240] Barth claims that placing the Sabbath at the head of all work is indicative of the whole character of good human activity, because it is a deliberate, responsible, obedient acknowledgement of the sovereignty of God's action, the necessity of God's grace, and therefore the "limiting of man's activity . . . his own work, his own understanding and achievement."[241] For Barth the decision of God to take a day of rest at the conclusion of God's creative work reveals the divine purpose for creation: "Man is created to participate in this rest."[242] God's act of creation demonstrates that God wills fellowship with a distinct reality, and that God desires to enjoy the satisfaction of co-existence with this other reality.[243] Hence "The goal of creation, and at the same time the beginning of all that follows, is the event of God's Sabbath freedom, Sabbath rest, and Sabbath joy, in which man, too, has been summoned to participate."[244] As such, the Sabbath has an eschatological point of reference, since the rest, joy

236. Nimmo, *Being in Action*, 123.
237. Tanner, "Creation and Providence," 117.
238. III/4, 3.
239. Ibid., 47. See also, Gorringe, *Karl Barth against Hegemony*, 212–13.
240. III/4, 47ff.
241. Ibid., 50. See Cocksworth, *Karl Barth on Prayer*, 41–42; Webster, *Barth's Ethics of Reconciliation*, 79.
242. III/1, 98.
243. Ibid., 214; Cocksworth, *Karl Barth on Prayer*, 43.
244. III/1, 98.

, and freedom granted through this particular historical form of obedience to God's lordship points us towards the ultimate rest, joy, and freedom that God will grant in the eternal consummation of covenant history.[245] In the eventfulness of Jesus's saving history, in which we are given a share, we are drawn into this freedom to rest through the "retrospective pull back to the first Sabbath . . . and the prospective push towards the final Sabbath."[246]

If the observation of the Sabbath is the beginning of human participation in the freedom for fellowship with God granted in Christ, then this Sabbath rest must subsequently inform all that we actively do; it must create the "moral space" in which we exercise our freedom. Keeping the holy day may be the "most visible" form of our "special responsibility" before God in which we acknowledge the dependence of our freedom upon the prior sovereign freedom of God, but there is secondarily an "invitation and obligation of man to bear express witness to God," and this witness is exacted through confession and prayer.[247] Barth claims that confession is "the confirmation, declaration and impartation of what is known."[248] The special confession commanded by God, then, includes a two-fold activity in which everything we do and say is both the unashamed proclamation of the Gospel,[249] and the responsible protest against and denunciation of all that stands opposed to the Gospel.[250] We saw that God actualizes God's freedom by gracefully electing Godself to relationship with humanity. Here, in confession, humanity is called to actualize its own freedom for sanctified participation in this fellowship by correspondingly acknowledging the reconciled relations with God to which humanity too is elect in Jesus Christ. Confession is that activity of human freedom in which humanity obediently responds to the command of God which "summons him to confirm [covenantal fellowship] on his side."[251] In the encounter between God and humanity actualized in the history of Jesus, God not only wills "as Lord of this history" that humanity will "be the object of His action and the recipient of his blessings" but also that in this encounter humankind will become "a responsible partner."[252] The freedom of a responsible partner of God is

---

245. III/4, 56.
246. Cocksworth, "Attending to the Sabbath," 264.
247. III/4, 73.
248. Ibid.
249. Ibid., 73, 78.
250. Ibid., 78–79.
251. Ibid., 74.
252. Ibid., 75.

> The freedom of those who have something to relate about [God], the freedom of confessors who cannot keep silence but must speak of Him, their freedom to expose themselves to His glory, to commit themselves to His honour with clear and definite words . . .[253]

Finally, human freedom before God is exercised in the activity of prayer. Prayer is for Barth perhaps the primary site of human freedom, since it is here more decisively than anywhere else that the human individual acknowledges the lordship of God, and that she is utterly dependent upon God's grace for her entire existence.[254] Prayer bears witness to God's lordship even more clearly than confession, "because in its decisive sense prayer obviously consists less in man offering something to God and doing something for Him than in turning to Him, seeking, asking and accepting from Him something he needs"—namely, fellowship.[255] As in confession, prayer represents the actualization of a freedom corresponding to God's primary free self-determination for fellowship, since the very possibility of prayer is granted by God's turning to humanity in Jesus Christ. We can "apply" to God only because God has first applied Godself to us, has made us God's concern. Hence the freedom of prayer is rooted in the doctrine of election: "God elects Himself to be gracious towards man, to be his Lord and Helper."[256] The only appropriate response, therefore, is to acknowledge our determination as those God wills to help, and to turn to God in grateful, obedient, and humble petition.[257]

Barth reiterates that the actualization of our human freedom to become responsible pray-ers does not rest ultimately with us, but with Jesus Christ, who fulfils the command to pray vicariously on our behalf, inviting us to participate in Christ's prayer. Humanity, in its sinfulness, will continually fail to pray to God; it will fail to become the responsible partners of God through the supplication of obedient petition. But "in His Son God has become man, and therefore has actually taken our side and become our Brother."[258] Through this divine taking up of our cause "we ask *comme*

---

253. Ibid., 75.

254. Gorringe, *Karl Barth against Hegemony*, 194, 210; Migliore, "Freedom to Pray," 97.

255. III/4, 87.

256. II/2, 510.

257. See Cocksworth, *Karl Barth on Prayer*, 64.

258. III/4, 108. Cocksworth notes that the "the physical circumstances of Gethsemane are particularly revealing of this aspect of Christ's vicarious action" (Cocksworth, *Karl Barth on Prayer*, 68). Christ prays alone, in our place, with no one to help (IV/1, 267–68). See also, Jones, "Karl Barth on Gethsemane," 148–71.

par sa bouche (Calvin)."[259] But it is also precisely this becoming of Christ which is already the answer to our prayers: for petition is "simply the taking and receiving of the divine gift and answer as it is already present and near to hand in Jesus Christ."[260] Christ is at once human prayer and divine response: as true man He humbly asks God for a share in the covenant; as true Word He grants humanity eternal fellowship, life at the heart of God's triune depths.[261]

Conclusion

The chapter commenced by asking how Barth might overcome the dualistic tensions inherent in his theological ontology and epistemology, with a view to repairing the apparent disjunction between divine objectivity and subjectivity, and consequently the relation between divine and human action. Subsequently Chapter 2 traced Barth's gradual movement away from a theological ontology which one-sidedly emphasized the separation of God and humanity through a stress on the infinite qualitative distinction. The chapter concluded with a consideration of Barth's highly participative theology of human freedom as it develops from II/2 onwards. I have demonstrated that for the mature Barth God wills to be God only in relation to humanity. I argued that the event of the knowledge of God is also the history of the eternally willed actualization of the covenant, and not simply a subjective manifestation of God's *Doppelgänger*. And it was seen that humanity has its ground and liberty in God's eternal determination to be the God of the covenant. On the basis of Barth's mature Christocentric divine and human ontologies, it may be concluded that the freedom of God and the freedom of humanity are freedoms *for* one another. It is this conclusion, reached in departure from some of the criticisms of Barth's early work highlighted in Chapter 1, which facilitates a detailed investigation into IV/3. This part-volume, it shall be argued, is Barth's most highly participative and anti-dualistic work. It is in IV/3 that Barth extends his mature understanding of the Christocentric divine and human freedoms to new levels of theological sophistication. And this occurs on the basis of Barth's radical integration of being and act, being and knowing, and object and subject, which, as I have shown throughout Chapter 2, he began to unite boldly in his writings from 1936 onwards.

259. III/4, 108.
260. III/3, 274.
261. Webster, *Barth's Ethics of Reconciliation*, 77; Migliore, "Freedom to Pray," 99.

Part B

DIVINE AND HUMAN FREEDOM IN ASYMMETRICAL RECIPROCITY IN *CHURCH DOGMATICS* IV/3

3

DIVINE AND HUMAN FREEDOM IN ASYMMETRICAL RECIPROCITY

Being, Act, and Knowledge in *Church Dogmatics* IV/3

God Himself says I in this Other, so that, whether we realise it or not, the decision is made that God will accomplish His personal life-act only together with us, and we can accomplish ours only together with God.

—Karl Barth[1]

God, for our sakes, "risks" his very identity, his continuity with himself. And if we are to take this at all seriously, the kinds of assumption about the freedom and lordship of God with which Barth is working in I/1 will need radical revision.

—Rowan Williams[2]

---

1. IV/3, 41.
2. Williams, "Barth on the Triune God," 176.

Part B: Divine and Human Freedom in Asymmetrical Reciprocity

Introduction

Having traced the development of Barth's understanding of divine and human freedom in Part A, I now come to the core argument of the book. In this chapter it is argued that IV/3 represents the denouement of Barth's engagement with the concept of freedom, offering his most fully participative and integrated vision of divine reality and human flourishing. Explicating Barth's treatment of Christ's prophetic office, Chapter 3 describes the divine and human realities as being ordered for freedom in asymmetrical, covenantal reciprocity. That is, the freedom of Christ the God-man represents a dialectical and unified freedom of God and humanity for one another. And the deeply participative nature of this text is grounded in a more thoroughgoing integration of the objective and subjective categories than in any other of Barth's works.

In Chapter 1 it was argued that the early Barth posited something of a sharp distinction between God's eternal objectivity (the divine essence *in se*) and God's historical subjectivity (the revelatory existence *ad extra*), one-sidedly emphasizing the non-objectivity of God. This was intended to safeguard an appropriate distance between God's sovereign being and fallible human subjects in the description of the event of theological knowledge. The result, however, was that Barth was unable to do justice to the historicity of God's being-in-act. Moreover, Barth's concern was rather exclusively with the question of theological knowledge, without also being sufficiently focused on the implications of God's economy for God's very identity. In IV/3 Barth treats of the *munus propheticum*, handling the relation of divine ontology and theological epistemology explicitly for the first time since volume I of the *Dogmatics*. By locating both of these themes in the history of the God-man, in a radical, actualistic way that was not achieved in the doctrine of revelation, Barth is able to say that the revelatory aspects of Christ's life-act form a concrete part of the divine ontology, and not just an analogical repetition or divine self-interpretation. Barth thereby insists that the event of human flourishing through the knowledge of God is itself integral to God's self-determination in covenantal lordship.

In this chapter I shall show i) that Barth overcomes some of the dualistic elements in his earlier works by stressing the irreducible importance of the simultaneity of Christ's divinity and humanity. And ii) that this non-competitive vision of divine-human relations in IV/3 is underwritten by a willingness to view the revelatory subjectivity of the risen Christ and the Holy Spirit (the noetic aspect of reconciliation) as a function of God's free ontological determination of divine and human reality in a pattern of reciprocity. In short, Jesus Christ's self-witness as God-man not only reveals that

God and humanity are reciprocally related, but, more specifically, that this revelatory history is the time in which Christ brings His own divine-human life-act to consummation by taking up human subjects into the event of God's own life.

Jüngel is right to find that IV/3 "is Barth's starting-point for overcoming the 'object-subject schema.'"[3] This observation indicates that in IV/3 something distinctive is taking place in Barth's theological conception. In this text he is thinking in terms that take the subjective to be a function of the objective: "the revelatory dimension of the event [of reconciliation] . . . is not to be separated from that event."[4] It is not simply the case, as (it shall be seen below) numerous inadequate readings of IV/3 have suggested, that for Barth Christ vicariously achieves the unity of God and humanity in the incarnation and the cross, subsequently returning on Easter Sunday to relay dogmatic information about this event. Nor, as has also been erroneously suggested by some commentators, is human subjectivity simply the cognition of a series of soteriological propositions that mirror brute ontological facts actualized in abstraction from the event of human faith. Barth's conceptualization of Christological and human subjectivity is far more sophisticated than such interpretations of IV/3 allow.

The development of Barth's eschatology suggests that the divine-human unity established in Jesus Christ is not only a set of affairs to be cognized by human subjects, but a participative event taking place in the midst of complex world-occurrence, into which we are attracted by the Holy Spirit. As such, IV/3 sets up an asymmetrical reciprocity between Christ's objective and subjective functions as mediator. The latter, whilst not identical with the former, is ingredient in it. The event of human subjects being attracted into participation in Christ's life (through His revelatory power) is an integral part of His ontic actuality as God-man, and therefore part of the history in which God determines not to come to Godself without also coming to humanity. Taken together, and triadically (which is to say, as two distinct terms that form a mutually explicating pair), the objective and subjective sides of covenantal mediation serve to indicate that God and humanity may only be adequately thought in the historical unity in which they are reciprocally actualized through Jesus Christ. It is my argument (throughout Chapters 3, 4, and 5) that once readers of Barth overcome a false opposition between the function of the objective and subjective categories in his soteriology (meaning the erroneous attempt to conceive of

---

3. Jüngel, *God's Being Is in Becoming*, 14 n1.

4. Ibid., 13 n1. In Chapter 4 we shall return to this point in detail, exploring the distinctiveness of Barth's theological conceptuality in IV/3.

one in separation from the other), they shall start to see the ontic and noetic aspects of Jesus Christ's mediatorship in triadic, rather than binary terms. I contend that it is a consequence of offering a triadic, rather than dualistic or binary, interpretation of Jesus's mediatorship as described by Barth, that the flourishing of humanity is driven back into the very structures of God's sovereign freedom. On this reading, God may not be thought as being eternally free from humanity, but as having the freedom to give human subjects a share in the covenantal history in which God's being is in becoming.

Re-assessing the Importance of *Church Dogmatics* IV/3

The value of IV/3 has, hitherto, gone largely unappreciated in scholarship. There may be several reasons for this. Perhaps the most obvious explanation is the sheer difficulty of interpreting the volume. As Webster articulates, IV/3 is "a highly complex text . . . The depth and range [of Barth's moves] are acutely difficult to capture; and Barth's peculiar rhetoric, now more than ever composed of layer after layer of variation and recapitulation of primary themes, will not yield to linear restatement."[5] But the more damaging explanation is that IV/3 has often been regarded as being of no particular theological value.[6] Consequently, scholars tend not to invest their interpretative energies in this (the largest) part-volume of the *Dogmatics*, when it is thought that the main doctrinal moves have been elucidated in prior volumes.

This may not be of great surprise, since Barth insists that IV/3 cannot develop "our material knowledge of the event of reconciliation" because everything that has to be said of the content of the story of Jesus Christ "is exhausted" by what has been set out in IV/1 and IV/2.[7] Yet this observation is misleading, if left unqualified, because it suggests, firstly, that the consideration of Christology from the perspective of the "God-man" can contribute no further development of our knowledge of Jesus Christ; and it also implies that an examination of the *munus propheticum* can only help to clarify the nature of Christ as high priest and king, without itself adding another vital layer to the explication of Christ's saving reality. Barth's com-

---

5. Webster, "Eloquent and Radiant," 126.

6. Gunton explicitly articulates this view (see Gunton, "Salvation," 151, and Gunton, *The Barth Lectures*, 212), but the paucity of literature on IV/3, by contrast to the surfeit of attention paid to IV/1 and IV/2, also suggests a wider tacit consensus in scholarship that IV/3 is of limited interest. The most obvious example of this is Hunsinger's essay, "Karl Barth's Christology," 127–42, which offers substantive reflection only on IV/1 and IV/2.

7. IV/3, 7.

ment was intended merely to reflect the fact that the divine and human natures are fulfilled in Christ's two-fold identity as the self-abnegating *Deus pro nobis* (the *status exinanitionis* explicated in IV/1), and as the exalted royal human (the *status exaltationis* developed in IV/2),[8] and that Christ's being-in-act as such is "intrinsically perfect and unsurpassable,"[9] requiring no augmentation, nor indicating the synthesis of the divine and human natures into a higher third.[10] Yet the third part-volume, whilst refusing any suggestion of a third Christological nature, and therefore adding no new "material" Christological content, does constitute an original and valuable development of Barth's Christology, soteriology, and the understanding of the divine and human natures. Where scholars fail to take note of the "God-man" Christology and of the function of the *munus propheticum* within the *munus triplex*, they are liable to fail to notice the radically participative nature of Barth's mature theology of freedom.

Chalcedonian Christology?

Commentators who read the mature Barth as consistently upholding an axiomatic disjunction between God and humanity are unlikely to be able to do justice to the place of IV/3 within Barth's Christological architectonic, since this text not only claims that the true natures of God and humanity are revealed in the history of Christ, but that the historical mutuality, simultaneity, and reciprocity of Christ's two natures is itself determinative of His identity as the subject of election. The interpretative emphasis placed

---

8. See, Jones, *The Humanity of Christ*, 122.

9. IV/3, 7 rev.

10. Gorringe is right to indicate that Barth made increasingly less use of Anselm's phrase "God-man," because he was afraid that a certain conception of Christ as God-man obscures Christ's dialectical "historicity" (Gorringe, *Karl Barth against Hegemony*, 233). Barth insisted that Jesus's humanity and divinity are not resolved into a third, higher "state" but are the "event of the co-ordination of the two predicates" (IV/2, 115). Barth says that the one history of Christ represents the mutuality of two distinct partners and not the dissolution of the individual identities of the two into a third, which would destroy the reciprocity of the covenant which Christ came to secure; the mere synthesis of God and humanity would simply extinguish the relationship that Christ serves by obliterating the distinction of the two who relate. Nevertheless, Barth had used the term in his soteriological survey: "This is Jesus Christ . . . very God, very man, very God-man [*Gottmensch*]" (IV/1, 126 = KD IV/1, 139). As long, therefore, as it is remembered that the formula refers to the event of the reciprocal simultaneity that occurs in the history of Christ between two distinct covenantal partners, there is no reason why the term might not be retained to characterize Barth's ambitions in the theology of mediation in IV/3. In fact, Barth does continue to use the term in IV/3, despite his wariness of it: see, for example, IV/3, 66, "[Jesus Christ] is the God-man."

on the separation of God and humanity is perpetuated by the common assumption that Barth operates with a standard "Chalcedonian," two natures Christology in the doctrine of reconciliation.[11] The most sophisticated reading of volume IV in this vein is Hunsinger's essay "Karl Barth's Christology: Its Basic Chalcedonian Character," where the author argues that central to Barth's Christology is the Chalcedonian formula's implication that "The relation of Christ's two natures . . . suggests an abiding mystery of their unity-in-distinction and distinction-in-unity."[12] For Hunsinger, Barth imposes a juxtaposition of the divine and human in Christ through the alternation of Alexandrian and Antiochene Christological statements, the purpose of which is to "comprehend the incomprehensibility of the incarnation precisely in its incomprehensibility."[13] Hunsinger rightly undercuts the ease with which some commentators have charged Barth both with docetism and Nestorianism, and suggests that to interpret his Chalcedonianism in one-sidedly Alexandrian or Antiochene terms is to miss the genuinely dialectical nature of his thought, by which he sought "to provide as descriptively adequate an account as might be possible of an event that was, by definition, inherently ineffable."[14] Hunsinger reads this Chalcedonian juxtaposition as the reaffirmation of Barth's claim in I/1 that

> It is impossible to listen at one and the same time to the two statements that Jesus of Nazareth is the Son of God, and the Son of God is Jesus of Nazareth. One hears either the one or the other or one hears nothing. When one is heard, the other can be heard only indirectly, in faith.[15]

Hunsinger's work represents an excellent overview of Barth's Christology, yet it subtly perpetuates a slightly misleading distortion of Barth's mature actualism, failing to see that Christ not only reveals who God and humanity are in historical relation to one another, but that this historical mutuality itself provides the ontological terms in which God and humanity are determined in asymmetrical reciprocity. It is telling that Hunsinger reads Barth's mature Christology in basic continuity with the rudimentary Christology of the *prolegomenon*; this suggests that he has placed an emphasis on the divine-human "distinction" over their historical "unity" and

---

11. See, for example, Torrance, *Karl Barth: Biblical and Evangelical Theologian*, 169; 198–201.
12. Hunsinger, "Karl Barth's Christology," 129.
13. Ibid., 130.
14. Ibid., 132.
15. I/1, 180. Hunsinger, "Karl Barth's Christology," 131.

reciprocal determination, and that he has not, therefore, sufficiently accounted for Barth's Christological development after II/2.

This is not to say that Hunsinger is inattentive to the strongly participative elements of volume IV, and he rightly insists that the event of Christ's life forms an embodied, historical "mutual participation"[16] between God and humanity—a covenantal *koinonia*.[17] Indeed, Hunsinger correctly concludes that the humiliation and exaltation that occurs in the divinity and humanity of Christ on the cross is meaningful only when considered as "the moment of their supreme simultaneity."[18] Hunsinger's "juxtaposition" thesis cannot therefore be equated with Prenter who accuses Barth of undulating between the imposition of a Nestorian gap between the two natures,[19] and movement in a monophysite and semi-docetic direction.[20] Hunsinger's essay is in fact a concerted effort to guard against both poles of such criticism. Moreover, Hunsinger is right to identify Barth's qualification of the personal simplicity of Christ by doing full justice to the sheer agential complexity suggested by the two natures.[21] Nevertheless, his reading of Barth's mature Christology is informed by a commitment to the "formal" conception of divine freedom of the first volume of the *Dogmatics*, which sought to protect the sovereignty of God's isolated being *in se* from any implication of historical necessity. God's being *pro nobis* cannot, for Hunsinger (as we saw in Chapter 2), be said to impact ontologically on God's being *in se*. Rather, the former corresponds to the latter only in the analogical sense that God re-iterates or interprets Godself for a second time in the history of revelation.

McCormack and Jones have recently called into question the adequacy of describing Barth's Christology in volume IV as Chalcedonian, on the grounds that "Barth's later Christology does not so much constitute a revision of the meaning of the terms employed in the formula as it does the substitution of an altogether different ontology which makes continued use of the term 'Chalcedonian' misleading as applied to him."[22] For McCormack the Apollinarian (an extreme example of Alexandrian Christology) and

---

16. Hunsinger, "Karl Barth's Christology," 134, citing IV/2, 117.
17. Hunsinger, "Karl Barth's Christology," 134.
18. Ibid., 135.
19. Prenter, "Karl Barths Umbildung der traditionellen Zweinaturlehre in lutherischer Beleuchtung," 28.
20. Ibid., 79.
21. See also, Jones, *The Humanity of Christ*, 103.
22. McCormack, "Karl Barth's Historicized Christology," 201 n1.

Nestorian tendencies in Chalcedonian interpretations of the *communicatio idiomatum* share a common problematic basis:

> Their source is a process of thought which "abstracts" the Logos from his human "nature" in order, by turns, now to make the human "nature" something to be acted upon by the Logos and now to make of that "nature" a subject in its own right in order to seal the Logos off hermetically from human experiences such as death. In both cases, the Logos has been "abstracted" from the human "nature" and made into an abstract metaphysical subject (the Logos *simpliciter*).[23]

In other words, both the Alexandrian and Antiochene interpretations of the Chalcedonian formula seek to protect divine immutability by emphasizing a metaphysical gap between the human and divine, so that God's being *in se*, above and behind revelation, cannot be infringed upon by creaturely finitude. Hunsinger's "juxtaposition" thesis rightly wants to do justice to both sides of the formula dialectically, but carries over the metaphysical abstraction latent in each because it is concerned to protect God's being *in se* from any thoroughgoing ontological continuity with humanity.

Hence one can *either* consider Jesus Christ as the revelation of God (the divine self-interpretation in a second, historical form), *or* one can consider Christ as the appropriate human response to the loving God. Indeed, one can hold this either/or dialectically together, but in both cases reflection on the two natures functions as explication of the relation established between two radically discontinuous partners in the history of revelation, not as a deeper ontological claim that this co-inherence of two natures in one person is the historical actualization of God's eternal determination of the covenant. By reading volume IV in continuity with Barth's Chalcedonianism in I/2, Hunsinger seeks to protect the claim that God's "Word would still be His Word apart from this becoming, just as Father, Son and Holy Spirit would be none the less eternal God, if no world had been created."[24] But as we saw in Chapter 2, for the Barth of II/2 and beyond it is precisely this "becoming" which is ontologically constitutive of God's being-in-act, and the *logos asarkos* is to be interpreted as a volitional "placeholder (*Platzhalter*)"[25] for the name Jesus Christ. On Hunsinger's "juxtaposition" interpretation, as in the Alexandrian and Antiochene readings of Chalcedon from which it is derived, "a wedge is driven between 'essence' and 'existence' in such a

---

23. Ibid., 206.

24. I/2, 135 rev.

25. II/2, 96 rev. = *KD* II/2, 103; see also, Jones, *The Humanity of Christ*, 95; see also, Jüngel, *Karl Barth*, 130.

way that whatever happens on the level of existence has no effect on that which a person is essentially."[26] In other words, the personal simplicity of Christ's historical existence, in which two distinct agents are mutually and simultaneously embodied, has no bearing on what the second person of the trinity most essentially is, viz. the one who elects God and humanity to covenantal fellowship. The subjectivity, actuality or eventfulness of Christ's objective identity, disclosed as the meeting or dramatic encounter between God and humanity in covenantal reciprocity, is undermined by the need to abstract the ontological identity of God's being *in se* from God's historical becoming *ad extra*.

It is not surprising that on Hunsinger's reading there is a tacit downgrading of the importance of IV/3 to Barth's soteriological architectonic, which he omits almost completely from his introduction to Barth's Christology.[27] The ontological significance for God and humanity of Christ's divine-human simultaneity is under-emphasized in an attempt to protect against interpretations of Barth that take the co-incidence of divinity and humanity in Christ's historical existence to impact on the eternal essence of God. By moving back and forth between Alexandrian and Antiochene considerations of the two distinct natures Hunsinger can "bear witness to the desire to say that Jesus Christ is 'complete in deity' and 'complete in humanity'" but he cannot do justice to the Chalcedonian prefix "one person in two natures." Accordingly, "Hunsinger effectively leaves to one side the first element in his definition because he never treats the problem of the ontology of the *subject* of the twofold history of humiliation and exaltation."[28] For McCormack, Hunsinger fails to see that in volume IV Barth affirms the basic values of the Chalcedonian formula, but does so "only by replacing the category of 'nature' with the category of 'history' and then by integrating 'history' into his concept of 'person.'"[29] And why does Barth substitute the "two natures" ontology for a historicized, Christological actualism? It is because the Chalcedonian language of "nature" does not correspond uniformly to Barth's mature intention not simply to declare that Jesus Christ reveals the nature of God and the nature of humanity, but more powerfully

---

26. McCormack, "Karl Barth's Historicized Christology," 211.

27. Hunsinger does offer some useful reflections on IV/3 in the epilogue to *How to Read Karl Barth*, and it must be noted that in that passage he takes efforts to stress the participative tones of this text. Nevertheless, Hunsinger's reflections, whilst lucid and informative, fail to emphasize the radicality of the ontological significance of the unity of Christ's two natures.

28. McCormack, "Karl Barth's Historicized Christology," 222–23 n52.

29. Ibid., 222.

that the singleness of the history of God and humanity existing mutually in Christ is itself the ontic ground of all reality, divine and human:

> The unity of what might seem to be two distinct histories finds its ground in the "primal decision" of God in election. The unity here is not the unity provided by an abstract metaphysical subject; it is the concrete unity of a decision in which God gives both to himself and to humanity his and their essential being and does so with respect to one and the same figure, Jesus of Nazareth. It is in and through this *one* history of the man Jesus that what is essential to both God and humanity is concretely realized.[30]

Jones expands on the reasons for Barth's movement away from the Chalcedonian language of "two natures": "The word [*physis* (*Natur* or *Wesen*)] is simply not one that appeals to [the mature] Barth. It chafes against his preference for language that conveys concreteness, actualism, and sheer eventfulness of biblical descriptions of Christ; it struggles, more particularly, to depict the integration of Christology and soteriology basic to the New Testament."[31] Barth prefers instead, to speak of the "name" Jesus Christ, which is the biblically testified "true witness" to the unity of the free God and free humanity existing simultaneously in their historically actualized freedom for each other. This name reveals that in

> the meeting of God and man which constitutes His existence [*Existenz*], there naturally stands an inner *connexion* [*innerer Zusammenhang*] . . . [which] consists in the fact that on both sides freedom is the form and character of the intercourse between true God and true man . . . It is in this way and this way alone, in this reciprocal *freedom* [*in beiderseitiger Freiheit*], that this intercourse corresponds to the relationship between God and man and man and God by which the existence of this man is constituted.[32]

To do justice to the eternal election to essential mutuality signified by this name, one must not only hear by dialectical turns now the divine, now the human, but must hear them both in their eventful simultaneity and mutual actuality. Thus in IV/3 Barth seems to modify his claim in I/2 that

---

30. Ibid., 228.

31. Jones, *The Humanity of Christ*, 32. See Butin, "Two Early Reformed Catechisms," 206–7, who explains that Barth "recommends . . . the dynamic and more narrative approach to Christology used originally by Calvin" because of the "abstract definition" of Christ's natures that had been proposed in Reformed orthodoxy.

32. IV/3, 381 = *KD* IV/3, 441.

"it is impossible to listen at one and the same time to the two statements that Jesus of Nazareth is the Son of God, and the Son of God is Jesus of Nazareth," by saying that it is precisely as one hears these two together (that is, triadically, where there are two distinct terms *and* the relation between them, necessary for an identification of each) that the freedom of God and the freedom of humanity are disclosed.

The Historical Simultaneity of Christ's Divinity and Humanity

Barth adverts to his commitment to thinking of God and humanity in their Christologically actualized togetherness in the well-known lecture on "The Humanity of God," delivered in 1956 whilst preparing IV/3.[33] Here Barth reflects on the shift that has taken place between his early theology and his mature theology of freedom.

> What began forcibly to press itself upon us about forty years ago was not so much the humanity of God as His *deity*—a God absolutely unique in His relation to man and the world, overpoweringly lofty and distant, strange, yes even wholly other.[34]

This, Barth now admits, had compromised the account of God's faithful relationality. "Unmistakably for us the *humanity* of God at that time moved from the centre to the periphery, from the emphasised subordinate clause to the less emphasised subordinate clause."[35] Barth now realizes that the appropriate site for the location of divine freedom is in God's freedom for humanity, willed in eternity and actualized historically in Christ:

> [T]he *deity* of the living God . . . found its meaning and its power only in the context of His history and of His dialogue with *man*, and thus in His *togetherness* with man . . . Who God is and what He is in His deity He proves and reveals not in a vacuum as a divine being-for-Himself, but precisely and authentically in the fact that He exists, speaks, and acts as the *partner* of man, though of course as the absolutely superior partner . . . And the freedom in which He does *that* is His deity.[36]

Barth insists that in and of itself the attempt to protect God's sovereignty had not been a mistake, since with the rise of liberalism "man was

---

33. Karl Barth, "The Humanity of God," 33–64.
34. Ibid., 33.
35. Ibid., 34.
36. Ibid., 42.

made great at the cost of God."[37] Nevertheless, a qualified "revision" of the early theology was now in order.[38] It was incumbent upon the mature Barth not to sacrifice the sovereign ontological priority of God in God's freedom, but to indicate that God's transcendent sovereignty is actualized in God's historical relationality, and is not therefore to be protected over against it.

Barth had suggested in II/2 that God's sovereign divine freedom for self-determination is exercised in His self-election to relationship with humanity. He now takes this point to a further depth, stressing the historicity of the divine-human simultaneity in Christ. "In Jesus Christ there is no isolation of man from God or of God from man. Rather, in Him we encounter the history, the dialogue, in which God and man meet together and are together, the reality of the covenant *mutually* contracted, preserved, and fulfilled by them."[39] For the Barth of IV/3 the simultaneity and mutuality of the essential determination of God and humanity is itself ontologically significant. God will not determine or reveal Godself apart from God's historical encounter with humanity; nor does God determine human being for God other than through the moment of God's own self-determination in Christ. In the theology of *Romans* II Barth had claimed that God is free as the divine "I" who stands absolutely over against the human other. By IV/3 Barth is able to say of God that

> God Himself says I in this Other, so that, whether we realize it or not, the decision is made that God will accomplish His personal life-act [*Lebenstat*] only together with us, and we can accomplish ours only together with God. This co-existence [*Zusammenleben*] may take different forms. But the fact the Jesus lives as attested in the biblical testimony to this history means that there is this union [*Verbindung*] between God and each of us men, and that it is indestructible [*unzerreißbar*].[40]

Since the doctrine of reconciliation considers Christ's history from three perspectives, by reflecting on the mutuality of Christ's divinity and humanity in IV/3 Barth subtly modifies the claim that, as Jüngel puts it, there can be "no humanlessness of God" and "no absolute godlessness of humanity,"[41] by demonstrating that salvation does not comprise two events,

---

37. Ibid., 36–37.

38. Ibid., 38. As Jüngel has insisted, the fourth volume of the *Dogmatics* constitutes "a great recapitulation, but also revision of Barth's entire theology" (Jüngel, "Einführung in Leben und Werk Karl Barths," 53).

39. Barth, "The Humanity of God," 43.

40. IV/3, 41 = *KD* IV/3, 43.

41. See Jüngel, "Keine Menschenlosigkeit Gottes," 332–47.

Divine and Human Freedom in Asymmetrical Reciprocity   119

but one single event mutually actualized. Whereas IV/1 looks "upwards, to God who loves the world... [in the] divine and sovereign act of reconciling grace," and IV/2 "downwards, to the world which is loved by God... [and] to the being of man reconciled with God in this act," IV/3 concerns itself with the "middle point between them" which is the presupposition of the two.[42] For Barth,

> It is only from this middle point that we have been able to look upwards and downwards... [And] that one thing in the middle is one person, Jesus Christ... In Him that turning of God to man and conversion of man to God is actuality in the appointed order of the mutual inter-relationship, and therefore in such a way that the former aims at the latter and the latter is grounded in the former.[43]

When Christ is considered not just as very God, nor as very man, but as the historical actualization of the two in simultaneity as the God-man, we see that "the sovereign act of the reconciling God and the being of reconciled man are one."[44] IV/3 is the keystone in the architectonic of the doctrine of reconciliation because it addresses itself explicitly to the significance of "the unity of the two natures of Christ as the divine-human person and the unity of the two states of exaltation and humiliation,"[45] a point assumed throughout IV/1 and IV/2 but explored in depth only now.

Barth therefore affirms that

> The Creator, God Himself, exists only as He does so together with this One who also exists as man, and each and everything in the created world exists only together with this One who also exists as man. As God exists only together with this One, and so too the world, His existence is as such the fact in which God and the world, however much they may oppose or contradict one another, are not of course one and the same, but do exist together in an inviolable and indissoluble co-existence and conjunction [*in unangreifbarer und unauflöslicher Koexistenz und Verbindung*].[46]

As the co-existence of God and humanity, Christ is objectively (i.e. ontologically) the mediator. The eternal determination of divine and human

42. IV/1, 122.
43. Ibid.
44. Ibid., 123.
45. Webster, *Barth*, 116.
46. IV/3, 39–40.

beings is described as being actualized in historical simultaneity, in the single event of reciprocal divine-human becoming in Jesus Christ. In a key passage Barth describes the objective mediation of Christ between creator and creature in some of the most overtly relational and actualistic terms used hitherto:

> That Jesus Christ lives [tells us] that His existence is act [*sein Dasein ist Akt*]; that it is being in spontaneous actualisation . . . the actualisation of being in absolutely sovereign spontaneity, after the manner in which the Creator, God, actualises Himself, so that His life-action is identical with that of God Himself, His history with the divine history. Again, however, we must add that the actualisation is also after the manner in which it is given to the creature to actualise itself . . . As Jesus Christ lives, there takes place in Him both creative actualisation of being, yet also in and with it creaturely actualisation; creative and creaturely life together, without the transformation of one into the other . . . or separation or division between them . . . [In Jesus Christ, God and humanity] live together (though not in identity) in the indestructible conjunction [*in unzerstörbarer Verbindung*] of the differentiated act in which both Creator and creature exist.[47]

Jesus Christ is, for Barth, the historical ground of reality insofar as all being, divine and created, is ordered for relationship in the actualization of the covenant in Jesus's life-act. Christ's mediatorial life is not that "of a negotiator running to and fro between two parties and now speaking for the one, now for the other. It is that of the One who is both Yahweh and Israelite, both the Lord and His Servant . . . in one and the same person."[48] God, Barth tells us, "is not content merely to be with man as in some sense his great Neighbour . . . [Rather] He goes and comes to him, [takes] him to Himself in His own person, not merely as one who is conjoined with Him, but as one who is His faithful covenant-partner."[49]

Barth's mature understanding of the relation of divine and human reality may therefore be appropriately described as Christocentric *asymmetrical reciprocity*. The word "reciprocal" in grammar expresses mutual action or relationship; in mathematics a "reciprocal" refers to a quantity or function so related to another that their product is unity. Importantly, in both the grammatical and mathematical senses of the word, reciprocity does not indicate simple equality or symmetry, but rather complex mutuality. This

---

47. IV/3, 40 = *KD* IV/3, 42.
48. IV/3, 51.
49 Ibid., 43.

is the manner in which we ought to consider Barth's understanding of the "oneness" (*Einheit*) that exists between God and humanity in their Christic mutual implication. The two partners are reciprocal in that the essence of each can only be thought in the expression of the relationship in which they exist; yet the relationship is ordered asymmetrically. God does not yield to the being and act of a partner on equal footing, being conditioned by the creature in the same way that God conditions all reality, but rather takes the sovereign decision not to exist on any other terms than those of a relationship for which the other is essential.

In this respect Barth remains consistent with a basic principle that had governed his references to freedom from the start of his theology, namely, the primacy and self-determination of God in God's lordship. Barth still insists that "There is no question of binding obligation ... No question of a binding necessity arises."[50] God retains God's "own initiative" even "in His overflowing kindness towards [humanity]."[51] It does mean, however, that Barth limits the way in which we can speak of God's lordship, because the free self-determination of God has a definite, historical character. The reciprocity of God and humanity within this historical event is such that we cannot think of God's being as an objective essence existing in an eternal continuity only with itself, in relation to which the history of the world is ontologically arbitrary. We may only think of God's essence in terms of God's existence as the supreme subject (i.e. the primary enactor) of the covenantal history with the world actualized in Christ the God-man. To abstract theological speech from the contours of this reciprocal actualization of being is to imagine a no-god; it is to try to think God as if God were not this God.

The Integration of the Objective and Subjective Categories in *Church Dogmatics* IV/3

Criticisms of *Church Dogmatics* IV/3: Object–Subject Disjunction

At this point, however, questions arise as to whether Barth does indeed conceive God and humanity as existing in an authentic covenantal reciprocity. For although Christ is objectively (i.e. ontologically) the mediator between two fractured parties, it has been suggested that Barth's texts neglect an authentically active role for humanity in the life of the covenant. Yes, we are liberated upon receipt of the knowledge that God is free for us; but this liberation, the event of human flourishing, appears to be entirely accidental to,

---

50. Ibid., 383.
51. Ibid., 382.

and perhaps even obliterated by, God's free self-determination on the cross. Critics have questioned just how participative Barth's doctrine of reconciliation is. On this reading, IV/3 is said to add little to Barth's real soteriological contribution in IV/1 and IV/2, and represents nothing more than a noetic addendum to Barth's soteriology. Gunton surmises as much, saying

> [T]he third part-volume . . . cannot be said to add much to Barth's understanding of salvation, except to reinforce his contention that it is a finished act. It is the part-volume devoted to what can be called the "mediatorship of Christ," to that focus of his one saving action that sees him as both God and man mediating between loving God and lost humankind. In what does the mediatorship consist? It is largely a matter of revelation.[52]

According to Gunton, the theology of IV/3 has little to do with the objective content of salvation, and merely represents the "subjective" revelation of the salvation achieved "objectively" in Christ's priestly and kingly offices. On Gunton's reading the consideration of Christ *qua* prophet simply serves to "bring home a past work";[53] Christ reveals contemporaneously what He has already achieved once for all through the incarnation and the cross.[54]

Gunton is right that Barth does not emphasize the language of bodily participation;[55] indeed, the primary images Barth employs to describe soteriological mediation are overly externalistic, epistemic, and non-corporeal, and do not therefore serve to indicate sufficiently that Barth is increasingly ready to think of God and humanity as existing in a dramatic, bodily unity in and through Jesus Christ the God-man.[56] For example, he says that "as the world is told, not merely what is resolved concerning it, but what has

---

52. Gunton, "Salvation," 151.

53. Gunton, *The Barth Lectures*, 212.

54. So Bloesch: "what has already been achieved and enacted must be apprehended and acknowledged in the here and now" (Bloesch, *Jesus Is Victor!*, 111).

55. Gunton, "Salvation," 152.

56. In IV/3 the leading metaphors employed by Barth are knowledge, truth and falsehood, witness, proclamation, acknowledgement, recognition, speech, the word, revelation, light, and so forth. Barth seems therefore to prefer a Johannine lexicon to the Pauline imagery of the body. Taken alongside Barth's provocative, and often misunderstood, interrogation of the ecclesial language of the "sacraments" in IV/4, it is perhaps unsurprising that the mature Barth has been read as upholding a radical disjunction between God and the world, in line with his somewhat dualistic early thought (Barth came to insist that "sacraments are nothing whatever but response" (Barth, "An Outing to the Bruderholz," 88), and that baptism must be regarded as "an act, a confession . . . not as a 'means' of grace and salvation, not as a 'sacrament'" (Barth, "Letter to H. Bizer, 29 March 1963," in *Letters 1961–1968*, 96).

already been done for it . . . as it is thus given news concerning itself, it has to decide whether it will accept this information or not."[57] Such moments do not cohere well with the actualistic direction in which he was moving, *pace* the early attempt to draw a sharp distinction between God and the world. It suggests that the risen Christ merely conveys dogmatic information that concerns us without really involving us.[58] Yet I argue that an alternative reading of IV/3 is possible, where the revelation of salvation is integral to the covenant's historical actuality. Interpreters have often failed to appreciate the radically participative currents in IV/3, with the consequence that they are forced to downgrade the role of this part-volume within Barth's soteriological architectonic. And this under-appreciation rests on the reticence of some scholars to re-evaluate the way we think theologically about the object-subject paradigm.

The critics' oversight of IV/3 tends to have its roots in the identification of two related "object-subject" disjunctions in Barth's so-called "soteriological objectivism":[59] i) a disjunction of Christ's contemporaneous, subjective mediation and appropriation of salvation from the objective content of His atoning identity as very God, very man; ii) the separation of human subjectivity (that is, our knowing and acting) from the objective content of Christ's vicarious salvation. These two disjunctions represent two sides of the same coin: one downgrades the subjectivity of Christ's prophetic agency to the mere communication of epistemic propositions, and the other takes human participation merely to be the cognitive acknowledgement of such propositions. Both fail to recognize that the divine-human history of subjectivity

---

57. IV/3, 186.

58. At times Barth appears to fall under the bracket of Rahner's criticism, levelled against Western theology (particularly that of Protestant traditions), that all too often the resurrection and ascension are divorced from the crucifixion, such that whilst the cross bears transformational ontic significance, the Easter *kerygma* can serve only as noetic confirmation and revelation. See Rahner, "Dogmatic Questions on Easter," 121-33.

59. This term refers to Barth's anti-Pelagian position that Christ achieves covenantal reconciliation "by Himself" *de jure* (IV/1, 15), without any need of a further contribution or completion by human subjects (IV/1, 76), regardless of the *de facto* human recognition of its vicarious completion (IV/2, 511). See also, Hunsinger, *How to Read Karl Barth*, 103ff.; Bloesch, *Jesus Is Victor!*, 32ff. Barth's soteriological objectivism is informed by a consistent critique of Bultmann's existentialism (IV/1, ix; see also, Hunsinger, *How to Read Karl Barth*, 139), which in Barth's view threatened the unique sovereignty of Christ by setting up the interpretative agency of the human subject as a necessary component in the mediation of divine grace (see Yocum, *Ecclesial Mediation in Karl Barth*, 98). However, as I shall demonstrate, it is wrong to read in Barth's critique of Bultmann a blanket interdiction against the subjective participation of human agents in the event of salvation and even in God's being itself (see Neder, *Participation in Christ*, 47).

is itself ingredient in the objective, ontic identity of God, undermining the point that God's being is bound up with God's activity (becoming) in the world.

Firstly, some scholars find that the subjectivity or activity of Christ in His prophetic office has, to a significant degree, been externalized in relation to the objective content or brute actuality of reconciliation achieved in His priestly and kingly offices.[60] Hence whilst the priestly and kingly offices achieve the material, ontological reconciliation between God and humanity, the contemporaneous activity of Christ in His prophetic office is ultimately accidental to the core of His saving achievement.[61] If there is a double aspect to the mediatorship of Christ—His ontological mediation between two fractured parties, and the subjective mediation of knowledge about this material reconciliation—then the first is seen as having been fully explicated in IV/1 and IV/2, and the second (IV/3) is not itself considered ingredient in the historical consummation of the former. Come, for example, questions "whether the communication of the gospel to men . . . (the prophetic office of Christ, IV/3) is really part of and the fulfilment of Christ's work of reconciliation or whether the communication is of a past event completed on the cross and now needs only to be told about."[62] Gunton cites a popular criticism which identifies a tendency in Barth's Christology to see "Jesus Christ as a kind of Platonic form of humanity, so that salvation is universally achieved *already*, and its appropriation only a matter of knowing that we are saved."[63] The "noetic" mediation and appropriation of salvation is thus read

---

60. See Gunton, "Salvation," 153–54; see also, Torrance, *Karl Barth: Biblical and Evangelical Theologian*, 134, who finds that the contemporaneous mediation of salvation is undermined by a slightly dualistic and docetic tendency in Barth's soteriology.

61. There may be a systematic reason underlying the criticisms of IV/3 as subjectivistic and soteriologically extraneous. Barth reverses Calvin's "prophet-king-priest" ordering of the *munus triplex*, so that the prophetic work of Christ may be seen as being a noetic afterthought to the priestly and kingly offices. (See Calvin, *Institutes*, 494ff.; Butin, "Two Early Reformed Catechisms," 197) But this was in fact the opposite of Barth's architectonic intention; Butin has argued convincingly that it was Barth's "strategy for giving the prophetic aspect of Christ's office the prominence he feels it deserves . . . to accord it the final place in the Christological sequence . . . Barth wants to avoid the minimising or 'tacking on' of the prophetic office which he has already criticised in the earlier tradition" (Butin, "Two Early Reformed Catechisms," 203–4; see also, IV/1, 137ff; 527; IV/3, 14ff.). Barth was suspicious of the risk, latent in the post-Reformation treatment of the *munus triplex*, that "the prophetic office threatens to become isolated from its incarnational and soteriological context . . . [and he thus] pushes the *munus propheticum* much more deeply into the structure of Christology and soteriology" (Webster, "Eloquent and Radiant," 131).

62. Come, *An Introduction to Barth's "Dogmatics" for Preachers*, 161.

63. Gunton, "Salvation," 155. See also, Gunton, "No Other Foundation," 71; see also, Jenson, *Alpha and Omega*,168; and Prenter, "Karl Barth's Umbildung der traditionellen

as being detached from the "ontic" reality of Christ's life-act, even if Gunton acknowledges this is not Barth's intention.[64]

The second disjunction is of a piece with the first, and concerns the relation of our human subjectivity to the objectivity of salvation achieved in Christ's priestly and kingly offices. Just as Christ's risen and ascended contemporaneous revelation is rendered external to salvation's prior, ontic accomplishment on Golgotha, so too our own subjective, agential participation in the salvation event is often construed in dualistic rhetoric. Some readings of volume IV have tended to assume rather simplistically that the divine-human fellowship willed by God has been achieved objectively in Christ, and that this once-for-all, completely vicarious accomplishment is subjectively made known or reiterated through the communication of knowledge to human subjects, whose agency comprises little more than a retrospective cognitive glance back to Christ's passion, and a prospective looking forward to a time when Christ's truth will universally be known.[65] On this line, human subjectivity is rendered basically external and accidental to God's work in Christ and to the historicity of God's self-determining freedom, ultimately jeopardizing the authenticity of human agential responsibility and its relation to divine agency. Bloesch, for example, follows Brunner and Come saying,

> Barth does not succeed in doing justice to the subjective dimension of salvation or in holding both dimensions in balance. The

---

Zweinaturlehre in lutherischer Beleuchtung," 1–88 (esp. 75ff.). This so-called platonic disjunction between Christ's soteriological "objectivity" and "subjectivity" can also be described in eschatological terms as the divorce of what Christ completed for us "there and then" from what Christ means for us "here and now." Admittedly, Gunton questions whether this line of criticism is as much of a problem as others have maintained when one sees that time and space are at every point bound up in God's eternity, and on this basis he notes that the vicareity of Christ's particular, earthly history is not to be divorced from its contemporaneous mediation. "God's eternity means here His contemporaneity to all times, and the application of a simple 'before' and 'after' is therefore impossible" (Gunton, "Salvation," 156).

64. Gunton accepts that for Barth we are not given knowledge merely of Christ's "effects," as Melanchthon had insisted (a belief re-capitulated by Bultmann, to Barth's doctrinal chagrin), but of His being (Gunton, "Salvation," 153; see also, II/1, 259; ChrL, 87).

65. Bloesch, *Jesus Is Victor!*, 106; Macken, *The Autonomy Theme*, 86. Gunton accepts that for Barth human subjectivity does not entail mere cognition of information, since the discovery of what Christ has done for us effects a genuine transformation on the level of being. But he does not think that Barth allows sufficient space for human participation in the actualization of the drama of reconciliation itself, and therefore locates in Barth a "non-participatory conception of knowledge." (See Gunton, "Salvation," 151–52).

paradox of salvation is ever again sundered in his emphasis on the objective to the detriment of the subjective. The crucial decision takes place outside ourselves in the suffering and death of Christ, where our situation and destiny are irrevocably altered, irrespective of personal faith.[66]

Salvation is something that happens to us and for us (*pro nobis*), but not in, with and through us (*in nobis*),[67] and, to put it in eschatological terms, the openness of our future orientation to the covenant is shut down by the Platonic vicariousness of Christ's duplex being.[68] For Willis, Barth's soteriological "transcendentalism" nullifies the particularity of the Christian community's existence, since there is little but an epistemological difference between Christians and non-Christians: "Man *is* reconciled now, whether he realises this fact or not . . . The distinction between the Christian community and the world is epistemological, not ontological, in nature."[69]

It will be noted that there is a direct inversion here of the criticism lodged by Bonhoeffer (see Chapter 1) that Barth over-emphasized the subjective at the expense of the objective. Now it is claimed that Barth onesidedly emphasizes the objective soteriological category thus jeopardizing the integrity of the subjective side of salvation. Yet both criticisms share the same ground, having their roots in the complaint that Barth seeks to posit a strong separation between divine being and human knowing and acting, consequently resulting either in the non-objectivity of God (early Barth), or in the over-objectification of his soteriology (mature Barth). Such criticisms of Barth's soteriology tend to read the mature Barth essentially in continuity with the early Barth, by suggesting that he does not allow the historical *qua* historical to impact ontologically either on God's being or on the state of affairs between God and humanity.

It is true that Barth insists that the reconciliation of God and humanity is completed once for all by Christ's death on the cross.[70] In IV/3 Barth

---

66. Bloesch, *Jesus Is Victor!*, 110; see also, Come, *An Introduction to Barth's "Dogmatics" for Preachers*, 158ff; Brunner, *Dogmatics Volume I*, 348–50; see also, Berkouwer, *The Triumph of Grace*, 287–88.

67. See Willis, *The Ethics of Karl Barth*, 435.

68. McDowell terms this criticism the "eschatological 'christomonistic' problem," according to which "The future has already come in Christ (ontic), whether one is aware of it or not (noetic), by virtue of Christ's incarnate and high-priestly inclusion of us in himself" (McDowell, *Hope in Barth's Eschatology*, 165). For the charge of "Christomonism" see Althaus, *Die Christliche Wahrheit*, 56–57; Prenter, "Karl Barths Umbildung der traditionellen Zweinaturlehre in lutherischer Beleuchtung," 73; Zahrnt, *The Question of God*, 112ff.; Bloesch, *Jesus Is Victor!*, 66.)

69. Willis, *The Ethics of Karl Barth*, 436.

70. IV/1, 244ff.

reminds readers of his soteriological objectivism, maintaining that Christ's saving achievement requires no completion, re-iteration, or augmentation by human subjects.[71] God does not only become for us as and when we come to know God, but is *Deus pro nobis* regardless of the adequacy of our theological knowledge.[72] Yet we misunderstand Barth if we view Jesus's incarnation, ministry, passion, death, and resurrection as a series of events which are then represented in the communication of dogmatic propositions which must simply be recognized and gratefully received—even if such acknowledgement effects a genuine agential transformation and correspondence in our own lives. To restrict talk about human participation in Christ's covenantal life-act to the analogical grammar of "correspondence" (as Barth admittedly himself often does[73]) is to perpetuate a one-directional linear reading of Barth's ontology that does not quite do justice to the radically participative elements in his mature actualism.[74] The mature Barth wants to say that "Participation is two-sided or reciprocal; it is not uni-directional," though of course he "finds it necessary to distinguish the *kind* of participation we are dealing with" on the divine and human sides.[75] Without jeopardizing the sovereignty of Christ's grace Barth wishes, in IV/3, to emphasize that we have a genuine and active share in His life-act (a share that extends beyond the posteriority and passivity of dogmatic acknowledgement), and that we are commissioned for authentic agential responsibility in relation to the covenant established, restored and completed in and through Christ. We are not the authors, executors or guarantors of God's covenantal will: Christ alone carries this responsibility in his three offices. As McCormack insists, human participation in the covenant cannot mean "deification"; but it can signify deep involvement "in a concrete history in which both the 'essence' of God and the 'essence' of the human are . . . *made real*."[76] In other words, human subjects are not merely spectators in the dramatic and reciprocal "making real" of the divine and human essences. God's story, whilst com-

---

71. IV/3, 8.

72. See also, IV/1, 229–30.

73. See for example, IV/1, 98; 634; 742; IV/2, 312; 529; IV/3, 532.

74. McDowell therefore rightly concludes that Barth's consistent use of the language of correspondence is not participative enough, having "all too little sense of the divine movement in and through the human" (McDowell, "Openness to the World," 276 n. 24). So also Mangina complains that, "the logic of 'correspondence' . . . is also highly problematic, since while it affirms God's enlistment of creaturely realities as witnesses to Jesus Christ, it just as firmly *excludes* the co-incidence of divine and human agency" (Mangina, *Karl Barth on the Christian Life*, 87).

75. McCormack, "Participation in God, Yes, Deification, No," 353–54.

76. Ibid., 349.

plete in eternity and actualized once for all in and through Jesus Christ, is not over, but continues to unfold to the extent that our histories form part of Christ's drama:

> [T]he kingdom of God come and the will of God done in Him ... while it is complete in itself, is only moving towards its fulfillment, i.e., not to an amplification or transcending of its content or declaration, which is neither necessary nor possible, but to a supremely radical alteration and extension of the mode and manner of its occurrence.[77]

The Integration of the Objective and Subjective Categories in *Church Dogmatics* IV/3

Barth opens his reflections on the *munus propheticum* by indicating the importance of turning to the history of Christ from this third perspective, in development of the first two Christological statements. If the Christological examination were to be broken off after IV/1 and IV/2, it would be evident that "Jesus Christ lives, as very God and very man, as Lord and Servant in all the singularity of the act of His existence," but it might well be concluded that the "supremely wonderful" life that Jesus lives "has no particular relevance to the state of things between God and man."[78] In such a case the Christological description from the first two perspectives might indicate that God has restored "co-existence" with humanity in an abstract ontological sense, but it would not be able to do justice to the fact that God desires living covenantal fellowship with humanity, and that as such the particular history of Christ must be and become a history which takes place in, with and through "the rest of world-occurrence."[79] If Christ's objective identity as mediator of the covenant between God and humanity is to be fulfilled in an actual and not merely "Platonic" sense, if it is to be "true" and not merely "real," then He must live His life-act in such a manner that binds up other human histories and subjects into the covenantal story of His being. Or as Barth says, "If Christology ... is to be anything more than an obscure metaphysics, in all its parts and aspects it can be only the unfolding of a drama."[80] Barth insists that

---

77. IV/3, 903.
78. Ibid., 42.
79. Ibid., 42.
80. Ibid., 136.

Jesus Christ does not live for Himself. His divine-human existence as divine-human act [*Sein göttlich-menschliches* Dasein *als göttlich-menschlicher* Akt], i.e., His life as we have so far described it, is not an end in itself. What kind of a Lord would He be, and what kind of Servant, if as such, for all that He has His life in common with others, He finally lived it in isolation in their midst, His lordship and servanthood in the creaturely world and humanity meaning only that He was unmistakably present in their midst, and that by His life the co-existence of the Creator with His creature, of God with man, was inviolably secured? In the New Testament the life of Jesus is naturally not seen in this abstraction. If it were, its witness could not be called good news. It might perhaps be described as the interesting disclosure of an ontological reality. But it could not be called . . . good news.[81]

The *de jure*, vicarious actualization of asymmetrically reciprocal relations between God and humanity in Christ is not an end in itself, but has its basis and its goal in God's desire to exist in authentic covenantal fellowship with all of humanity. Corresponding to what I have called a triadic interpretation of Jesus's divinity and humanity, it is also necessary to offer a triadic view of the relation of Jesus's saving being and action to His prophetic call after the resurrection. What Jesus has achieved in and of Himself (objectively), and how He communicates this truth (subjectively) to humanity at Easter and contemporaneously are certainly distinct terms, and must not be passed into one another if we are to avoid obscuring the New Testament's witness to the historical Jesus of first century Israel. Jesus is not just an idea to be grasped; nor does He merely communicate a spiritual or ethical message. But each term (what Jesus did, and how we come to learn of it) can only be understood when viewed in relation to the other. To offer a binary reading of Barth's texts in which Jesus's objective and subjective roles are taken in separation from one another, is to obscure *who* Barth's Jesus is in IV/3.

God not only says "Yes" to humanity in Jesus Christ, but also "stands by His Yes,"[82] faithfully guaranteeing that God shall not cease to affirm God's creatures, but shall conclude and confirm "His covenant with man, maintaining it and carrying it to its goal in spite of every threat."[83] As such, it belongs to Christ's objective identity as mediator that He attests the covenantal event of His being, in a form that allows other humans to become

81. Ibid., 41 = *KD* IV/3, 44.
82. IV/3, 3.
83. Ibid., 3.

actively implicated in the drama of grace. It is inclusive in the efficacy of Christ's saving identity that what He is objectively—viz. the truth of God and humanity existing in covenantal fellowship—must become true for the world. And since Christ's objective identity is emphasized in IV/3 as taking the form of an encounter or reciprocal drama, simply by living this life-act Jesus's identity takes place in a self-manifesting, mediating manner. As such the form of Christ's life is fundamentally expressive and attractive, manifesting and extending the content of His covenantal truth throughout the world, drawing others into the heart of its historical actualization.

> Because [Christ's] is the life of grace, it is this eloquent and radiant life. Grace would not be grace if it were to remain mute and obscure, or could try to be in and for itself alone. It would be a contradiction in terms if it did not mean self-disclosure and self-impartation.[84]

The prophetic office of Christ therefore belongs to the objective efficacy of Christ's reconciling activity alongside the priestly and royal offices, as form belongs to content, and as expression belongs to truth. As Jüngel says, "the prophetic office of Jesus Christ discloses his being in his work of reconciliation as a speech-event."[85] Reconciliation takes place as an event of divine speech, and is not therefore anterior to Christ's revelatory proclamation but bound up in it. This is why Barth insists that "reconciliation is indeed revelation . . . [Revelation] takes place as reconciliation takes place; as it has in it its origin, content and subject."[86]

This identification of revelation with reconciliation signals the extension of Barth's Christocentric actualism in IV/3. Since act and event are Barth's chief ontological categories, the "perspicuous and vocal" "How" of Jesus's life-act itself modifies the "What" of His divine-human truth, demonstrating that the reconciliation of the covenant is not only ontologically "real" as a vicarious, Platonic ideal to be acknowledged by human subjects, but is "true" for human subjects simply as it takes place in historical world-occurrence. To suggest that reconciliation is a fact established in the past and to be cognized contemporaneously is to miss Barth's contrast of organic truth and static reality, and to obscure his claim that the event of our subjective reception of the covenantal truth occurs only insofar as we encounter the living Christ. It is not that Christ lived the covenant in the past, and now reiterates what He lives. Rather, it is as He lives the encounter and unity of

---

84. Ibid., 81.
85. Jüngel, *God's Being Is in Becoming*, 14 n1.
86. IV/3, 8–9.

God and humanity here and now that the salvation drama occurs, and in a thoroughly expressive and attractive character:

> We understand His life as act . . . The divine and human act in which He lives is also as such His Word. As He performs it, He constitutes Himself a sign in which He faithfully repeats it in exact correspondence with its reality, meaning and purpose, correctly representing it, authentically sharing it, declaring it in such a way that it demands obedience, making it public and obligatory.[87]

It is here that the prophetic office forms a concrete part of Christ's saving identity; for as Christ lives the covenantal event of His being, He attests Himself. Or, put differently, Christ's prophetic proclamation of the reconciled covenant—His subjective mediation of salvation—is simply identical with the living event of His being, the objective actualization of the divine-human encounter that takes place in Him. As Hunsinger articulates, Christ "lives as the one who identifies himself *by means* of this history, and this history is the *content* of his self-identification."[88] Christ's prophetic revelation of salvation is quite simply eventful *self*-manifestation. "He does not need to look or point beyond Himself to attest the fulfilment of the covenant . . . The actualisation of His own life is coincident with [it]. In form and content His witness can only be self-witness: "Come unto me"; "I am" the way, the truth, the life, the door."[89]

As such, Christ is the fulfilment of the prophetic history of Israel. The prophets of Israel had a "mediatorial" function,[90] insofar as they attested the "living divine-human unity."[91] As witnesses of a sinful history, however, the prophets of Israel could only point indirectly to the covenant, speaking "as witnesses of the co-existence, but also of the constant and gaping contradiction within the co-existence, of Yahweh with Israel."[92] By contrast, Jesus Christ, as true prophet and true witness, may declare the truth of God and humanity in their unity, because He is, objectively, this truth, living it in perfect fulfilment, and allowing others to enter once and for all into the covenant without fear of a divine covenantal renunciation.

---

87. Ibid., 47.
88. Hunsinger, *How to Read Karl Barth*, 236.
89. IV/3, 51.
90. Ibid., 62.
91. Ibid., 63.
92. Ibid., 50.

> [W]hat distinguishes Him from them is that He stands on the basis of the fulfilment of the covenant. The abyss of the contradiction is no longer before but behind Him . . . What he attests is the peace made in the co-existence of God with His people . . . The prophecy of Jesus Christ is no mere indication. It is direct declaration.[93]

What I have been dealing with here is the first object-subject split identified above; namely, the complaint that in volume IV Christ's subjectivity as prophet and mediator is divorced from His soteriological objectivity as very God, very man. Careful reflection on the place of IV/3 in Barth's Christological architectonic demonstrates that the "subjectivity" of Christ in His prophetic office is an integral function of His "objectivity" as mediator between two fractured and distant parties. Hence, as Webster explains, "the 'subjective' aspect of reconciliation—its effectiveness in human knowledge—is a function of itself."[94] We cannot divorce the event of human knowing from the objective event of covenantal actualization, since the latter, if it is to be the establishment of a living covenant and not merely an "ontological reality," includes the former in itself.

At this point it is necessary to consider the second object-subject disjunction identified above, which is of a piece with the first. According to the critics, since Christ's subjective proclamation of the covenant is external to His objective reconciliation between God and humanity, human subjectivity can only be rendered in non-participative terms. Accordingly, we are spectators of the covenant's actualization, and whilst we are included vicariously in Christ's high-priestly representation, and although we may grapple cognitively with the event of Christ's being, our own knowing and acting is not itself ingredient in the realization of salvation. However, we have already begun to see that Barth actually locates Christ's subjectivity under the canopy of his soteriological objectivism, paving the way for the inclusion of human agency within Christ's own covenantal identity.

It is true that Barth maintains the sovereignty and primacy of divine subjectivity, and that he thereby denies the claims that God's being, the ontic actualization of salvation, or the revelation of these are conditioned by human subjectivity. "Barth consistently denies that describing the revelatory character of God's work involves us in a shift of subjects, by introducing . . . a theory of cognition or human readiness."[95] The event of human participation remains firmly relativized by the objectivity of Christ's truth: "[Christ]

---

93. Ibid., 51.
94. Webster, "Eloquent and Radiant," 132.
95. Webster, *Barth*, 131–32.

lives, and the believer lives by the fact that Jesus Christ lives, and not *vice versa*."[96] Hence, there is a distinction and asymmetry between being and knowing, for all their mutual implication:

> [I]n the history in which knowledge is grounded, and in the Christian knowledge grounded in it, neither the ontic and objective nor the noetic and subjective elements is absorbed or swallowed up by the other . . . In the real intercourse and exchange between them their mutual relationship is always irreversible and their connexion unequal. Precedence is always taken by the *esse*, by the objective occurrence of reconciliation . . . [Moreover, Christ] is always the primary acting Subject. He can only be followed by the *nosse* as the work of His prophecy, by the subjective occurrence of knowledge, by Christians.[97]

Whilst, therefore, the event of covenantal reciprocity by definition includes the incorporation of human histories into the eschatological consummation of its truth, there remains "a strict correspondence between the mode and object of theological knowledge . . . [T]his correspondence means that, since Jesus as prophet is self-manifesting, knowledge of his self-manifestation is a function of his revealing activity, not of human cognitive proposing."[98] If, therefore, Barth has modified his understanding of the object-subject pattern by integrating the noetic within the shape of the ontic, he has in no way jettisoned his consistent rejection of natural theology as an epistemological foundation; the efficacy of divine revelation is guaranteed not by the cognitive prowess or spiritual piety of the individual believer, but by the authoritative power of Christ's light, which shines irrespective of the darkness in which human sinners shroud themselves. He reminds the reader that

> This *objectivity* [*Objektivität*] of even its revelatory character must be emphasised so expressly because misunderstanding can so easily creep in, as if the problem of the knowledge, understanding and explanation of reconciliation . . . were really a problem of the theory of human knowledge and its spheres and limitations, its capacities and competencies, its possible or impossible approximation to this object.[99]

---

96. IV/3, 45.
97. Ibid., 213-214.
98. Webster, "Eloquent and Radiant," 136.
99. IV/3, 10-11 rev. = *KD* IV/3, 9.

The efficacy of salvation's revelation and appropriation therefore also has its authenticity in Christ, and not in the individual believer. "As prophet, he attests his own reality, and, therefore, is the active subject in our apprehension of him."[100] This may chafe against those critics who find here a devaluation of the importance of the human subject's responsibility for decision.[101] Barth is acutely wary of Bultmann's interpretation of John 1:4-5, according to which the "light" of Christ and the "darkness" in which it shines are two existential possibilities of "self-understanding."[102] The risk of Bultmann's interpretation, for Barth, is that it allows the sovereignty of Christ's life-act, in the last resort, to be authenticated, validated and confirmed (or indeed, to be rejected and denied) by the human individual. But for Barth, Christ's incorporation of human subjects into the event of His covenantal light is powerful and efficacious because it is His light; He is not proven to have power by virtue of the event of human individuals coming to knowledge of Him, but *vice versa*.[103]

> As Jesus Christ lives, He also shines out, not with an alien light which falls upon Him from without and illuminates Him, but with His own light proceeding from Himself. He lives as the source of light whose shining gives light without . . . As He lives, He is the light which comes and gives sight to all the eyes which as such are created and destined to see Him and everything which He discloses . . . so that all verification of its occurrence can only follow its self-verification, all interpretation of its form and content its self-interpretation.[104]

The light of Christ's covenantal truth "may and therefore will be received" but the actual occurrence of this light's shining, and its ever-increasingly powerful and radiant splendor, "is independent of our actual reception, being the sovereign basis of all reception and therefore conditioning our reception but not [being] conditioned by it."[105] Whether or not we accept the truth of Christ's light, it will continue to shine, in irrepressible brilliance.

---

100. Webster, 'Eloquent and Radiant,' 134.

101. So Brunner: "the real decision only takes place in the objective sphere, and not in the subjective sphere . . . Whether they know it or not, believe it or not, is not so important" (Brunner, *Dogmatics Volume I*, 351).

102. IV/3, 9; see, Bultmann, *The Gospel of John*, 40ff.

103. IV/3, 9.

104. Ibid., 46.

105. Ibid., 8.

This objectivity of Christ's subjectivity, it seems to some commentators, undermines the authenticity of human agency, and apparently signals the disjunction of truth's objectivity and its subjective apprehension. Christ's saving truth, and the event of its revelation, stands as a brute force over against the individual believer, who is attributed no responsibility for decision, knowledge, or response. However, to read IV/3 in such binary terms is to miss the holistic character of Barth's approach to truth and the triadic integration of the objective and subjective in historical and eschatological terms. It is to see truth as standing over against the human subject as a proposition to be (arbitrarily) accepted or rejected, and to see the event of Christ's prophetic agency as the mere communication of a series of dogmatic facts. But upon closer reflection one realizes that for Barth the objectivity of reconciliation's revelation does not shut down the authentic participation of human agency in the event of Christ's covenantal truth, but renders it possible.

It is here that Barth's eschatological explication and intensification in IV/3 helps to expound how human subjects are given a genuine, though relativized, share in the event of Christ's covenantal truth, and therefore how Christ facilitates an authentic divine-human reciprocity, not only existing in Him but also between God and the world as such. The fact that knowledge of the covenant occurs in the contemporaneous drama of Christ's risen life precludes any interpretation of Barth's soteriological epistemology as "mere cognitive impartation" across the historical divide stretching out between the "here and now" and Christ's earthly "there and then."[106] Barth has in mind a far more dynamic and complex understanding of reconciliation's revelation, organized around the Easter *kerygma*. For Barth the resurrection guarantees the final validity of Christ's covenantal truth, confirming that what has taken place between God and humanity in Him will become true not merely for Him and for God, but for all of humanity.[107] The risen "Jesus is Victor."[108] As He lives His risen life, He continues to make known the truth of the covenant, binding others up into its history. And because Christ has defeated death, He will continue to live in and alongside all human histories, drawing them into the event of His covenantal victory, until the Kingdom of God has been universally established on earth:[109] "The history which here begins cannot grow old in time. It cannot become past

---

106. McDowell, *Hope in Barth's Eschatology*, 160.
107. IV/3, 44, 227; 281ff.; 296ff.; 312ff.
108. Ibid., 165.
109. See ibid., 301-2.

history."¹¹⁰ As the risen Christ encounters human subjects in the particularity of their own lives He is confronted continually by human beings who do not accept His truth, and who advance their untruth against Him, resisting participation in the reciprocal event of His body.¹¹¹ The "here and now" of Christ's risen life therefore issues in an eschatological "not yet,"¹¹² the coincidence of an historical actuality and provisionality, of an ultimate and a penultimate, in which Christ has consummated the truth of the covenant, both in time and in eternity, but has yet to realize the universal knowledge of and participation in this reality.¹¹³ Participation in Christ's covenantal freedom must therefore be described as a "dynamic teleology."¹¹⁴ For Barth, there is neither a dualistic equilibrium existing between the light and darkness, "as though darkness had the claim and power finally to maintain itself against light," nor a Christomonistic obliteration of the provisional and limited power of darkness in the here and now.¹¹⁵ Rather, there is a complex history being enacted, where the end of history has already been anticipated and disclosed "proleptically," but has not yet arrived.¹¹⁶ In the intervening history, Christ wills that as He encounters us in eloquent and radiant being, we would follow Him, allowing ourselves to be "drawn into His sphere, into what takes place in Him."¹¹⁷

Whilst, therefore, we continue to live under the threat of darkness—the "contradiction" of His covenantal truth by the falsehood and opposition of sinful humanity to its elected and actualized liberation—the testimony of John 1:5 cannot be surpassed: "The light shineth in darkness; and the darkness comprehended it not."¹¹⁸ In Christ's contemporaneity as the subject of His own truth, "A history is here taking place; a drama is being enacted; a war waged to a successful conclusion."¹¹⁹ The radiance of Christ's light, the efficacy of its shining, and the acceptance of His covenantal truth is in no way conditioned by or ultimately dependent upon the subjectivity of

---

110. Ibid., 227.

111. Ibid., 375.

112. Ibid., 327; 903ff.

113. McDowell, *Hope in Barth's Eschatology*, 160 (see also, ibid., 153). As Barth said in *Dogmatics in Outline*, "The Christian perfect is not an imperfect; but the rightly understood imperfect has the force of the future" (Barth, *Dogmatics in Outline*, 132).

114. IV/3, 168.

115. Ibid.

116. See McDowell, *Hope in Barth's Eschatology*, 153.

117. IV/3, 182.

118. See ibid., 167.

119. Ibid., 168.

Divine and Human Freedom in Asymmetrical Reciprocity 137

fallible humans.[120] Yet the eschatological guarantee of Christ's victory, revealed proleptically at Easter Sunday and Pentecost, in anticipation of the final *parousia*, ensures the certainty that what is true of Christ will become true also for the whole world. "In the Easter event as the commencement of the new coming of Jesus Christ in revelation of what took place in His life and death, it is also revealed that the time which is still left to the world and human history and all men can only be the last time, i.e., time running towards its appointed end."[121]

Quite what this drama will look like for each individual remains an eschatological mystery veiled by the provisionally abiding power of sin; it is not for us to know here and now how it is that Christ's covenantal truth will become a universal reality, nor for us to count upon an *apokatastasis* as if it were simply inevitable.[122] Nevertheless, Christ's prophetic guarantee and the promise of His Spirit permits us "to hope and pray . . . that in accordance with His mercy which is 'new every morning' He 'will not cast off for ever' (La. 3:22f.; 31)."[123] Hence Barth's account of human subjectivity is underwritten by his theology of hope; the authenticity of our participation in the covenant is guaranteed not by a noetic or pietistic responsibility attributed to us, but by the mysterious hope inaugurated on Easter Sunday that Christ's victory shall not fail, and that the world entire shall be brought into the event of Christian truth. "In hope that which the Christian cannot reach is already near for all its farness. In hope, that which is unknowable is not alien but already known."[124]

The attraction into Christ's proleptical truth amidst the eschatological "not yet" secures the authenticity of human agency, *pace* Barth's critics who say there is no room for genuine human freedom. For the "not yet . . . opens up for the creature which is reconciled but not yet redeemed and perfected a field on which it can and should demonstrate its freedom."[125] Why is it the case that "Easter Day" was not also "at once and as such . . . the last day"?[126] "Why have we still to wait?"[127] Quite simply because it belongs to the "good will of Jesus Christ" to procure for reconciled creation "time and space, not merely to see, but actively to share in the harvest which

120. See ibid., 288-89.
121. Ibid., 295.
122. Ibid., 478.
123. Ibid.
124. Ibid., 923.
125. Ibid., 334.
126. Ibid., 330.
127. Ibid., 320.

follows."[128] It belongs to the self-electing freedom of God, actualized in the history of Jesus Christ, not only to co-exist with humanity, but to live in authentic covenantal fellowship with them. God does not reconcile creation "in order that it should vanish and dissolve in Him" but in order that it may "be free."[129] Hence the summons to covenantal participation which is issued in Christ's subjectivity, and the knowledge of God through which humankind is liberated to follow Him, is ingredient in God's freedom to be God of the living covenant and not otherwise. In the prophetic office of Christ divine being and human knowing, God's sovereign freedom and the corresponding flourishing of humanity, are interwoven in a pattern of covenantal, asymmetrical reciprocity. In this history God "does not will to be alone or without us, [nor] to go over our heads, [but] wills to give us a share in His work in our independence as the creatures of God summoned to freedom."[130]

As such, Barth refuses to force a binary choice between a human subjectivity in which the authenticity of Christ's saving efficacy rests ultimately with the decision of the believer (existentialism), or a subjectivity in which knowledge arbitrarily conforms to the object of salvation conceived as a vicariously rendered Platonic ideal, irrespective of our decision (uncritical soteriological realism). Barth actually suggests *both* that the appropriation of Christ's truth to the world rests solely upon His prophetic power as mediator, *and* that the event of this power includes the attraction of human subjects into their own, active freedom for the acceptance of, response to, and participation in the actualization of the covenant. That is a consequence of seeing His objective and subjective aspects as mediator of salvation in triadic terms, which take the two distinct aspects of Jesus's saving reality (its ontic establishment and noetic revelation) as a mutually informing pair.

A generous reading of IV/3 will affirm that informing the asymmetrical reciprocity that belongs to God and humanity in Jesus Christ is a methodological asymmetrical reciprocity, or triadic logic, between the objective and subjective categories. The concrete objectivity of Christ's actualization of divine-human unity is differentiated from and ontologically prioritized over the appropriation of this truth in human history; yet this objective power of Christ is performative and expressive, such that it belongs to Christ's life-act that what is true in Him is historically unfolding as the truth of the whole world. One cannot, therefore, think of Christ's reconciling life-act, or the power of His prophetic agency, without also understanding the

128. Ibid., 331.
129. Ibid., 332.
130. Ibid.

event of human subjectivity and knowledge as being ingredient within it. According to the asymmetrical reciprocity of the objective and subjective categories, being is not static, and knowing is not posterior to being. Rather, for Barth, Christ's being as God-man is an event taking place in an intrinsically knowable form, and the event of human knowledge of the covenant is a function of Christ's very identity. So Barth says, there is a

> relationship and reciprocity between the reconciliation which in its character as revelation establishes Christian knowledge and the knowledge which is established by it and thus participates in its occurrence . . . The ontic or objective element [*Ontische oder Objektive*] implies as its consequence the noetic or subjective [*Noetische oder Subjektive*] established by it. Conversely, the noetic or subjective element implies as its presupposition the ontic or objective which establishes it.[131]

Furthermore, Barth stresses that the event of reconciliation's revelation and appropriation is not the communication of soteriological propositions, but has the character of personal encounter with Christ.[132] Hence, the objectivity of Christ's subjectivity as conceived by Barth does not undermine the authenticity of human participation in the actualization of truth, because in the self-manifestation of Christ to human subjects we are dealing not with the presentation of ideas about Him, but with an embodied, personal encounter through which we are commissioned for an active role in the history of His covenantal truth. We do not assume control of the encounter with Christ, yet our being summoned to His presence is an irreducibly important factor in the actualization of the covenant's dramatic occurrence in world-history; Christ calls us as disciples to take up our "highly practical recognition of His existence and commitment to it."[133] As Gunton says, "In order to know God, we must be where he makes himself known."[134] Consequently, the mediation of salvation is not merely humanity's being made aware of an ontological proposition or brute fact established externally to us, or in an isolated and abstract historical "pocket." Rather, as Christ lives among us, making Himself known to us, the dramatic encounter between God and humanity continues to take place, being actualized contemporaneously through the

---

131. Ibid., 215 = *KD* IV/3, 245.

132. McDowell, *Hope in Barth's Eschatology*, 161; see also, Hunsinger, "Truth as Self-Involving," 41–56; Gunton, "No Other Foundation," 61–79, esp. 70ff.

133. IV/3, 585.

134. Gunton, "No Other Foundation," 71.

conjunction of the prophetic here and now with the high-priestly and royal there and then of Golgotha.[135] As Barth said in IV/1,

> We must realise that the Christian message does not at its heart express a concept or an idea, nor does it recount an anonymous history to be taken as truth and reality only in concepts and ideas . . . [I]t recounts this history and speaks of its inclusive power and significance in such a way that it declares a name, binding the history strictly and indissolubly to this name and presenting it as the story of the bearer of this name . . . the name of Jesus Christ.[136]

On the basis of this teleologically dramatic, personalistic, and thoroughly participative theological epistemology, Barth laments the "constant and widespread devaluation of knowledge," and he explicitly denies "that Christian knowledge can be regarded and described as mere acceptance or reflection."[137] For the Barth of IV/3 the event of human knowing has been driven into the heart of God's elective freedom, epistemology into the actualistic ontology, and as such "knowledge" cannot be described in propositional terms, but only as event, history, drama, and participation. This helps to overcome the criticism in Chapter 1 that for Barth the primary purpose of theology is to describe the human acquisition of information about God. Rather, to "know" God, for the Barth of IV/3, is to live in God, and therefore to take up one's place in the heart of the divine drama.

> We cannot impress upon ourselves too strongly that in the language of the Bible knowledge (*yada*, γιγνώσκειν) does not mean the acquisition of neutral information, which can be expressed in statements, principles and systems . . . What it means is the process or history in which man . . . becomes aware of [God's history] in such a compelling way that he cannot be neutral towards it, but finds himself summoned to disclose and give himself to it in return . . . We can and should say even more emphatically that knowledge in the biblical sense is the process in which distant "*object*" [*Objekt*] dissolves as it were, overcoming both its distance and its objectivity [*Objektivität aufhebt*] and coming to man as acting "*Subject*" [*handelndes «Subjekt»*], entering into the man who knows and subjecting him to this transformation.[138]

135. IV/3, 279.
136. IV/1, 16–17.
137. IV/3, 218.
138. Ibid., 183–84 = *KD*, IV/3, 210.

Divine and Human Freedom in Asymmetrical Reciprocity

According to the mature Barth's participative rhetoric, the "divine noetic" has the "full force of the divine ontic."[139] On one level this indicates that the event of knowledge has an ontological effect on the condition of the human agent, issuing in a transformation not only of her "intelligence and imagination," but of her "heart and will."[140] But if the actualistic reading that has been pursued throughout this book is correct, then there is also a deeper ontological implication for the event of human knowledge rooted in the doctrine of election. If God has determined Godself only to be God in relationship with humanity, freely coming to Godself by coming to the world, then it belongs to God's own freedom for the covenant that "The Word of God does not return to Him void (Is. 55:11),"[141] but finds its response in God's covenant partner, first in Christ, and secondarily and analogically in humanity as such. Perhaps it is for this reason that, as McDowell observes, "Barth expresses a weariness at having to deal again with the highly unoriginal objection that 'the future brings "nothing new," "only" something noetic.'"[142] The future does indeed bring something new; it is the covenantal field opening up in which Jesus Christ encounters human subjects, bringing them into the event of His divine-human freedom through knowledge of His life, and therefore allowing them to participate in God's life just as God participates in theirs. Barth's mature epistemology does not isolate the divine objectivity in the way that the earlier works did, but in fact suggests that the history of human knowing is ingredient in the elective history of God. God will be and become this God not only with Jesus Christ, the true witness, but through Christ's utterly compelling prophecy with all human witnesses. The thinkability of God is therefore integral to the freedom of God, and Christ's prophetic history incorporates the event of human knowledge into the event of the covenant's historical actualization.

On the basis of this inclusion of human subjectivity within the account of the God's self-determinative freedom, Barth speaks of a divine ontological *risk*:

> He does not will to be in the heights without also being in the depths of this man [Jesus]. He does not will to be God without Him, but only with Him. This involves a risk [*Risiko*]. There is no telling what might become of Himself and His deity in undertaking it. But He does not fear any of the imaginable dangers

---

139. IV/3, 298.
140. Ibid., 183.
141. Ibid., 298.
142. McDowell, *Hope in Barth's Eschatology*, 166, citing Barth, "Letter to Tjarko Stadtland, 18th January, 1967," in *Letters, 1961–1968*, 235.

of this enterprise. He has no suspicions in relation to this man. He simply says Yes to Him.[143]

This inclusion of divine self-risk in the theology of freedom is rooted in the radical transition that occurred in II/2 where, as Busch reminds us, Barth suggested that "When one considers that God wants to coexist with sinners, then his freedom includes his willingness 'for the sake of man' to 'hazard Himself wholly and utterly.'"[144] Yet Barth can speak of this divine self-risk and self-limitation because of his confidence that "Jesus is Victor." Although God elects Godself to a freedom which in a (qualified) sense necessitates human flourishing, it is *God* who has elected Godself as such, and there can be no doubt as to what the final outcome of this prophetic history might be.[145] The ineluctability of God's redemptive victory should not be equated with a static inevitability, for God does not will to live alongside a creature who has been coerced into fellowship, but rather guides the world into an authentic freedom for covenantal flourishing.

Barth is now able to propose his most participative language of anywhere in the *Church Dogmatics*, insisting that "the one who participates in this knowledge participates in the event of salvation itself."[146] Whilst the Barth of IV/3 retains his anti-Pelagian soteriological Christocentricity, there is no doubt that in departure from the somewhat dualistic and oppositional bent of the early epistemology, in the third part of the doctrine of reconciliation the event of human subjectivity has been interwoven into the depths of divine ontology, with the result that a genuine human reciprocity with God is conceived, albeit in a qualified and asymmetrical sense. Notably, Barth even accepts that whilst the term "synergism" is ordinarily used "polemically and critically to denote the Pelagian and semi-Pelagian doctrine of a *liberum arbitrium*," and whilst there is only limited justification for saying that the New Testament encourages the use of the term soteriologically, yet "we cannot say that its use is forbidden."[147] For the Barth of IV/3 there is a legitimate "co-operation" of human subjects in the historical actualization of covenantal reciprocity, because it is ingredient in the freedom of God that human subjects are liberated for an authentic share in the divine-human fellowship willed from eternity and consummated through Christ's historical life-act.

143. IV/3, 379 = *KD* IV/3, 438. See also, IV/3, 431.

144. Busch, *The Great Passion*, 115; see also, II/2, 164.

145. IV/3, 197.

146. IV/3, 217. See also, Webster, "Eloquent and Radiant," 143; McDowell, *Hope in Barth's Eschatology*, 161.

147. IV/3, 600.

> If Christ lives in him and he in Christ, if this common life is not just the action of Christ but his own action, then, although the Christian is certainly not the subject and in no sense the author of the history of salvation which takes place in the action of Jesus Christ, although he is not himself the reconciler or even the co-reconciler . . . yet he certainly has a part in that history as a co-operating subject, and in its own place and manner this part is not merely apparent but real . . .[148]

Corresponding to the asymmetrical reciprocity between God and humanity enacted in Christ's life-act is its extension and parallel in the particular histories of individual creatures.[149]

> Whether we think down from Jesus Christ to His people, or up from His people to Jesus Christ, we must respect and bring out the relationship and reciprocity [*Beziehung und Reziprozität*] which always characterise the intercourse [*Verkehr*] between God and man inaugurated and ordered by Jesus Christ. To be sure, there is inequality. This is inevitable when on the one side we have as the primary acting Subject Jesus Christ in His prophecy and on the other as the secondary acting subjects those who receive His Word . . . But for all the inequality they are mutually related [*aufeinander bezogen*].[150]

Conclusion

In this chapter it has been argued that IV/3 provides the resources for Barth's most participative theology of freedom. This part-volume not only conceives Christ's being from the perspective of His divine-human simultaneity, mutuality, and reciprocity, but also sees the prophetic subjectivity of Christ as itself an integral part of the actualization of this reciprocal identity. Since Christ is the God-man, the divine-human subject, it belongs to the objective truth of His being-in-act that other humans will be attracted into the covenantal reciprocity taking place in Him. Hence, the subjective mediation of Christ, and the subjectivity of human agents, is described in IV/3 not so much as the communication of propositions about what has taken

---

148. Ibid., 599.

149. "The familiar pattern which describes the person of Jesus Christ in particular is, by correspondence and extension, the very pattern which describes all relations more generally between God and the world, for *all* such relations are inviolably and indissolubly centered in and mediated by him" (Hunsinger, *How to Read Karl Barth*, 238).

150. IV/3, 215–16 = *KD* IV/3, 246.

place ontologically in Christ, but as the drama in which humanity is drawn into the reciprocal life of the covenant embodied in Christ. The next chapter continues to develop this reading of IV/3 by arguing that the work must be read through the lens of a non-propositional, triadic logic in which the account of Christ's truth takes the objectivity of His identity and the subjective communication of theological knowledge to be mutually implicated.

4

THE PARTICIPATIVE LOGIC OF *CHURCH DOGMATICS* IV/3

Placing Barth in Conversation with Hegel

Everything turns on grasping and expressing the True, not only as Substance, but equally as Subject[1]

—G. W. F. Hegel

Introduction

The unification of the objective and subjective sides of salvation, achieved by Barth in IV/3, indicates, as Jones suggests, that the "elaboration of the *munus propheticum* amounts . . . to a Christological *Aufhebung* of the theological epistemology of *Church Dogmatics* I."[2] Theological knowledge cannot any longer be viewed as the communication of propositions in a revelatory history accidental to God; and the thought of God's being can-

---

1. Hegel, *Phenomenology of Spirit*, 10.
2. Jones, *The Humanity of Christ*, 252.

not be abstracted from the thought of God's coming to human knowledge. Rather, the history of revelation, in which God becomes thinkable, must itself be the ontological stage on which the drama of God's being is played out. Hence, the event of human knowledge of salvation is ingredient in the event of divine self-determination. And it belongs to Christ's inclusive, saving and graceful truth as God-man, that He attest His truth simply by living it in an attractive and expansive form, consummating His own identity by allowing others a share in it.

Where commentators simplistically view the mediation of Christ, as described in IV/3, as the communication of knowledge about what He objectively achieves externally to us, they demonstrate an inability to reconceive the object-subject relation "triadically" (that is, as reciprocally related but distinct terms within a pair) in line with the direction in which the mature Barth was moving. These commentators take the covenantal truth of Christ, and therein the objective reality of God, to be something existing in isolation "over there," over against human subjects; Christian knowledge is then described as the acquisition of doctrinal information about whom we have abstractly become in Christ. But Barth indicates that the event of human beings actively coming to know Christ itself forms part of Christ's actualization of the mediation between God and humanity, and the zenith of salvation history. The subjective side of salvation described in IV/3's theology of mediation (its communication to humans, their appropriation of it, and their participation in it) is absolutely integrated with the objective side described in IV/1 and IV/2, as two reciprocal elements in the single Christocentric divine-human truth. I argue, therefore, that Barth's mode of theological conception has shifted since the epistemology of *Church Dogmatics* I, and that readers' interpretative strategies must demonstrate a corresponding level of flexibility. This requires further investigation of what is meant by the object-subject relation in the mature Barth.

Chapter 4 places Barth in conversation with Hegel. This serves to draw attention to the way Barth's theological conceptuality has developed by IV/3, allowing him, to a large extent, to avoid two related dualistic tensions that we have been tracing throughout this study: the first is a general dualism between God and the world; the second is an underlying dualism between the categories of objectivity and subjectivity. Where the early Barth made critical use of a quasi-Kantian epistemology in order to protect divine being from the fallibility of human knowing (and in so doing unwittingly perpetuated a divine-human disjunction, by isolating the historicity of divine act from the eternal truth of God's being), the Barth of IV/3 seems to have integrated the object-subject relation in a participative and historical manner more closely akin to the triadic logic displayed in Hegel's texts, than in the object-subject relation that the earlier Barth derived partly from his reading of Kant. Reading Hegel alongside Barth serves to draw attention to the way a participative theology of freedom refuses to think God and humanity in isolation from one another. Below, I argue that we ought not to conceive the event of divine being in abstraction from the history of human knowing, and that instead we should view both as mutually implicated in Christ's divine-human truth. Consequently, I shall demonstrate that the subjective side of reconciliation in IV/3 is not to be seen as the arbitrary communication of soteriological propositions, according to which human beings "find out" what happened vicariously for them in Jesus Christ. Rather, it is the event by which we are drawn into the drama of Jesus Christ's covenantal being.

Being and Knowing in Hegel

Why Read Hegel Alongside Barth?

I opened Chapter 1 with a discussion of Kant, the purpose of which was to introduce the challenge facing modern theologians, and to show that Barth does not respond to the post-Kantian theological tradition without also taking Kant seriously and appropriating some of the key themes in his critical epistemology. And I found that Barth's quasi-Kantian epistemological instincts contributed to a theological *modus operandi* that was, in some ways, problematic. The earlier works of Barth unwittingly introduced a sense of competition between God and the world by holding apart the concept of God's being in and for Godself and the account of God's historical revelation and human knowledge of God. This served to protect a "formal" and negative concept of God's sovereign freedom from external manipulation, but could not do justice to the historicity of God's freedom for covenantal self-determination and self-limitation. Moreover, it failed to provide an authentic theological space for describing human participation in the life of God.

If, as I have argued, Barth has moved away from the somewhat abstract and competitive understanding of the relation of divine and human agency, might it be that the mature Barth is thinking in fundamentally different terms than those characterizing the works leading up to and including *Church Dogmatics* I? The present chapter calls on Hegel to draw attention to the ways in which the mature Barth regards the relation of the divine and human realities in asymmetrical reciprocity. The chapter only makes very limited use of one aspect of Hegel's work in order to illuminate the nature of Barth's actualistic development in IV/3. No attempt is made at a "genetic-historical" reading of Barth's methodological transformation with reference to Hegel. In fact, despite his somewhat disingenuous comment that "I myself have a certain weakness for Hegel and am always fond of doing a bit of 'Hegeling,'"[3] Barth shows little direct interest in or sensitive engagement with Hegel's work, and the occasional references to him in IV/3, as elsewhere, are largely (and somewhat naively) critical.[4] Nonetheless, it is contended that a particular reading of Hegel can help to identify the shift that has taken place in Barth's thinking. Whereas Barth was not explicit about the logical architecture supporting his doctrinal claims, Hegel's philosophy seeks to identify problems with certain kinds of thinking, and then to repair them by rehearsing patterns of thought that may be more generative for Christian theologians. Of particular significance to this study is Hegel's interest in the relation of pairs of terms such as object and subject, being and thinking, and so on. Where Hegel finds that the relation between two terms has been mishandled, he seeks to repair the way we think about their mutual implication. This logical process of diagnosis and repair is pertinent to our study of Barth because it provides us with an apparatus which helps identify the shift in Barth's thinking towards an actualism in which the integrity of ontology and epistemology, of divine being and human knowing, forms the basis for a participative theology of freedom. Although Barth did not deliberately pursue a "Hegelian" method, his *Dogmatics* demonstrate a sustained critical struggle with various approaches to the question of knowledge inherited from post-Enlightenment thought, the

3. Barth, cited by Busch, *Karl Barth*, 387.

4. See, IV/3, 171; 703. See also, Welker, "Barth und Hegel," 307–28. Welker has argued convincingly that Barth probably did not read much more than about 200 pages of Hegel's first and third volumes of the *Philosophy of Religion* (Barth read Georg Lasson's edited harmonization of Hegel's four lecture series, based heavily on manuscript transcripts of Hegel's 1827 lectures (see Barth, "Hegel," in *Protestant Theology*, and Adams, *Eclipse of Grace*, 168), as well as some extracts from the *Phenomenology of Spirit*, in preparation for his essay on Hegel in *Protestant Theology* (Welker, "Barth und Hegel," 310–11). After writing this chapter in December 1929 (although Barth mistakenly recalls writing the chapter in 1932 (see Welker, "Barth und Hegel," 310) Barth did not return to Hegel. He says "Hegel has not claimed much of my time since I wrote about him in 1932" (Barth, "Letter to Dr. Carl Gunther Schweitzer, 27th January 1964," in *Letters: 1961–1968*, 149). Barth had Charlotte von Kirschbaum extract key terms from Hegel's texts and place them on index cards, and then consulted these index cards as he wrote his chapter on Hegel. Barth also made use of these index cards, compiled thematically, in the following years when he addressed himself to their themes in the *Church Dogmatics* (Welker, "Barth und Hegel," 311–12). Adams finds that Barth's reductive essay on Hegel in *Protestant Theology* is "wholly inadequate as an introduction to Hegel" (Adams, *Eclipse of Grace*, xv) since it is "largely based on a questionable reading of a dated edition of a single work. Barth's essay is easy to read, magisterially confident in tone, and neatly places Hegel as a modern Pelagius" (Adams, *Eclipse of Grace*, 3).

result of which is something far closer to a Hegelian method than a Kantian one. Barth's attempt to "replace the Enlightenment project with something different . . . was not altogether successful, for there are many remnants of the old syndrome."[5] Indeed, attempting to understand the relation between divine being and human knowing, between the objective essence and subjective existence of God, and between the divine subject (Jesus Christ) and ordinary human subjects is extremely complex, because Barth occasionally lapses into internal conflict and ambiguity. Yet by IV/3 Barth's achievement represents "something of a *tour de force*, plucked from the intellectual air by an act of intuitive genius";[6] his theological instincts led him to work out a method quite distinct from that characterizing the quasi-Kantianism of his *Romans* II commentary. Chapter 4 highlights some instances where Barth's mature work on the reciprocal freedom of God and humanity seems to echo Hegel's reparative recommendations for Christian theology after Kant. In so doing it shall tacitly call into question the ease with which some scholars assume Barth is consistently "Kantian" in his philosophical orientation, even if Barth himself did not explicitly acknowledge a qualification of his basic Kantian commitments.[7]

Before I proceed, it is important to qualify the nature of my engagement with Hegel in order to allay some of the inevitable anxieties that might arise. There is almost unanimous agreement in Barth scholarship that Barth attempts to evade "Hegelianism," and scholars work assiduously to avoid their own interpretations of Barth being labelled "Hegelian," where this is taken to be synonymous with various kinds of anthropomorphism. This trend in Barth scholarship is perhaps unsurprising when one considers Hegel's atypical use of quasi-theological language, in conjunction with Barth's own criticisms of Hegel in his essay in *Protestant Theology*. It seems clear to some theologians that Hegel is guilty of collapsing all distinctions between God and the world, and that anthropomorphic idolatry is inevitable in such a system. As Barth says, "Hegel's living God . . . is actually the living man."[8] Hegel's "theology" must be resisted at all costs, and Barth

---

5. Gunton, "No Other Foundation," 64.

6. Ibid., 64.

7. For McCormack, once Barth had adopted a Kantian framework, he never saw "any serious reason to question this basic epistemological commitment later" (McCormack, *Orthodox and Modern*, 12). Yet McCormack correctly acknowledges that "In *CD* IV especially, [Barth's] thinking about Christology began to draw nearer to Hegel" (ibid., 13). Likewise, Willis insists that Barth came to replace "Kant (for the most part) with Hegel" (Willis, *The Ethics of Karl Barth*, 429). Unfortunately, neither McCormack nor Willis unpacks the similarities between Barth and Hegel.

8. Barth, *Protestant Theology*, 405.

scholars who otherwise stand at opposing poles of the theological spectrum can at least agree upon this (even where some scholars level the supposedly damning charge of "Hegelianism" against those who resolutely protest their innocence).[9] Even Jüngel, a sophisticated and sympathetic reader of Hegel, echoes Barth's critique, saying that "Hegel's God needs man, who thereby becomes divine himself" and that whilst Hegel's "theological accomplishment" was "grand," his doctrinal efforts must ultimately be treated with suspicion.[10] Some philosophers seem to be in agreement with the theologians that Hegel addresses himself to a "speculative reconstruction of Christian theology,"[11] and on this reading Hegel is inevitably cast as a "stalwart opponent" of "traditional forms of Christian theology" who "abhorred both theism and deism."[12] Desmond goes as far as to express "dismay" at "Hegel's power to infatuate religiously gullible admirers" who have been taken in by a Hegelian "'God' who is not God."[13]

9. Van Driel and Molnar have charged McCormack with slipping into the "Hegelian" mistake of making creation and incarnation necessary and essential to God (see van Driel, "Karl Barth on the Eternal Existence of Jesus Christ," 45–61 (esp. 53–54), and Molnar, *Divine Freedom and the Doctrine of the Immanent Trinity*, 61–64, 81). McCormack, in response to such criticisms, insists that "unlike" Hegel, he has made no such mistake, and certainly avoids the "Hegelian" heresy of setting aside the ontological distinction between God and humankind (see McCormack, "Seek God Where He May Be Found," 70, and "Grace and Being," 99ff.). Molnar, however, has since re-affirmed that McCormack (and Hector, whom Molnar takes basically to be in support of McCormack's position) "still has not escaped the Hegelian dilemma," despite the acknowledgement that McCormack is "at pains" to refuse any link with Hegel (see Molnar, "Can God be God without us?," 218, and "The Trinity, Election, and God's Ontological Freedom," 301). Molnar finds that McCormack's work demonstrates amply, to Molnar's urgent distress, that the doctrine of God stands under threat "in this time when Hegel's thinking remains such an appealing temptation" (Molnar, "Can the Electing God be Without Us?," 221). Finally, Hunsinger has echoed Molnar's insistence that Barth "always took care to avoid making Hegel's mistakes," particularly the gross error of making "God's triune being depend on his relationship to the world." For Hunsinger, Barth developed a "strategy for avoiding Hegel's errors while he indulged in a little 'Hegeling'" (Hunsinger does not identify what this "Hegeling" might mean if it does not mean making the doctrine of trinity dependent on the doctrine of election, which is the theological position Hunsinger tacitly takes to be the result of "Hegelianism"). Hence, Hunsinger takes care explicitly to distance himself from "the theological followers of Hegel" (see Hunsinger, "Election and the Trinity," 190). Hunsinger concludes his theological theses with the claim that to take the Barth of volume IV as arguing for the "dialectical identity" of the immanent and economic trinity "would be like looking at Barth's doctrine of the Trinity through a funhouse mirror, where the funhouse was owned and operated by a character named Hegel" (Hunsinger, "Election and the Trinity," 197 n22).

10. See Jüngel, *God as the Mystery of the World*, 94.
11. Hodgson, *Hegel and Christian Theology*, v.
12. Beiser, *Hegel*, 43; see also, ibid., 145.
13. Desmond, *Hegel's God*, ix.

The question of Hegel's legitimacy as a theologian is well-established in Western theological circles and will continue to be debated in scholarship. Following Adams, however, it is suggested here that interpreters who assess Hegel's contribution to theology by reading his work as constructive Christian doctrine are likely to obscure the diagnostic and reparative nature of his thought, and it is these elements of his oeuvre that are pertinent for this study. For Adams, "The answer to the question, 'does Hegel collapse the distinction between divine and human action?' is 'the question arises from a misconception about the kind of discussion Hegel offers.'"[14] Adams suggests that Hegel's interest in theology is best understood not as seeking to make constructive doctrinal and ontological claims, but rather as endeavoring philosophically to investigate the "forms of thinking" that guide theology, and as identifying the problematic relation of pairs of terms such as "being and thinking" in a number of philosophies and theologies.[15] Hegel helps us to identify some of the problems introduced into Christian thought with Kant's Copernican shift, and provides some suggestions, seemingly (if unwittingly and cursorily) paralleled in IV/3, about how Christian theology ought to repair the object-subject and being-knowing patterns.

Hegel's texts are useful for investigating the shape of Barth's theology because they reveal a concern to distinguish between what Adams calls "triadic" and "binary" logics, and to identify the types of thought to which each logic is appropriate.[16] This process of logical discernment is germane to my project because it provides the interpretative tools—not themselves explicitly adverted to in Barth's texts—necessary for making sense of Barth's doctrinal claims. It is my argument that Hegel helps to display the consequences of seeing a "binary" or "oppositional" logic as being performed in the soteriology of mediation in IV/3. To find that talk of the mediatorship of Jesus in His prophetic office should be governed by a triadic, non-propositional, and non-oppositional logic is not to suggest that there is no place in Christian thinking for oppositions or propositional logic. For example, as Adams points out, different biblical texts reveal alternative ways of characterizing Jesus: the Jesus of the Synoptics is more often oppositional than He is in John's Gospel. And there are plenty of instances in which Jesus communicates propositions entailing the "knowledge that." Good theological exposition will require a "further" triadic logic, which governs how we select between the use of oppositional and participative logics them-

---

14. Adams, *Eclipse of Grace*, 218.

15. This is one of the core arguments of Adams's work. See, for example, ibid., 11–12, 172, 178.

16. Ibid., 53.

selves.[17] But Hegel does insist that when speaking of object and subject, and consequently of the relation between divine and human action, one should be guided by a participative and triadic, not oppositional and binary, logic.[18] This is because

> when one's account of subject and object is guided by opposition, the result is a series of failures which stimulate a reassessment first of the object and then of the logic itself. He also insists that when one's account of God is guided by opposition, the result is an insufficiently participative account of human action.[19]

It is my argument that once we have established the nature of Barth's triadic pattern of thinking about divine and human action in IV/3, a recovery of Barth's *Church Dogmatics* IV/3 within his architectonic is possible, because it too will be read "triadically" in relation to IV/1 and IV/2. What is to be understood about Jesus's salvation, for Barth, is not only how Jesus determines both to be God for humanity, and to be the faithful creature of God, but that this actuality opens up a history of participation as the living performance of the relationship in which this reciprocal determination coheres.

Hegel's Critique of Kant and the Shape of Christian Thinking

Hegel thought that Kant's distinction between the thing considered *qua* in and for itself and a thing considered *qua* given to thought betrayed an uncritical abstraction which risked undermining his entire project.[20] Hegel was deeply respectful of Kant's claim that there is no such thing as simple being, but only being as it is considered by us, and he agreed with Kant that the conditions for knowledge are not objects which are simply "given" to thought; the human subject plays an active role in determining the shape of her experience because "we presuppose categories and concepts in all our dealings with the world."[21] However, for Hegel Kant's identification of a distinction between things as they really are and things as they appear in experience betrayed the remnant of an uncritical presupposition which

17. Ibid.
18. Ibid., 53.
19. Ibid.
20. See Hegel, *The Science of Logic*, 42.
21. Houlgate, *Freedom, Truth and History*, 7. See also, Houlgate, introduction to *The Hegel Reader*, 7ff.; Beiser, "Introduction: Hegel and the Problem of Metaphysics," 16; Pippin, "You Can't Get There From Here," 60; Adams, *Eclipse of Grace*, 22–23.

amounted almost to "a failure of nerve" to complete the critical revolution.[22] Hegel claims that the idea of a thing in itself is "utter abstraction, total emptiness,"[23] indeed a contradiction in terms, since "what something is in itself has actually to be conceived as inseparable from its relations to other things and from the way it appears."[24] We cannot think of something other than as it is related to other things, and as it appears to us. To attempt to do so would be to think of nothing at all; indeed, it would be to think of something as if it were not being thought, which is absurd.[25] Hegel's point is that there is no need to posit an opposition between pure being and being thought in order to insist that we acknowledge the active role of reason in determining the shape of being.

For Hegel, Kant's *noumena-phenomena* distinction is uncritical because "there is no good reason to contrast the appearance of a thing with what it is in itself, as Kant does."[26] Reason has no solid basis for assuming that the way things appear is not in fact the same as the way something truly is, because it could never get outside of itself to judge whether things are different in themselves to the way they are for thought.[27] As Houlgate says, for Hegel, when consciousness critically examines its own processes it "recognizes that it does not actually have any grounds for distinguishing between what belongs to it and what comes from things in themselves, and that, consequently, it is not able to make a clear distinction between what *we* know or understand there to be and what there really *is*."[28] To assume that being exists differently in and for itself than it does for us is to attempt to think the unthinkable; it is not only that we cannot know things in themselves, but that try as we might to conceive the possibility of distinguishing between pure being (*noumena*) and being for thought (*phenomena*) we are already bound up in a process of thought, from which we cannot abstract ourselves. There is only being for thought. Likewise, we cannot think without thinking being, because even the thought of "nothing" is the thought of that which *is* not.[29] Hence, Kant's distinction rests on an abstraction and a presupposition

---

22. Guyer, "Thought and Being," 171.
23. Hegel, *Hegel's Logic*, 72. See also, Hegel, *The Science of Logic*, 93–94.
24. Houlgate, *The Hegel Reader*, 13.
25. See Hegel, *The Science of Logic*, 93–94.
26. Houlgate, *The Hegel Reader*, 13.
27. See Pippin, "You Can't Get From There to Here," 61–62.
28. Houlgate, *Freedom, Truth and History*, 72.
29. See ibid., 53–54.

that amounts to a logical absurdity, and Hegel avers that being and thinking must always be conceived in their inseparable unity in distinction.[30]

Hegel's critique of Kant is not ontological *per se*. He is not attempting to propose an alternative description of reality. The point of contention is rather that Hegel is dissatisfied with an imbalance between the terms "being" and "thinking" which leads to the relegation of being to an unknowable ontic realm, and the consequent one-sided attention paid to the subject who is said "only" to have access to the thought of being, and not to being in itself. Kant's error, for Hegel, was not in the distinction between thinking and the world, nor in his desire to unite the objective and the subjective, but in positing an unwarranted and uncritical gulf between being and thinking, and resolving the contradiction between the two opposed terms one-sidedly in favor of the subject.[31] As Bowie explains, "Attempts to base philosophy on either the subjective or the objective aspect of existence . . . always leave the difficulty of connecting the two aspects and of establishing the priority between them."[32] In Kant's case, there is a "one-sided concern with the 'I' at the expense of the 'object' which is relegated to an unknowable 'thing in itself,' Hegel says."[33] For Hegel this leads to abstractions and presuppositions that impact negatively on the ability of theologians to think in a generative manner.

Hegel opens his *Phenomenology of Spirit* by performing a critique of the "simple, immediate consciousness of being,"[34] rehearsing what may be

30. For this reason it is appropriate to describe Hegel's project as stemming "from his desire to be even more *critical* than Kant . . . by assuming less to begin with about what it means to think . . . For Hegel, to be genuinely critical means not just to question the validity of the metaphysical claims that have been made about the world, but to question *all* determinate assumptions about thought and being and to seek to discover from scratch what it is to think and what it is to be" (Houlgate, *The Hegel Reader*, 17). Hegel's *Phenomenology* reaches the conclusion that "being cannot be regarded simply as confronting consciousness but must be thought as disclosing itself *within* thought itself" (Houlgate, *The Hegel Reader*, 127). Hegel then responds to his criticism of Kant in *The Science of Logic* which assumes nothing about the shape of thinking and being, but rather starts with the most simple thought of pure, indeterminate being, and then traces the relationship between the determination of being and the thinking in which it becomes determinate, through a taxonomy of "becoming." In so doing Hegel seeks to demonstrate that it is impossible to distinguish cleanly between being and thinking, and to show that you can only think one in relation to the other (Houlgate, *The Hegel Reader*, 128). As Adams says, "Being and thinking are a pair: they can (and must) be distinguished, but one can only do justice to each term by doing justice to its relation to the other" (Adams, *Eclipse of Grace*, 126).

31. Adams, *Eclipse of Grace*, 22.

32. Bowie, *Introduction to German Philosophy*, 79.

33. Adams, *Eclipse of Grace*, 136.

34. Houlgate, *The Hegel Reader*, 18.

called a "common sense" or "ordinary" mode of thinking about the relation of the self to the objective world in basically Kantian terms.[35] "The first three chapters all share the common assumption that 'what is true for consciousness is something other than itself.'"[36] Here Hegel is rehearsing the kind of distinction between the self and the world that we ordinarily take for granted. Both Descartes and Kant had perpetuated the notion that truth or reality is distinct from the knowing subject: "Descartes claims that there is *res cogitans* and *res extensa*, and these are quite separate. Kant claims (on certain interpretations) that there are concepts which guide judgment, and things which elude knowledge."[37] Hegel wants to say that when philosophy traces the way reason operates, it comes to realize that underlying both the Cartesian and Kantian logics is an unsupportable assumption that what we think and what there truly is are irreconcilably disjunct terms, as if naked being, substance, or essence could be taken as distinct from the manner in which it exists for us. To put it in Hegel's own terms, "everything turns on grasping and expressing the True, not only as *Substance*, but equally as *Subject*."[38]

> The commonest way in which we deceive ourselves or others about understanding is by assuming something familiar, and accepting it on that account ... Subject and object, God, Nature, Understanding, sensibility and so on, are uncritically taken for granted as familiar, established as valid, and made into fixed points for starting and stopping. While these remain unmoved, the knowing activity goes back and forth between them, thus moving only on their surface. Apprehending and testing likewise consist in seeing whether everybody's impression of the matter coincides with what is asserted about these fixed points.[39]

---

35. See Pinkard, *German Philosophy*, 229–30 n13; see also, Taylor, *Hegel*, 124. Hegel's texts are deeply performative (see Houlgate, *The Hegel Reader*, 18). This is because for Hegel philosophy or "science" must begin with "a total absence of presupposition" (Hegel, *Hegel's Logic*, 112). The task of the *Phenomenology of Spirit* is simply to strip thinking of its presuppositions, and thereby to pave the way for the *Science of Logic* which will explore the structures of thought from the very beginning of thought's journey (see Houlgate, *Freedom, Truth and History*, 71–72; see also, Adams, *Eclipse of Grace*, 18–19). Hegel claims to take nothing for granted, and says that his philosophical "view" can only be "justified by the exposition of the system itself," that is, by rehearsing the philosophical journey of spirit in a dramatic manner (Hegel, *Phenomenology of Spirit*, 10).

36. Pippin, "You Can't Get There From Here," 61, citing Hegel, *Phenomenology of Spirit*, 104.

37. Adams, *Eclipse of Grace*, 20.

38. Hegel, *Phenomenology of Spirit*, 10.

39. Ibid., 18.

Hegel calls this type of thinking "*Dogmatism*" which he defines as "the opinion that the True consists in a proposition which is a fixed result, or which is immediately known."[40] For Hegel this commonsense account of thinking is perfectly legitimate for ordinary questions such as "When was Caesar born?, or How many feet are there in a stadium?,"[41] but it is ill-suited to describe "philosophical truths," and it does not provide the basis for a healthy theological conceptuality, because it presupposes the meaning of terms such as "God" in abstraction from the event or form by which the content of such a term might become determinate for thought.

> *God* is the eternal, the moral world-order, love, and so on. In such propositions the True is only posited *immediately* as Subject, but is not presented as the movement of reflecting itself into itself. In a proposition of this kind one begins with the word "God." This by itself is a meaningless sound, a mere name; it is only the predicate [i.e. "eternal" etc.] that says *what God is*, gives Him content and meaning. Only in the end of the proposition does the empty beginning become actual knowledge.[42]

For Hegel this logic begins with a static proposition "God" and then gives content to the term by ascribing various predicates, but denies to the subject (God) a role in the determination of its own predicates. What God *is* is defined by the human knower who claims to have comported her cognition to locate the being "God." But by denying the subject "God" a concrete role in the event of its becoming determinate for thought, the knower has excluded in advance the very means by which such a subject could become known. The knower takes the word God to be "a fixed point" to which predicates "are affixed," instead of as a subject whose own involvement in the event of self-determination is bound up in the event of human knowing. Moreover, by assuming the immediate truth of the term God, the knower fails to take into account that it is only in the event through which this being becomes concretely knowable as "love" etc. that the proposition becomes actual knowledge. In other words, it has to be seen that the relationship between knower and known is not static, but unfolds by mutual implication.

For Hegel, Kant's is a philosophy that locates the quiddity of things as that which is off limits to reason, positing the truth, or the way things "really are" as a static proposition "existing over there" in isolation from the thoughts we have "in here."[43] Adams rehearses the way this common sense

---

40. Ibid., 23.
41. Ibid.
42. Ibid., 12–13.
43. Pippin reminds us that Hegel is not "shifting the focus from what's 'Out There'

logic operates: "There are the ideas in my head; there is the world out there: I wonder how these are related to each other."[44] In Chapter 1 I argued that when this reading of Kant is transposed into theology, the gulf between the most real (God as the *ens realissimum*) and the human thinker becomes absolute, so that the "in here" of human reason, by definition, could never have access to God who exists in an infinitely distant "over there."

> The fundamental principle common to the philosophies of Kant, Jacobi, and Fichte is, then, the absoluteness of finitude and, resulting from it, the absolute antithesis of finitude and infinity, reality and ideality, the sensuous and the supersensuous, and the beyondness of what is truly real and absolute.[45]

Thus reason "is deprived of the possibility of comprehending rationally its noblest subject."[46] For Hegel, Kant provides an "empty" account of reason, where reason is conceived as the *a priori* structures in place to systematize or order the manifold of experiences arising from the intuition of sense data.[47] And on this basis terms such as "God" can only be treated as regulative ideals, since the characteristics assumed of "God" in advance, such as transcendence, by definition cannot be given to experience. "The fact that reason depends upon sensibility, judged by understanding, for evidence of the actual existence of any objects is what condemns its ideas [such as God] to serving as mere postulates or regulative ideals."[48] In Hegel's view this results in the postulation of ideals of reason, including the concept of God, which are "utterly without content" and which therefore do not "constitute anything."[49] Since for Kant reason does not supply its own content, but merely organizes the information provided for it, once we have translated God into an infinitely distant concept, God can only be conceived as the ground of reason's organizational capacity, and not subject to it. We

---

as the guarantor of truth claims to what's all 'In Here'" as if all mention of externality or the independent reality of nature were prohibited (Pippin, "You Can't Get There from Here," 62–63). Hegel is not making an ontological claim, but a logical one. "The sensuous world does not 'vanish.' What vanishes is its status as wholly independent ground of experience" (ibid., 83 n23).

44. Adams, *Eclipse of Grace*, 182.
45. Hegel, *Faith and Knowledge*, 62.
46. Jüngel, *God as the Mystery of the World*, 69; see also, Hegel, *Faith and Knowledge*, 61.
47. See Guyer, "Thought and Being," 193.
48. Ibid., 194.
49. Hegel, *Faith and Knowledge*, 80.

cannot know God, because God cannot be "discovered" as an object in the world.

Hegel's critical response to Kant is the suggestion that when Christians claim to know God, the kinds of thinking that they display demonstrate a far more holistic and historicized relation between being and thinking than is ordinarily allowed. Being does not provide a foundation for thought; rather, being becomes determinate for thought, that is, it becomes concrete, particular, and meaningful, insofar as it takes place for thought as historical event. Being ought not to be conceived as a static, external brute fact which is then to be discovered by reason, but as becoming determinate in and through the event of its coming to knowledge. Being and knowing are mutually implicated in a deeply historical sense, since being without concrete determination by thought is an inadmissible abstraction, and thinking is not other than the event by which being becomes determinate.[50] This is not an ontological claim suggesting that being becomes only when it is created by thought. It is simply a logical claim which tries to express "a deeper sense of a notion of truth"[51] than was allowed in Descartes and Kant by indicating that truth does not stand neutrally before or behind the mediation of the object for thought. Rather, the category of mediation must itself be incorporated into our account of what it means for something objectively to be true. The logic displayed in Christian thinking about God is triadic, rather than oppositional, since being and knowing, and revelation and witness, are pairs of terms mediated by a third term such as history or event. That third term must not be divorced from the definition of either term within the pair. Consequently what we might call the "thirdness" of terms such as "mediation," "event," and "actualization" belong to the definition of "being," "objectivity," and "truth" (on one side of a set of related pairs) just as they belong to a definition of "knowing," "subjectivity," and "witness" (on the other side of the pairs concerned in accounts of revelation). Quite often in theology these terms are taken, erroneously, to relate only to the noetic side of the pairs.

To express this triadic logic in theological terms is to say that the truth of God is not an isolated fact existing "over there"[52] to be discovered empirically or represented by knowledge, but is an event. The same is true of the actualization of salvation. Truth *occurs*, since God's being and human knowing are mutually implicated in a history full of movement, whereby

---

50. For Hegel's holistic integration of being and thinking, see Hegel, *The Science of Logic*, 59ff.; see also, Houlgate, *Freedom, Truth and History*, 48ff.; and Burbidge, "Hegel's Conception of Logic," 94ff.

51. Pinkard, *German Philosophy*, 218.

52. See Houlgate, *Freedom, Truth and History*, 205.

God's being becomes determinate for human subjects through an encounter which is itself constitutive of that being. Likewise, salvation is an event and a living history. Hegel's is an idealism that seeks to subvert static, immutable accounts of identity, objectivity, and essence, and to indicate the fact that identity or truth is actively produced through the drama of becoming.[53] He states that spirit is

> not an essence that is already finished and complete before its manifestation, keeping itself aloof behind its host of appearances, but an essence which is truly actual only through the specific forms of its necessary self-manifestation.[54]

In the *Lectures on the Philosophy of Religion* of 1821 Hegel rehearses the kind of dynamic and eventful logic that he sees as being in play in Christian thinking, describing God rather enigmatically as "absolute idea . . . spirit," and then offering three clarifications of what such a term is designed to indicate:

> (a) It *is* only as the *unity of concept and reality*, so that the concept in itself is the totality, and likewise the reality. (b) . . . the idea of spirit is to be the unity of divine and human nature . . . (g) The truth cannot be expressed in a proposition . . . Spirit, therefore, is the living process by which the *implicit* unity of divine and human nature becomes *explicit*.[55]

Hegel is saying that according to the logic of Christianity it is illegitimate to think of who God "really" is and who God is "for thought" as being opposing entities, because Christian thought about God displays a concern with the inseparable unity in distinction of "reality" and "concept," as well as displaying "a concern with unity (*Einheit*) and process (*Prozess*)."[56] That is, unlike the version of Kantian logic Hegel rehearses, it refuses to give an account of the way thinking occurs by splitting the concept (our idea of God) from reality (the being of God in itself).[57] Reality (God's being in itself) is an *event*, not an immutable, fixed state, and to describe this reality in terms of a concept (our idea of God) is to make the claim that the knowing subject has been drawn into participation in the eventful becoming of reality, truth, and divine identity. When Christians claim to know God they are not, for Hegel, displaying a logic in which subjects gain access to and subsequently

53. See ibid., 33–34.
54. Hegel, *Hegel's Philosophy of Mind*, 3.
55. Hegel, *Lectures on the Philosophy of Religion*, 66.
56. Adams, *Eclipse of Grace*, 182.
57. Ibid., 182.

"name" a truth that stands "over there," external to them. Rather they display a mode of thinking in which truth is an event to be participated in, and which therefore insists that terms such as reality and participation, being and knowing, must be mobilized triadically in conjunction with each other. As Adams says, Hegel "refuses to think the 'being' of God independently of thinking the 'thinking' of human beings."[58]

The key to understanding Hegel's contribution to Christian theology, then, is to acknowledge his claim that Christianity displays a deeply participative account of the relation between divine and human agency, and it does so by integrating the determination of divine being with the event of human knowing in a non-competitive, non-propositional, historical, and dramatic account of truth. "The logic of Christian talk about the spirit is one in which truth is generated by spirit, for spirit, rather than being something over and against the thinking subject."[59] To put this in Johannine terms, Hegel is investigating what it means to say that we "have" the truth of God's reality only to the extent that the Spirit leads us into all the truth (John 16:13).[60] This Johannine investigation seeks to overcome the divine-human dualism prevalent in certain readings of Kant by refusing to conceive divine being as an abstract reality isolated from the capacities of human conceptualization, and replacing it with the account of a drama, an encounter, or an event, where the determination of being for thought is to be conceived organically. Adams summarizes Hegel's explication of the participative nature of Christian thinking about God:

---

58. Ibid., 14–15. This is not to say that when we think of God we are really thinking of ourselves in the manner of Feuerbach, or that human thought has infallible access to God's truth, or that God *is* only when God is thought properly. It is simply to say that when we account for the being of God we can do so only insofar as this being is understood as being for thought.

59. Ibid., 204. It is notoriously difficult to capture the various senses of what Hegel means to indicate by the term "spirit" (*Geist*). For our purposes, its importance lies in the fact that, as Fergusson notes, spirit denotes "movement, energy, and dynamism" and is therefore less static than being or substance. It engenders a concept of truth which is dramatic, not propositional, and a vision of reality as historically concrete and not abstract. "For Hegel, spirit is essentially self-communicating. It must reveal and reconcile itself to what it is not. Only by so doing does it become fully expressed and achieve its identity as spirit" (Fergusson, "Hegel," 62). Or as Adams suggests, "Talk of spirit displays a logic in which the false opposition between content and agent, object and subject, is overcome" (Adams, *Eclipse of Grace*, 197). To invoke the rhetoric of "spirit" in theology indicates that how God exists (form) is itself ingredient in what God is (content), and that to divorce form from content, acting from being, or existence from essence, is to conceive God in a fundamentally non-biblical manner.

60. See Adams, *Eclipse of Grace*, 199.

To speak of a unity of concept and reality is a sign that this alternative [i.e. participative and triadic] logic is operative. To speak of the unity of divine and human nature is a fruit of this alternative logic. To describe this unity as a process, which unfolds historically, rather than a state of affairs, which can be captured in a proposition, is to be guided by this alternative logic.[61]

Beyond the Propositional Logic of Spatial Distance: "Hegelian" Echoes in *Church Dogmatics* IV/3

Beyond the Logic of Spatial Distance

What Hegel is critiquing is what Gunton refers to as the modern logic of "spatial distance," according to which

> Knowledge is something (1) possessed by an *individual*, who (2) stands over against something which is conceived to be spatially distant. The spatial distance is bridged either by bringing the mind into conformity with the world ("realism") or the world into conformity with the mind ("idealism"). In either case (3), the intellectual bridge between the two is provided by the foundational axioms which are conceived to link the mind with the world.[62]

For Gunton, Barth moves away from the adherence to a modern logic of spatial distance characteristic of the *Romans* II commentary, towards a "post-critical" account of knowledge as personal acquaintance between knower and known. Gunton makes use of Michael Polanyi's thought to draw attention to this logical shift.[63] My own study has drawn on Hegel's philosophy because it performs the fruitfulness of what I have termed—following Adams—the triadic logic on display in Barth's theology of mediation in IV/3. Whether one uses Hegel or Polanyi to advert to the consequences of certain logics in Christian thinking, the crucial point is that in an "epistemology of spatial distance . . . the essence of knowledge is the proposition, in which the distant object is described in words which attempt to mirror what is there. The emphasis is on "knowledge that" rather than knowledge by acquaintance."[64] In *Romans* II, and even volume I of the *Church Dogmat-*

---

61. Ibid., 182.
62. Gunton, "No Other Foundation," 63–64.
63. See Polanyi, *Personal Knowledge*.
64. Gunton, "No Other Foundation," 64.

ics, Barth had one-sidedly emphasized an oppositional logic, at the expense of the more triadic lines of thinking necessary for an adequate account of human freedom. For example, he had stressed that "God is transcendent insofar as he stands outside of or on the boundary of ordinary human experience."[65] This brought with it an epistemology in which it is presupposed that the object, God, and human subjects are separated by an almost unbridgeable gulf, an absolutely infinite qualitative distinction. This gulf is then bridged by means of a vertical movement downwards of the object *qua* subject (Christ and the Spirit), representing or relating various theological propositions which correspond analogically (in an act of self-interpretation or re-iteration) to God's pre-existing being *in se*, by which the distant object is made known and the human subject moves "from ignorance to knowledge."[66] In fairness to Barth, by I/1 he was rightly insistent that God is known only to the extent that God is the living subject, and therefore that God becomes thinkable in the very eventfulness of God's being. But at that stage Barth's actualism was not yet fully developed, and the subjectivity of God was emphasized precisely in order to protect a quasi-Kantian critical separation of God's being in and for itself, and God's being for us. Whilst, then, the earlier Barth wanted to resist what he took to be Kant's relegation of God to an absolutely unknowable other, it was not until his later works, when he was able to integrate divine being and God's self-revelatory economy, that he could do justice to the deep-seated unity of God and the world in Jesus Christ. And it was not until IV/3 that this model was brought to fruition, since here Barth claims that the reconciling event of Christ, which itself has ontic significance for God, includes the event of salvation's revelation as an integral part of the drama in which God allows God and humanity to become mutually implicated.

Barth therefore moves towards a position in which there is a far greater "measure of reciprocity"[67] between the being of God and the knowledge of the human subject. "[I]nevitably, it is an asymmetrical reciprocity"[68] for the event of God's being and activity is not exhausted in the event of human knowing, and it cannot be controlled or conditioned by the latter; but neither can it be abstracted from it. In IV/3 Barth suggests that the event of human knowledge takes place in and with the event of God's ontological self-determination, so that the history in which God becomes *this* God, the God of the covenant, is identical with the event in which God becomes

---

65. Thiemann, *Revelation and Theology*, 47.
66. Gunton, "No Other Foundation," 68.
67. Ibid., 70.
68. Ibid.

thinkable. The gracefulness of the divine is such that precisely as the supremely ontologically distinct other, God is eternally faithful to Godself by coming to humanity historically, allowing the human pilgrimage into truth to be a part *of* the truth. It belongs to the objectivity of God's identity, and to the objective actualization of reconciliation, that the event of God's relational self-identification takes place in and with the mutual implication of human subjects by the prophetic agency of Christ. In IV/3, then, "Barth is insistent that, even when speaking of the knowledge of God, we are in the realm of personal relationships rather than being concerned with the conveying of information."[69]

To clarify my procedure at this point, I am not identifying a "Hegelian" theological ontology which is then repeated in Barth. Rather, I am using Hegel's investigation into the shape of Christian thinking to identify a better way of reading Barth's doctrine of reconciliation than the typical accounts, which tend to see the epistemology of IV/3 as simply being exterior to Barth's soteriological objectivism. Hegel helps theologians to see that to take the "objective" as a brute fact existing neutrally "over there," externally to the event of human subjectivity "in here," is to mishandle the relation of these terms, the doctrinal result of which is to abstract the thought of the being of God from the concrete history in which God may be known, leading to a dualistic conception of the God-world relation. I suggest that Barth's description of Christ's activity as the "Word of life" (1 John 1:1) and the "light of life" (John 8:12)[70] resists a theological ontology and soteriology in which the subjectivity of Christ and the event of human knowing could be taken as being posterior to and divorced from the objective content of His reconciling identity, as if the two were cleanly distinguishable. Barth seems to be indicating that to try to think God's being or the objective actuality of divine-human reconciliation in abstraction from the history of their coming to human knowledge through Christ and the Spirit would be to try to think a completely obscure reality, and not therefore the glorious and self-giving truth of God. It is for this reason that Barth insists in IV/3 that what Christ lives He lives not for Himself, but for the sake of our active participation in the life of God. IV/3 is Barth's attempt to balance his anti-Pelagian soteriological objectivism with the claim that God's life, and the

---

69. Ibid., 70. It is surprising that Gunton does not pursue his reading of Barth further; he often neglects IV/3 finding that Barth is over-noetic, concerned with the relation of information about what has objectively been completed in Christ. This book has argued that in fact Barth identifies a far more dynamic vision of divine being and human knowing, in which the two are reciprocally related within the space of a covenantal drama of mutual implication.

70. IV/3, 47.

performance of the covenant, are not lived out in abstraction from us, nor can they be *thought* as such, but must be conceived precisely in and through the history through which Christ and the Holy Spirit enable us, subjectively, to participate in them.

The critics' interpretations assume a "commonsense" or "oppositional" approach to Barth's account of mediation, according to which Christ is primarily and objectively the reconciler of God and humanity in the "there and then" of His earthly history, and only secondarily and subjectively the one who relates information about the event of His being in His prophetic "here and now." Commentators have not sufficiently identified the mature Barth's overhaul of the theological method prevalent in *Romans* II wherein it is presupposed that the divine object and the human subject are fundamentally opposed or disjunct, that this disjunction is first overcome by means of Christ's objective reconciliation, and that we are subsequently made to "find out" through the relation of doctrinal propositions what has happened on our behalf. They see the truth of God as existing in abstraction from the event of knowledge, and the event of knowledge as the naming of a brute fact which exists over against the subject. But in IV/3 Barth seems to say that the Christological event of divine-human truth—which is both the objective actualization of God's covenantal identity and the actualization of human salvation—is a drama taking place, and is known only to the extent that Christ facilitates human participation in it through attraction of subjects into His body, the Church. And whilst this truth is secured once and for all in Jesus, His history is not yet at an end, and therefore includes the time in which He guides particular subjects into all the truth. Hence, when Jesus Christ the prophet appropriates the event of His life-act for humanity contemporaneously, this is not the communication of propositions to be acknowledged, but the invitation to humanity to join God in the journey to the depths of a mutually forged covenantal reality.

This doctrinal point is the fruit of a triadic logic of participation which governs Barth's use of object and subject in IV/3. Daniel Hardy helps to explain the nature of the truth to which Christians attest through the pursuit of such a logic: "We use labels like . . . 'word in spirit,' or 'Trinity,' or 'God,' but these are not just labels for something that is there. They name that which of its nature is infinite, endless and expansive, to which the only possible response is not to name it but to follow it into the depths. You can say of it only that it is what attracts."[71]

The key to participative accounts of theological epistemology, divine and human agency, and freedom, then, is to see that in Christian speech

---

71. Hardy, *Wording A Radiance*, 46.

about God, being and thinking are a pair of terms that can be understood properly only when they are expounded in their mutual implication. To think God, and to think the event of salvation, is not to try to conceive of entities that exist neutrally in relation to us, or in abstraction from us, but rather to consider both from the standpoint of our historical involvement in them. Again, Hardy helps to explain this point:

> In quantum physics, the act of measuring the movement of photons, for example, also affects that movement, so that to measure is to enter into an actual relation to what is measured. There is no neutral or distant observation here: just as in ethnography, observation is participant-observation, so that the observer . . . participate[s] in and influence[s] the activity that is observed . . . [Similarly], for a life of pilgrimage, to know God is not to observe things "about" him from some neutral standpoint but to participate in his life in the world . . . [W]e are drawn into the measure of God in the degree to which we participate in his infinite nature.[72]

What God and salvation most essentially are can only be considered from the perspective in which we discover ourselves to be a part of their reality. These cannot be represented in propositions which try to conform themselves to neutral facts standing over against us.

It is true that Barth speaks of human knowledge of reconciliation simply as acknowledgement and gratitude (*eucharistia*), and he says that salvation is objectively secure (*de jure*) regardless of our subjective awareness of it (*de facto*). Such language is ostensibly externalistic, non-participative, and oppositional. Nevertheless, this study has presented an alternative reading of Barth's soteriological object-subject paradigm which both affirms that Christ alone can achieve the reconciliation of God and humanity and the actualization of God's covenantal reality, and that as the prophet, mediator, and true witness, Christ does not actualize these in abstraction from us, but in such a way that our gratitude and subjective acknowledgement is itself an irreducibly important part of the covenantal drama. Christ guarantees that the relationship between God and humanity is eternally secure. But in His prophetic history, Christ comes good on this promise by leading us into His truth. We cannot cleanly separate Christ's truth and our placement in it. As identified in Chapter 3, Barth insists that Christ's reality is not merely an interesting ontological reality but a truth and event taking place between God and humanity which is to be lived by all humans. And if this is so, it is necessary to take the mature Barth as conceiving the objective actualization

---

72. Ibid., 60-61.

of the covenant and the revelatory means by which it is made known as being part of one and the same Christological drama. Barth comes to realize that our knowledge of God must itself be considered from the perspective of our participation in God's life as event, and not as the mere reflection or representation of facts about a spatially distant truth. As Gunton says, "Barth rightly sees that the shape of our knowledge of God must correspond to the covenantal relationship in which we stand."[73] Describing God's truth as "speech-event," Jüngel therefore recalls an important passage in Barth's essay on Hegel, finding that

> if theology had not learned it from Hegel, it would have to let itself be reminded by Barth "that the source of knowledge of Reformation theology had been the word, the word of God, the word of truth. But this also means, the event of God, the event of truth . . . an event at which he for whom it is to be an event must be present; an event which by repetition, and by man's renewal of his presence, must ever become event anew."[74]

Hegelian Echoes in Church Dogmatics IV/3

Hegel helps to demonstrate that the theological result of thinking being and knowing as essentially separate is the thought of a divine-human disjunction. By contrast the result of thinking being and knowing triadically as mutually implicated within an organic history of truth is the conception of the unity of God and humanity. In IV/3 Barth refuses to think of the actualization of Christ's divine-human truth and the event of its revelation in disjunction. Neither the subjectivity of Christ in the *munus propheticum* nor the event of human knowledge can be abstracted from the covenantal space in which the being of God and humanity are reciprocally in becoming. To come to know Christ in the history of salvation is to journey deeper into His covenantal truth, and therefore to become a part of salvation history itself.

In IV/3 Barth explicitly signals his holistic approach to the covenantal truth of Christ's life and the event of its appropriation by human subjects. He says that this truth consists in a "drama" or encounter "in which man and his history are thus drawn into the history of Jesus Christ."[75] And as we have seen, Barth takes the expressive quality of Christ's prophetic life

---

73. Gunton, "No Other Foundation," 71.
74. Jüngel, *God's Being Is in Becoming*, 14 n1, citing Barth, *Protestant Theology*, 402.
75. IV/3, 187.

itself as being a function of the covenantal truth being performed in His existence:

> For as reconciliation is also revelation, the light of life, the covenant Word and Jesus Christ Prophet, the sphere is burst wide open where we shut ourselves off from Him . . . the fact that reconciliation is also revelation and Jesus Christ lives and works as Prophet means that objectively we cannot be remote from Him in a private sphere, but that we are drawn into His sphere, into what takes place in Him . . . We experience here what takes place there in the supposed but only apparent "there" which in reality encloses our here and in which our here is also there.[76]

The historicity of truth is perhaps the most obviously neo-Hegelian feature to be echoed in Barth's late work; the resemblance between Hegel and Barth's mature thought therefore signals that a decisive logical shift has taken place in the way Barth thinks about divine truth and human participation in the truth. In IV/3 Barth repairs the externalistic and oppositional logic that governed his early thought, expounding a dynamic divine reality in which God's truth is an event being actualized in the midst of the history of human agency, the content of which is the eternally willed fellowship of God and humanity. Barth says

> In the "is" which links the life with the light, the covenant with the Word of God, the reconciliation with revelation . . . there is concealed a drama. The "is" is thus to be understood in dynamic rather than static terms . . . All the concepts used refer to a history . . . Life, covenant and reconciliation all "are" as they take place. Similarly, light, Word and revelation "are" as that which is denoted by them occurs. Only as they happen, therefore, "are" they in this equation . . . That the covenant is also Word means that in its institution, execution and fulfilment it makes itself known as it is enacted.[77]

Here we see that the Word is no longer conceived by Barth as a one-sidedly immanent divine reality, existing in and for itself, whose repetition in human history is of little significance to its eternal content. Human history—the covenant between God and humanity willed by God—is itself the content of a truth which "is" only as it happens. Grammatically, the relationship between the verbal and the nominal in IV/3 is significant: Barth will only employ nouns prominent in the Christian lexicon such as "content,"

76. Ibid., 182.
77. Ibid., 165.

"truth," and "Word," where their use is governed by the verbs that qualify them, such as "occurs," "happens," "enacts," "executes" and "takes place." And this suggests that the historical form of Christ's mediating activity is itself ingredient in His covenantal truth.

Barth, like Hegel, draws particularly on the Fourth Gospel. In Barth's reading of John, as Eyeons has observed, the leading images of Christ as Word and truth preclude the presentation of Jesus "simply as an idea, or the bringer of an idea for us to learn. [Barth] describes Jesus Christ in personal, historical, dynamic terms."[78] Barth makes particular use of the "I am" sayings throughout IV/3 because these indicate that one cannot discriminate cleanly between form and content, between truth and the bearer of the truth, or between the effects of salvation and the one who saves.[79] The "I am" sayings inform Barth's actualism by indicating that as Christ lives, the truth occurs, such that the only means for accessing the truth is to encounter it, and to journey into it. To learn of Christ's truth is to be illuminated by His presence as light (John 8:12), to enter into Him (John 10:9), to be nourished by Him (John 6:35), to be guided as one of His flock (John 10:11), and to live in Him (John 11:25). It is not therefore simply to discover propositions relating facts which are first objectively true in Him, and only subsequently epistemologically communicated by the Holy Spirit as a kind of conveyance of soteriological information. On the contrary, as Barth says in III/2, the

> Johannine passages in which Jesus describes himself as the light, the door, the bread, the shepherd, the vine and the resurrection, point to pure process, to a being which is caught up in its products, so that it is impossible to distinguish between this being as such and its products, or to seek and find this being in itself or apart from these products, but only in them.[80]

Hegel was troubled not only by the claim that God cannot be known, but also by a range of theological responses to Kant that failed to re-think the object-subject disjunction. In the *Lectures on the Philosophy of Religion* of 1824 and 1827 Hegel is particularly concerned with the question of "warrants for belief."[81] For Hegel, theology was bound to fail in its response to Kant so long as it accepted the validity of a logic that assumes that "truth" has a reality "out there" regardless of the subject who "knows" the truth, and that this external reality of truth is something to be discovered or located by the subject. On this mode of thinking we are required to conduct various

78. Eyeons, "Retreat and Restructuring," 143.
79. See esp. IV/3, 231ff.
80. III/2, 60.
81. Adams, *Eclipse of Grace*, 204.

kinds of empirical investigation in order to account for our beliefs. We must find "facts," "external warrants" of various kinds, that would authenticate our claim to knowledge.[82] Hence, the primary theological question of concern was how, in fact, we might be able to demonstrate that we (human subjects) can, after all, have knowledge of this superior, transcendent object, God. Hegel is equally critical of those who take miracles to be warrants for faith, and of those who take them to be insufficient evidential propositions for belief. In both cases it has been assumed that God is an external object to be located, and that there may or may not be facts to verify the being of this unique external object for knowing subjects.[83] Hegel counters this way of thinking by identifying a logic in Christianity where the truth is not to be validated propositionally, but is simply to be participated in.

Barth adverts his commitment to a participative, actualistic, and non-propositional logic in his engagement with Pilate's question, "What is truth?" put to Jesus in John 18. Barth, echoing Hegel's Johannine logic of participation, takes the passage to be a refutation of the request for propositional warrants for belief. For Barth "We are certainly not asked whence Jesus Christ has that with which to prove that His life is light . . . If there were any need or ability to prove Him to be such, what is to be proved would slip through our fingers."[84] The divine-human reciprocity that constitutes His life-act is not a brute fact for which convincing evidence could be gathered and adjudicated as a foundation for belief. The human subject who finds herself encountered by Christ the prophet will find her mode of theological conception transformed in the event. For she will discover that the reciprocal truth of divine and human reality is not an empirically verifiable proposition to be cognized and consumed, a brute ontological state of affairs to be grasped, but is an event to be drawn into and lived in.[85] It is the event of the one who bears the name Jesus Christ. Hence, the Christian

---

82. Ibid., 330ff.; see also, Houlgate, *Freedom, Truth and History*, 184.

83. Adams, *Eclipse of Grace*, 172; see also, Hegel, *Lectures on the Philosophy of Religion*, 253-54.

84. IV/3, 77.

85. This point is entirely obscured by Willis, who charges Barth with falling back on "dogmatic assertion . . . [tending] to ignore the pressing question of evidence and verification" (Willis, *The Ethics of Karl Barth*, 431). Willis complains that Barth's axiomatic rejection of natural theology excludes any continuity of "ordinary epistemic modes" with faith (ibid.). In doing so, Willis reveals a commitment to a propositional logic that does not cohere with the mature Barth's method. Willis is therefore subject to Hardy's indictment against English theologians who are not well-placed to read Barth because "English norms involve the use of naturalistic human knowledge as determinative of what can be believed" (Hardy, "The Reception of Schleiermacher and Barth in England," 147). Where Willis assumes an approach to knowledge that does not cohere with

must not, may not and will not, then, put any more the question of Pilate: "What is truth?" He no longer has the false freedom to ask for special confirmations of the truth from without. Nor does he stand under the false compulsion of having to ask for such confirmations. It has of itself confirmed itself to him ... [A person] hears [Christ's] voice, and his only possible question, put to him by this voice, is not whether and how this voice will show itself to be the voice of truth, but whether and how he himself will show himself to be its hearer.[86]

On the basis of this Johannine view of truth, we might question whether standard interpretations of Barth's soteriological epistemology have done justice to the more participative aspects of his work. Whilst it is true that Barth sees Christ alone as the fulfilment and guarantor of divine-human covenantal truth, it is also crucial to understand that, for Barth, what Jesus Christ does alone He does not do in *isolation*, but in the intensity and brilliance of His risen presence with us and for us, and therefore in utter proximity to us and in perspicuity. Hence, our coming to know the truth cannot be viewed as the receipt of soteriological propositions or dogmatic information that correspond to some abstract ontological reality. Rather, we know the truth to the extent that through personal encounter with Christ, and in the illuminating presence of His light, we are drawn into the event of the truth.

It will be beneficial to readers of Barth to re-assess critically the way they tend to approach Barth's soteriology and theological epistemology in IV/3. Instead of asking two separate questions "what does Barth take to be the truth?" and "how does he take this truth to be communicated?" it may prove more generative to ask how, for Barth, the content of the truth and the form of its communication are mutually implicated in Jesus's "I am." To accuse Barth of seeing the divine-human truth as statically and vicariously completed in Christ, and subsequently mediated noetically in the form of dogmatic propositions, is to neglect important moments in his work which aim to balance the soteriological objectivism of IV/1 and IV/2, and to fail to see that for Barth, as for Hegel, we come to know the truth only insofar as we are of the truth. Only in the reciprocal encounter with Christ is humanity bound up in the event of the truth's mediation and appropriation, so that

---

Barth's, he inevitably takes Barth "either to conflict with or to stretch the bounds of what is considered possible," and criticizes him on that basis (Hardy, ibid.). But for Hardy, this is precisely what Barth had intended; the journey into theological knowledge is described as a journey into God's truth which will "unsettle" epistemic norms, and show that theological belief cannot be based on ordinary propositional foundations.

86. IV/3, 78.

one cannot divorce the content of the truth and its contemporaneous communication. As Christ lives out His being as God-man with us and for us, we find ourselves being drawn into participation in the covenant in which God and humanity reciprocally come to the fullness of their respective realities.

> [I]n this relationship to this man [Jesus] God is the true God, i.e., God in the authentic revelation of His divine nature, God as He is. And in this relationship to God man is true man, i.e., man in faithful confession of His humanity, man as he is. The meeting of this revelation of God and this confession of man is truth in the full sense of the term. For both, i.e. God as He is and man as he is, are the one, whole truth. As this man exists in this meeting, in the unity of God and man, He is the truth.[87]

There is no sign here of the operation of a binary theo-logic, no separation of God in God's eternal truth from the human history. Rather, "truth" is thought as the event of a "meeting," and to know the truth is to be drawn into this meeting, and to measure God's covenantal life from within that meeting. God's self-mediation in Christ does not dissolve the distinction of God and humanity; reconciliation is not homogenization, and God and humanity remain distinct, even in Christ's single person in two natures. There can be no claim to divine-human covenantal reciprocity without reference to its qualifying asymmetry. But by the same token, Christ, in the distinction of His two natures, does not represent two persons, but one, not two truths but one. This is the single truth of God and humanity, the truth that characterizes both their identities—namely, the Christocentric truth that God is not divine other than in relationship with humanity, and humanity is not human other than in relationship with God. This is the single truth of all reality, divine and human, willed by God in God's freedom.

> At no point does the difference mean separation. Nor are abstractions possible to the one who knows Jesus Christ. There is no place for a dualistic thinking which divides the divine and the human, but only for a historical, which at every point, in and with the humiliation and exaltation of the one Son of God and Son of Man, in and with His being as servant and Lord, is ready to accompany the event of the union of His divine and human essence.[88]

Reading IV/3 through a Hegelian lens helps to identify two points in particular that assist in overcoming readings of Barth that perpetuate an

87. IV/3, 379–80.
88. IV/2, 115.

air of competition between God and humanity on the basis of a sense of separation between the objectivity and subjectivity of the covenantal truth of Christ. The first point is that if we are to do justice to the subjective side of salvation, we must conceive it in relation to the objective side, and must not therefore see Christ's *munus propheticum* as the mere relation of facts, but as the attraction of human subjects into the event of His divine-human being. In other words, our thinking about thinking will have to become more participative and covenantal if we are to give IV/3 a more sophisticated reading than it has hitherto enjoyed. Barth will not take human thinking to be abstracted from the history of divine becoming, as if our coming to know God was isolated from God's objective coming to Godself (God's free self-determination). We may not think the event of human knowledge as if it takes place outside of the life of that which is being known, for to know God is to be in relation with God, and hence to enjoy the liberation that constitutes the entire purpose of Christ's identity.

Secondly, it is illegitimate to think God's being in abstraction from the historical realm in which God becomes thinkable, as if we could think God's being *qua* not being thought, and as abstracted from the self-witness of Christ and His Holy Spirit. That is, our thinking about being must also become more participative, and refuse the abstraction latent in the metaphysical traditions in theology and philosophy (which, on some readings, was carried over into Kant, and perpetuated by the earlier Barth). Once our thinking about thinking and being is allowed to be determined in utterly participative, historical, and relational terms, we shall start to do justice to the freedom of God and the freedom of humanity as they are mutually related in Jesus Christ.

Church Dogmatics IV/3: Implications for the Trinity-Election Debate

To conclude this chapter, it is worth noting the contribution that the final completed part-volume of the *Church Dogmatics* may make to the contemporary trinity-election debate, once we have allowed it a more subtle reading than it usually enjoys. The Barth of IV/3 does not, on the whole, try to think how God might be if God had not chosen to exist in this covenantal way; such an effort would display the operation of a logic in which God's essence is thought in separation from God's concrete existence, and in which, therefore, divine and human subjectivity are considered the mere explanation and cognitive acknowledgement of—not ingredient components in— the actualization of living covenantal fellowship. We must not think God's being in disjunction from the act that constitutes, grounds, and reveals the nature of this being; and we therefore cannot even postulate a freedom of God in which God *might* have been another God, a God who was content to exist in and for Godself as eternally self-isolated truth. Barth articulates this point exactly:

> [God] acts of His own initiative . . . He wills of Himself to be the God of man and to have man as His man. He determines of Himself to begin this history common to Himself and His creature . . . [I]t is not accidentally, nor arbitrarily, nor under any constraint or compulsion of a reality distinct from Himself, but in His own freedom that He is this God, that He is God in this way and not another . . . The freedom in which, determined by nothing and no one else, He was and is and will be this God and not another; the execution and revelation of His own divine election—these are our concern in the history of Jesus Christ and therefore in the fact with the positing [*Setzung*] of which the history of light shining in the darkness begins . . . It [i.e. the "positing" of Christ's shining light] does not arise from any necessity, except that of the freedom of God to be this God and not another, or to be God in this way and not another [*Sie entspringt keinem Müssen: es wäre denn dem der Freiheit, in der Gott dieser und kein anderer Gott, so und nicht anders Gott sein will und ist*]. It is a free gift of this free God. Hence it is not subject to man's control or even to the reflection whether or not He might have refrained from it and therefore been another God.[89]

Whilst there are moments in Barth's texts that seem to give rise to a purely formal concept of divine freedom in order to protect the sovereignty of God from the suggestion of dependence upon creation,[90] I suggest, with Gunton, that it is "the *ontological* rather than *spatial* otherness of God which comes to expression in our awareness of the asymmetrical personal relationship between creator and creature."[91] But this otherness must be thought from within the divine-human reality in which the history of human knowing is participant.

It is of use, at this point, to turn to Jüngel, who has been able to articulate with greater clarity than Barth (who even in IV/3 fluctuates occasionally between the two poles of divine independence and divine relationality) the manner in which God's freedom can be described *both* as a freedom from necessity, *and* as a freedom for self-limitation in the humanity of Christ.

---

89. IV/3, 228 rev. = *KD* IV/3, 262.
90. See for example, IV/3, 81.
91. Gunton, "No Other Foundation," 76.

> [F]reedom has two sides: (a) self-determination as the opposite of external determination [*Selbstbestimmung als Gegensatz zu Fremdbestimmung*], but also (b) self-determination as the opposite of indeterminateness (arbitrariness) [*Selbstbestimmung als Gegensatz zu Unbestimmtheit (Beliebigkeit)*]. Freedom understood without the goal of determinateness would be an impermissible abstraction [*unzulässige Abstraktion*]. The will to determination is what makes self-determination, makes freedom something concrete. Thus freedom is something other than the state of free suspension which has no bonds or obligations. Faithfulness is constitutive of freedom. God, the free God, is the very opposite of something like an eternal state of free suspension. God determines himself [*Gott bestimmt sich*]. Only as one who is determined on the basis of his self-determination is God a concrete reality. As the faithful God he is the free God.[92]

Jüngel accepts that there can be no question of a divine dependence on humanity when we think God's divinity in terms of God's humanity. "The final result of our thought cannot be that ultimately man is necessary for God. That God does not want to come to himself without man does not make man the consummation of God. God perfects or consummates himself."[93] But Jüngel quite explicitly forbids any attempted protection against such divine dependence simply by saying that God in God's truth stands eternally prior to, and essentially detached from, God's self-determination in the event of Christ's human history, and he claims the whole of his book *God as the Mystery of the World* is presented in order to provide a theologically viable alternative to this conception of divine freedom. Jüngel recognizes that theology could "easily dispose" of the erroneous statement of human necessity to God

> by saying that God could come to himself without coming to man [*Gott könne eben auch, ohne zum Menschen kommen, zu sich selber kommen*], that, in fact, he is God by virtue of the fact that he has always come to himself without man and the world. But I regard this argument as godless [*Ich halte dieses Argument jedoch für gottlos*]. It conceives the freedom of God as mere self-possession [*bloßen Selbstbesitz*] and restricts the sovereignty of God, conceived of as the absolute having of being, to God himself, in that it sets aside the selflessness of love from this sovereignty and allows freedom to be derived from it as a distinct

---

92. Jüngel, *God as the Mystery of the World*, 36 rev. = Jüngel, *Gott als Geheimnis der Welt*, 46.

93. Jüngel, *God as the Mystery of the World*, 37–38.

and secondary factor. Basically the studies presented here are nothing other than a concerted attack [*ein einziger Angriff*] on the godlessness [*die Gottlosigkeit*] of this argument.[94]

The "concerted attack" Jüngel proposes must be applied to those parts of Barth's own thought where, in deference to a logic of spatial distance, Barth conceives the being of God's Godhead in abstraction from the humanity of God's act. One must also, therefore, question the interpretations of Barth's divine ontology offered by Molnar and Hunsinger, who, in a retreat to classical trinitarian scholasticism, attempt to secure the divinity of God by refusing the humanity of God a part in the eternal constitution of God's triune identity. It is true that Molnar and Hunsinger find support for their interpretations of Barth in his texts, which, as I have shown, admit of ambiguity in key passages. But in light of the reading of IV/3 developed in this book, such positions are appear to theologically problematic, for they refuse the participative kinds of thinking that Christianity encourages by positing a metaphysical gap between God's being and God's act, and by tearing the thought of God's essence away from the thought of God's human existence in Jesus Christ.[95] The emphasis placed on divine freedom as the negative freedom from all necessity, encouraged by Molnar and Hunsinger (although Molnar is keen to protest that he balances God's freedom from humanity with God's freedom for humanity[96]), does not do justice to the positive claim to God's freedom for self-limitation in the event of the crucifixion, and therefore protects an abstract divine essence at the expense of the biblical description of the faithful God. Such a negatively construed notion of divine freedom is not descriptive of the Christian thought of God. This conception of God's freedom not only reveals a one-sided concern for naked being over act,[97] but ultimately manifests a one-sided account of God's freedom *from* humanity, over against God's freedom *for* humanity. Moreover, it fails to account for the dynamic historicity of divine-human truth in which Christ's prophetic mediation of the covenant to the world is

---

94. Ibid., 37 n. 6 = Jüngel, *Gott als Geheimnis der Welt*, 47–48 n. 6.

95. As Jüngel says of such a notion of God's eternal freedom: "The tradition . . . took refuge in the Beyondness of God's being [*Seinsjenseitigkeit Gottes*] . . . The advantage of this thesis is that it distinguishes between God and being in favour of God. But we found it to be deficient because it rendered it impossible to speak *positively* of God and instead only expressed God as the one who is actually unspeakable and unthinkable" (Jüngel, *God as the Mystery of the World* 381 = Jüngel, *Gott als Geheimnis der Welt*, 522).

96. See, for example, Molnar, "The Trinity, Election, and God's Ontological Freedom," 300–301.

97. McCormack has articulated this point. See McCormack, "Theses in Response to George Hunsinger," 205.

envisaged as a core component in the unfolding of the drama in which God and humanity reciprocally become most essentially themselves.

Conclusion

This chapter has built on the argument of Chapter 3 in order to counter standard readings of IV/3 by drawing attention to the somewhat static and binary approach to the question of theological knowledge assumed by some commentators. I have drawn on Hegel's critique of Kant to suggest that when reading the mature Barth we are required to employ an altogether different mode of theological conception than that used when reading the early Barth. In place of the logic of opposition that marked Barth's critique of religion and natural theology, one sees that the theology of mediation in IV/3 is characterized by a far more participative and triadic logic. Part of the motivation for this chapter was my agreement with Nicholas Adams that as long as students of theology are not given sufficient training in comparative logic, they will be likely to obscure certain creative and generative ways of approaching the most significant and complex texts in theology.[98] One such failure, I suggest, has been the neglect of *Church Dogmatics* IV/3, which I take to be one of Barth's finest theological accomplishments, and an excellent example of where the consistent application of a binary and oppositional logic to a text whose central concern (soteriological epistemology) requires a triadic one for its appreciation can result in the almost universal oversight of that text. I have argued that where Barth scholars fail to revise their "common sense" understanding of the object-subject pattern (as Hegel might call it), the more interesting and generative features in IV/3 will continue to be obscured.

Since, in this chapter, it has been argued that the event of Christ's mediatorial agency draws human subjects into the asymmetrically reciprocal truth of His divine-human identity, it remains to be seen how Barth conceives the shape of human flourishing in and through that mediation. In what way are we liberated for participation in the covenantal life of the free God by Jesus's prophetic call? It is to this question that I turn in the final chapter.

---

98. See Adams, *The Eclipse of Grace*, 12.

5

CALLED TO LIBERTY

Human Flourishing in *Church Dogmatics* IV/3

Now the Lord is the Spirit, and where the Spirit of the Lord is, there is freedom.

—2 Cor 3:17

Introduction

If the liberation of humanity for covenantal participation is an integral part of the drama in which God's being is in becoming, then it is necessary to investigate the shape of human flourishing as Barth sees it in IV/3. The difficulty Barth faces in his mature theological ethics is trying to do justice to the space God wills to give human creatures to exercise their freedom for authentic covenantal participation, whilst upholding his strongly anti-Pelagian commitment to a Christocentric description of divine and human reality. As I shall argue below, some commentators have read Barth as positing an ontic-noetic divide, which they then take as evidence that the human situation with God is resolved ontologically in Christ and is merely to be accepted epistemically by human creatures. This is then viewed as underwriting a pneumatological, ecclesiological, and ethical abstraction, where the Spirit and the Church cannot really contribute anything to the drama of the covenant of grace.

In departure from this criticism, this chapter describes Barth's actualism as providing a space for human participation in the body of Christ. Since Christ's elective, reconciling, and redemptive being is in action, it is reductive to view Barth as holding a sharp distinction between the *illuc et tunc* ("there and then") of Christ's earthy life and its achievement, and the *hic et nunc* ("here and now") of His risen life in ecclesial contemporaneity. Furthering the main argument of this book, the chapter suggests that by positing a more fluid relation between the objective and subjective categories, and between world-history and eschatology in IV/3, it is possible to bring to the fore the share Barth attributes to the Church in the consummation of the covenant. Hence the freedom of God and humanity in asymmetrical reciprocity is not merely one lived solely by Christ, to be passively accepted by humanity. The very nature of Christ's being-in-action as the God-man means that our active participation in divine-human relations is a feature of Christ's mediatorial mission. In order to see how this is so, I shall pay particular attention first to Barth's pneumatology, and then to his doctrine of vocation, demonstrating that it is reductive to view these in overly noetic and externalistic terms. When one assumes a binary rather than triadic mode of conception in interpreting Barth's Christology it becomes impossible not to see the work of the Spirit and Church as extraneous to Christ's salvation victory. Interpretations of IV/3 on these lines take terms such as crucifixion and revelation, Jesus's self-witness and human reception, and salvation and ecclesial ministry, to be construed in basically competitive terms, where one is over-emphasized at the expense of the other. What is proposed in this book is that on a triadic view of Barth's way of thinking in IV/3, the two terms in each pair are related non-competitively and non-exclusively, so that it is entirely meaningful to speak *both* of the complete objectivity of salvation in Jesus *and* of the place of the Holy Spirit and the life of the Church in the exercise of the covenant's actuality. The two pairs of terms are reciprocally related, without any sense of the latter needing to "complete" or "augment" the former. The argument presented here is that the complaint that Barth has under-emphasized the Spirit and the Church in his soteriology is a sign that a binary and competitive, rather than triadic and actualistic, reading of his Christology is operative. On the triadic and actualistic reading of IV/3 offered in this book, what is fulfilled in and through Jesus, (*Sola Christus* so to speak), has not actually been achieved objectively if it does not also manifest subjectively in the call of the Church issued by the animating work of the Spirit. To apply Barth's actualism to IV/3 is to acknowledge that what happens in the ways and works of God in the world has repercussions for the self-identification of God in eternity. The reception of, and witness to, the Gospel by the Church, as inspired through the Holy Spirit, is anything but ancillary and accidental to the triune life of God and the eternal election of an authentic, historical, and genuinely contingent covenant.

The History of Human Freedom: The Promise of the Spirit

For Barth, the Holy Spirit governs the Christian life, in pursuit of which human subjects exercise their Christ-centered liberty to become most fully themselves as obedient covenantal partners with God. In order to grasp Barth's account of human freedom, therefore, I shall explicate the strong pneumatological and ecclesiological currents in his mature thought. However, a number of scholars, such as Robert Jenson, Eugene Rogers, Colin Gunton, Thomas Smail, and Philip Rosato have provided robust critiques of Barth's pneumatology, and if one is to do justice to the role of the Spirit as the driving force in human flourishing, careful engagement with these critics is needed. In this section I shall find that many of the commentators' criticisms introduced in Chapter 3 are recapitulated from a pneumatological perspective. In what follows, the main argument of this book is advanced once more: renewed attention to the object-subject relation in Barth's theology of freedom helps to mitigate against some of the more damaging complaints lodged by many critics, and therefore to capture the radical sense of reciprocal freedom between God and humanity envisioned by Barth.

Criticisms of Barth's Pneumatology

Jenson finds that frequently the Holy Spirit does not appear in the *Church Dogmatics* as one would expect in line with what the New Testament has to say about the Spirit's agency, and that "long stretches of Barth's thinking seem rather binitarian than Trinitarian."[1] For Jenson and Rogers, Barth particularly neglects the Spirit in IV/3's account of human freedom in the passages on the proclamation of salvation (§69), and the mission of the Church (§72), despite his ostensible intention to conduct pneumatological

---

1. Jenson, "You Wonder Where the Spirit Went," 296. So argue Rogers, "The Eclipse of the Spirit in Karl Barth," 173; and Smail, *The Giving Gift*, 43.

investigation in these paragraphs.² For Jenson, everything that happens *pro nobis* is conducted by the Son in relation to the Father,³ and Barth simply pays lip-service to the Spirit, who is associated merely with a function of the Son.⁴

The diagnosis Jenson offers for this neglect of the Spirit turns on an analysis of the trinitarian foundation (I/1).⁵ For Jenson, Barth's mistake lies in his thoroughly "Western-style trinitarianism" which sees the triune God as a person, and the three members of the trinity as impersonal "*parties of divine action*."⁶ When God's being is identified with God's action, the one personal God is seen as acting in three different modes of being, but not as three individual persons acting individually in inseparable community.⁷ This becomes especially problematic when the inner trinitarian activity of God's one being in three modes is described as "two-sided."⁸ The Father commands and the Son obeys. This immanent pattern is the foundation for God's activity *ad extra*, where everything that is to be actualized historically is decreed eternally by the Father-Son relationship, without any real space for the Spirit.⁹ Following Augustine, the Spirit is described as the *vinculum amoris*, the bond of love, between the Father and Son. It is no surprise, the critics maintain, that Barth cannot develop "a specific salvation-historical initiative of the Spirit" in the doctrine of reconciliation because "the Spirit is condemned by the *vinculum*-doctrine to remain a *modus* only."¹⁰ And, says Gunton, "because the [Spirit's] function is defined so narrowly—almost wholly christologically—such a move maintains an effective *ontological* subordination of Spirit to Son and militates against an identification of the Spirit's specific *persona*."¹¹

---

2. Jenson, "You Wonder Where the Spirit Went," 298; see also, Rogers, "The Eclipse of the Spirit in Karl Barth," 174.

3. Jenson, "You Wonder Where the Spirit Went," 302.

4. Ibid., 303. This complaint is lodged by numerous scholars. See Rogers, "The Eclipse of the Spirit in Karl Barth," 173; Gunton, "God the Holy Spirit," 106; Smail, "The Doctrine of the Holy Spirit," 93; Rosato, *The Spirit as Lord: The Pneumatology of Karl Barth*, 160.

5. Jenson, "You Wonder Where the Spirit Went," 296.

6. Ibid., 301.

7. See Torrance, *Persons in Communion*, 111–19.

8. Jenson, "You Wonder Where the Spirit Went," 300; see also, Gunton, *Theology Through the Theologians*, 106; I/1, 504.

9. Jenson, "You Wonder Where the Spirit Went," 300.

10. Ibid., 300; 302.

11. Gunton, *Theology Through the Theologians*, 106.

In IV/3, Jenson complains, the proclamation of the Gospel and the formation of the Church are responsibilities of the Son, and not the Holy Spirit, despite what Scripture has to say about the life of the Spirit in this regard.[12] Jenson thinks Barth is right to secure the objectivity of the Gospel's proclamation as "external" to its reception by the human subject,[13] but he suspects Barth deliberately avoids giving the Spirit a central role in the appropriation of salvation by human agents because he has identified the agency of the Spirit entirely with the "subjective," that is, with the performance of a noetic function.[14] This point is re-iterated by Rogers who says of §69.4 "Everywhere in these passages, the Spirit is the condition for the possibility of human knowledge of God."[15] And Jenson also suspects that Barth does not want to give the Church a concrete role in the "objective" mediation of the covenant (fearing the synergism he felt characterized Roman Catholic ecclesiology), and therefore associates the pneumatic life of the Church with the subjective reception of a message or truth which is ontologically secure in Christ.[16] Barth, Rogers adds, is wary of a perceived anthropomorphic subjectivism in Schleiermacher where "the Spirit of the Lord has become identified with the spirit of the human."[17] The Spirit is thus described as the agency or capacity of Christ to make Himself known, but is not Himself described as an independent agent.[18] Jenson asks critically, "Does Barth suppose that an act of the Spirit cannot transcend subjectivity?"[19] And Rogers continues, "It is true that the Spirit is *responsible* for human reception of revelation. But the Spirit is not therefore *reducible* to the subjective."[20]

The danger inherent in such a perceived error, as Smail argues, is that human freedom, mediated by the Spirit, is all too narrowly defined as the acquisition of knowledge about what Christ has done for us. This minimizes any agential space in which human freedom is viewed as authentic, active participation in the life of the covenant: "the work of the Spirit [according

12. Jenson, "You Wonder Where the Spirit Went," 298.
13. Ibid., 298.
14. Ibid.
15. Rogers, "The Eclipse of the Spirit in Karl Barth," 174.
16. Jenson, "You Wonder Where the Spirit Went," 302.
17. Rogers, "The Eclipse of the Spirit in Karl Barth," 176.
18. Jenson, "You Wonder Where the Spirit Went," 303; see IV/3, 869–70: "the Holy Spirit is the godly power unique to the being of Jesus Christ." The Spirit is what happens when "Jesus Christ makes use of his power." See also, Rogers, "The Eclipse of the Spirit in Karl Barth," 175; 179: there is no "interval" between the Son and Spirit, so that whatever is said of the Spirit is said through the Son.
19. Jenson, "You Wonder Where the Spirit Went," 298.
20. Rogers, "The Eclipse of the Spirit in Karl Barth," 184.

to Barth] is to convince us that Christ has vicariously responded to God on our behalf, rather than bringing us to respond *for ourselves* to what Christ has done."[21] Rosato finds that on the basis of the subordination of pneumatology to Christology and the disjunction of the ontic *prius* from the noetic *posterius* the doctrine of sanctification is absorbed by the doctrine of justification.[22]

Retrieving the Subjective

One suspects that the critics' complaints hit close to the mark, given the relative inattention paid to the Spirit in Barth's theology, and the decision to subsume pneumatology largely within the scope of Christology.[23] As Gunton says, Barth is too fine a dogmatician to eclipse the Spirit completely, "But in dogmatics, a proper distribution of weight between the various topics is important, so that the underweighting of the place of the Spirit in relation to the humanity and ministry of Jesus" is out of kilter with Barth's attempt to do justice to Scripture and its concerns.[24] Nevertheless, this study contends that Barth's predominant Christological concern represents more of a grammatical than a systematic devaluation of the third person. Despite Barth's anti-Pelagian polemic, there is a burgeoning desire, lying beneath the doctrinal surface, to give the Church a concrete freedom for participation in the fulfilment of the covenant inaugurated by Christ, and it is to possible recoup some of the pneumatological losses in order to provide a more explicitly Spirit-oriented basis for human liberation once we review the way the object-subject pattern functions in Barth's mature actualism. In Chapters 3 and 4 it was argued that the objective actualization of the divine-human covenantal truth was not to be viewed simply as external and prior to its subjective appropriation by human beings; it was asserted that Barth's view of Christ's truth can be viewed as being more participative than is often acknowledged once one takes the history of human subjectivity and the *munus propheticum* not as subsequent to the actuality of the truth, but as being ingredient in the dramatic history of it.

---

21. Smail, *The Giving Gift*, 174. See also Rosato, *The Spirit as Lord*, 161.

22. Rosato, *The Spirit as Lord*, 164.

23. In Barth's defense, the New Testament does not tend to view the agency of the Holy Spirit in abstraction from the life, work and futurity of Jesus Christ, so that it is difficult to know how to bind Christology and pneumatology together in a satisfactory manner without reducing the Spirit simply to a Christological parenthesis. Rogers also makes this point (Rogers, "The Eclipse of the Spirit in Karl Barth," 177).

24. Gunton, "Salvation," 152.

Called to Liberty

Jenson is only half right to say that Barth wants to avoid giving the Church a concrete role in mediating salvation history. Barth does not wish to say that the Church can win its own salvation, but he does see the event of Christ's actualization of reconciliation as an ongoing drama, mediated by the Spirit in the contemporaneous life of the Church. Barth's anti-synergistic position causes him at times to downplay the role of the Spirit, and the association of the Spirit with the "noetic" side of reconciliation appears to limit the ontic space for a concrete pneumatological contribution to the unfolding of salvation. Barth invites criticism of this nature by saying, for instance, that "the work of the Holy Spirit is merely to 'realise subjectively' the election of Jesus Christ and His work as done and proclaimed in time, to reveal and bring it to men and women."[25] And in IV/3 Barth says that those who do not yet believe in Christ are those among whom the Holy Spirit "is not yet present and active . . . in the subjective realisation corresponding to [Christ's] objective reality."[26] This perpetuates the notion commonly assumed by Barth scholars that the objectivity of Christ's divine-human truth stands in neutral priority to its communication, and there is no genuinely divine-human reciprocity because human subjects may only accept epistemic propositions about the covenant, rather than being an integral part of its story. Barth clearly wants to avoid the dangers he perceives in Roman Catholic ecclesiology and Bultmannian existentialism in which the mediatorial function of human agents might be said to be ingredient in the winning of salvation for individuals.[27] Yet it is also evident that Barth wants to affirm the irreducible importance of the revelation of reconciliation to its historical fulfilment,[28] and the mediation and appropriation of Christ's achievement through the Spirit in the Church, without which Christ's reconciling mission does not come to historical fruition.[29] The ecclesiological and pneumatological avenues pursued in volume IV, especially in IV/3, IV/4, and *The Christian Life*, indicate that Barth simultaneously wants to avoid pneumatologically disguised synergism (where the Spirit is used as a thin veil for humanity's accomplishment of their own salvation) and pneumatological subordinationism (where the Spirit is not accorded a particular

---

25. IV/1, 667; see also IV/1, 295–96. Nimmo takes this as evidence that Barth never conceives of the being-in-action of the Spirit to add anything objective to the work of atonement accomplished in the cross of Jesus Christ (Nimmo, "Barth and the Election-Trinity Debate," 169).

26. IV/3, 353.

27. See Yocum, *Ecclesial Mediation in Karl Barth*, 98–100; Webster, *Barth's Ethics of Reconciliation*, 126–27.

28. See Hunsinger, "The Mediator of Communion," 178.

29. See Rosato, *The Spirit as Lord*, 112.

salvation-history initiative of His own), so that the Spirit's gathering (IV/1), building (IV/2), and sending (IV/3) of the Christian community in the form of Christ's risen body is utterly intrinsic to, though not reducible to, the Christological fulfilment of God's elective desire for the covenant of grace. In other words, Barth is trying to navigate pneumatologically and ecclesiologically between Christomonism and anthropomonism,[30] though it is often complained that he lapses into the former.

The only way to do justice to the importance with which he views the Spirit and the Church in the ongoing consummation of the covenant—which is proleptically actual and teleologically provisional in Christ—is to begin to see the subjective or noetic side of reconciliation, actualized by the Spirit in the Church, as being utterly integrated with, though distinct from, the objective or ontological side of the same soteriological coin. As Webster identifies, Barth is attempting to resist the temptation of several alternative theologies of mediation which are "predicated on a sense of the disjunction between Jesus and the world of contemporary experience, with the disjunction variously identified as one between past and present, objective and subjective, transcendent and worldly."[31] By extension of the argument in Chapters 3 and 4, then, it is suggested that where commentators continue to read the mature Barth through a "common sense," "non-participative," or "oppositional" logic, they will be unable to do justice to the concrete role of the Spirit in the mediation of salvation and the foundation of human flourishing. Christ's actualization of covenantal reconciliation is not, for Barth, simply a static, brute fact to be passively accepted by human subjects "as spectators"[32] on the basis of the Spirit's epistemic function, as many commentators somewhat simplistically assume.[33] Christ's ontic actuality as divine-human truth is a dynamic, historical, expressive event, and as such this being-in-action is expansively inclusive of human agents, the source of "our true and highest activation";[34] thus the Spirit's contemporaneous mediation of Christ's truth—in which the situation between God and humanity, as resolved in the God-man Jesus, is made known and made real for human agents in the Church—is itself a key component in the onto-historical consummation of the covenantal drama. So Webster argues, "The objective is not a complete realm, separate from the subjective and, therefore, standing in need of 'translation' into the subjective. Rather, the objective includes the

---

30. See ibid., 109; and Webster, *Barth's Ethics of Reconciliation*, 98; 137–38.
31. Webster, "Eloquent and Radiant," 128.
32. IV/1, 15.
33. See Rosato, *The Spirit as Lord*, 160ff.
34. IV/1, 15.

subjective within itself."³⁵ It is therefore not as problematic as many commentators suggest that the Spirit is given a primarily "noetic" soteriological function, since this does not necessarily entail the abstraction that many take it to. It is surely reductive to lament that "The role of the Spirit and man is reduced to that of noetic and subjective compliance with the ontic and objective reality of Jesus Christ."³⁶ In Barth's mature works, the relationship between the objective and subjective categories is far more holistic than this binary reading permits (even if at times Barth grammatically slips back into a one-sided emphasis on objectivity).

In IV/3, Christ's objective truth and its noetic mediation are integrated as part of the same drama, distinct but inseparable, such that the noetic function of the Spirit is itself a part of the objective history in which Christ fulfils the elective desire of God: "I shall be your God, and ye shall be my people."³⁷ As a "predicate of this Subject [Jesus Christ]" the Church is formed by the Holy Spirit and "sent in the same direction as He is" in order to "correspond to what He Himself is and does in the time which hastens to its end but is still left to the world. It can thus consist only in the fact that He gives it to them to take a ministering part in His own prophetic work."³⁸ As Nimmo suggests, the noetic, ontic, and telic bases for theological ethics are mutually implicated in Barth's actualistic ontology, so that the "vertical" dimension of human freedom in which the ethical question has "already been answered by the grace of God in Jesus Christ"³⁹ intersects with a "horizontal" dimension "as part of a history of encounter in the covenant of grace."⁴⁰ Since for Barth the being of Jesus is an event, although Jesus alone determines what humanity may be and become, the epistemic discovery and subsequent ontological transformation of the particular human agent does not occur in a de-particularized posteriority to this Christ event, but in and with it in the particularity of its concrete contemporaneity, through a lived encounter with Jesus mediated by the Spirit. The intersection of the vertical and horizontal, and the actualistic integration of the ontic, noetic, and telic bases for human freedom, means that the ethical event "takes place in the history of God with this man but also with all other men."⁴¹

35. Webster, *Barth's Ethics of Reconciliation*, 128.
36. Rosato, *The Spirit as Lord*, 161.
37. IV/3, 753.
38. IV/3, 791.
39. Nimmo, *Being in Action*, 43.
40. Ibid., 45.
41. ChrL, 5.

It is for this reason, as we have seen, that Barth insists that the divine noetic has the full force of a divine ontic.[42] The Spirit's noetic is the power in which we are actively and participatively included in the dramatic occurrence of Christ's covenantal truth. The Christological ontic is not static, but dynamic. It is as Christ's truth is lived and expressed amongst the Church by the mediation of the Holy Spirit that Christ's objective covenantal actuality becomes efficacious in our own particular lives, liberating us for dignified life in creaturely obedience to God. Without the Spirit, therefore, and in abstraction from the Church, the so-called objective and vicarious actuality of Christ's truth would be a mute and obscure ontological fact without covenantal significance. Hence, when speaking of the basis of the Church's life, Barth refuses to separate the "ontic" and "noetic" foundations in Christ and the Holy Spirit, and instead describes the Church's "noetic as its ontic and its ontic as its noetic."[43] For Barth the names "Jesus Christ" and the "Holy Spirit" underwrite "two strictly related statements which mutually complement and elucidate one another."[44] The first "Christologico-ecclesiological"[45] statement says Jesus Christ is the ontological foundation of the Church in the sense that the Church is a "predicate or dimension" of Christ's body.[46] "[T]he community exists only as He exists. 'Because I live, ye shall live also' (Jn. 14:19)."[47] The Church is given a concrete share in the covenant of grace quite simply because Christ elects and is elected not only to live divine-human harmony in Himself and "abstractly in heaven," but also "with the community on earth, [as] the heavenly Head of this earthly body."[48] The first statement is therefore derived from the testimony of 1 Corinthians 12:27, "Ye are the body of Christ."[49] But this first "objective" and Christological statement makes little sense without "the second statement concerning the mighty work of the Holy Spirit" as its explanation.[50] Barth insists that "the second statement tells us that the relationship of the being of Jesus Christ to that of His community is not static nor immobile, but mobile and dynamic, and therefore historical."[51] In other words, we are not objectively included

42. IV/3, 298.
43. Ibid., 751.
44. Ibid., 752.
45. Ibid., 758.
46. Ibid., 754. See also, ibid., 791.
47. Ibid., 754.
48. Ibid., 757. See also, ibid., 790–91.
49. See ibid., 758.
50. Ibid., 759.
51. Ibid.

in the truth of Christ's risen body by some externally established, static, and Platonic ideal. We become a feature of Christ's divine-human embodiment of the covenantal truth to the extent that the Holy Spirit "causes His community to become what it is."[52] Barth says,

> the work of the Holy Spirit . . . creates, upholds and governs . . . this particular people of witnesses, causing it to come to be and to exist as such, to exist as Jesus Christ exists, giving it a share in His being, endowing it with the power, freedom and capacity to do its human work, to bear the witness entrusted to it.[53]

The temptation in scholarship is to see the "objective" reality of Christ's divine-human truth as being all that matters for Barth, so that the "subjective" mediation of this truth in human knowledge is merely a noetic addendum, the experiential receipt of knowledge about something that has happened externally to us. But Barth explicitly denies a "Christomonist solution" in which "the *in nobis*, the liberation of man himself, is a mere appendage, a mere reflection, of the act of liberation accomplished by Jesus Chris in His history, and hence *extra nos*."[54] He wants to say that the objectivity of Christ's truth is dynamic and expressive, that is, subjective in its quality, and that this Christocentric vertical and ontic dimension of salvation-history intersects perfectly with the pneumatological horizontal, noetic, and telic dimension. Only as the Holy Spirit takes the initiative to induct us into the expansive drama of Christ's divine-human reality can this objective reconciliation between God and humanity become meaningful and indeed be historically fulfilled. Similarly, the subjectivity of the Holy Spirit's agency is transformative and genuinely mediates the fulfilment of the truth embodied and eschatologically fulfilled in Jesus Christ—hence its achievement is objective in quality. Thus the human acquisition of knowledge of the covenant by the subjective power of the Spirit is not merely the passive cognition of soteriological propositions concerning us, but rather the forceful awakening of the whole of one's being for obedient participation in the actuality of Christ's bodily truth, and therefore the summoning to free responsibility for the state of affairs between God and humanity. "As disclosed by the Spirit, in other words, the knowledge of Jesus is not something merely cognitive, for it claims those who are addressed by the gospel as whole persons."[55] And quite apart from diminishing the importance of active human participation

---

52. Ibid.
53. Ibid.
54. IV/4, 19.
55. Hunsinger, "Mediator of Communion," 182.

in Christ's truth, the object-subject unity in distinction, as ordered dialectically in Barth's Christology and pneumatology, safeguards the authenticity of human agency. The fact that salvation happens objectively in Christ, *extra nos*, means that we are released from the burden of obligation to maintain the covenant (a task in which we have demonstrably failed throughout Israelite and ecclesial history). But that we are drawn subjectively into Christ's expressive history through the Spirit means that what happens *extra nos* "also works *in nobis*"[56] giving us the freedom genuinely to live as we ought to, and therefore to flourish in authentic covenantal reciprocity with God. As such, "human action is neither a superfluous appendix to the work of God, nor a struggle to somehow establish or guarantee our standing before God."[57]

Hence, whilst the objective and subjective categories are to be distinguished, and whilst the agency of Christ and the Spirit are not reducible to one another, yet Barth will refuse to speak of one in isolation from the other. Notice the triadic logic that governs his conception of the roles of Christ and the Spirit in the formation of the Church:

> Both [the Christologico-ecclesiological and pneumatologico-ecclesiological] statements denote one and the same reality. But neither renders the other superfluous. Neither can be reduced to the other. Hence neither is dispensable. Again, neither can be separated from the other. Neither can be understood to be true except as elucidated by the other.[58]

In spite of the critics' somewhat justified complaints, a more sensitive approach to the object-subject relation enables us to see that for Barth—as Gunton suggests is characteristic of any solid pneumatology—"there is a way of God's action towards us and his world which is not *separable* from his action in Christ, but not *reducible* to it either."[59] In this vein of interpretation Thompson says,

> Because the Spirit is active in this way it is therefore incorrect . . . to say that Barth has no ontic role for the Spirit . . . [While] the Spirit in the earlier writings of Barth has a purely subjective, noetic role . . . later there is a widening of vision to see the Spirit in a more active way, doing its own work, yet never divorced

---

56. IV/4, 21.
57. Webster, *Barth's Ethics of Reconciliation*, 108.
58. IV/3, 759.
59. Gunton, *Theology Through the Theologians*, 112.

from the living Lord. The Spirit is the power of the risen Christ reaching out to all, powerful in mission and in liberation.[60]

Building on Thompson, it might in fact be better to say that it is precisely in the Spirit's subjectivity that both the third person and the Church are seen as having an objective role in the historical fulfilment of the covenant. For whilst Christ alone can bring about the covenant's actualization, He does not do so in isolation or historical anteriority, and it belongs to His risen life-act that He sends His advocate and representative the Spirit to gather, build, and send the community to participate in the teleological, horizontal outworking of His mission on earth—not merely passively and cognitively, but actively and ontologically. A "true Christocentricity"[61] appropriately married with pneumatology views Jesus's history not simply as substitutionary, "but also and as such 'fruitful,' evocative, and generative of other histories."[62] Subjectivity ought not, therefore, to be viewed as the repetition or reiteration of soteriological facts. It is more like the generation of truth by the Spirit for human subjects, the fruit of which is active participation in Jesus Christ's divine-human reciprocity.

The Promise of the Spirit

This inseparable unity in distinction of Christ and the Spirit can be drawn out if we pay attention to the architectonic relation of Barth's soteriology to his eschatology. "Whereas from the standpoint of reconciliation, the work of the Spirit served the work of Christ; from the standpoint of redemption, the work of Christ served the work of the Spirit."[63] One must recall that for Barth, Christ's earthly fulfilment of reconciliation is not the end of the story.[64] Only when the world entire enjoys its Spirit-given freedom to live what Christ lives, as Christ's risen body in world-history, will the covenant be completed on earth as it is in heaven. As Rosato says, "The goal of the Father's redemptive turning towards man is achieved when Jesus Christ's alteration of mankind's status is not only acknowledged but also accepted. If it is through the Holy Spirit that this goal is assured, in the Christian community, then the Holy Spirit is God orchestrating the spatio-temporal

---

60. Thompson, *The Holy Spirit in the Theology of Karl Barth*, 104.
61. IV/4, 19.
62. Webster, *Barth's Ethics of Reconciliation*, 138.
63. Hunsinger, "The Mediator of Communion," 178.
64. Ibid., 178.

movement from Jesus Christ to man, overseeing the transition form His sphere to man's sphere."[65]

Barth clearly tries, in IV/3, to give the Holy Spirit its own concrete time in which to mediate and actualize the liberation of humans for flourishing at the heart of Christ's covenantal truth.[66] In the time between times the Holy Spirit has the "enlightening power" to draw, press, and impel human agents to take up their place within Christ's covenantal truth.[67] Whilst it does not belong to Spirit-led human agents to actualize or complete Christ's reconciling history, yet because the Spirit places subjects concretely in this history it is impossible to conceive the drama of Christ's truth as something that happens in abstraction from us. In the age of the Spirit, Christ's truth is, oxymoronically, both something He achieves without us and in absolute continuity with and through the Church as the contemporary form of His risen body. Barth repeatedly links the contemporaneous history of human freedom in the Spirit to Christ's promise and commission in Matthew 28:17–20.[68] It is Christ's promise, "Lo I am with you, even unto the end of an age," that forms the title of §69.4, "The Promise of the Spirit." The Holy Spirit guarantees Christ's promise to remain with us. It is the Holy Spirit who witnesses to Christ's living history, and it is therefore the Holy Spirit who draws humanity into historical participation in the event of Christ's truth, in which God and humanity reciprocally have their freedom to be and become most essentially what each is. In this section, Barth modified his conception of *parousia* to include Pentecost. Barth had intended in IV/1 and IV/2 to give the Spirit a proper role in the mediation of salvation-history, but his reference to the two-fold coming again of Christ at Easter and at the end of time, without reference to the significance of Pentecost in salvation history, hinted at a form of soteriological Gnosticism. There it sounded almost as if the role of the Spirit was to give us knowledge of what Christ did for us in the past, and of what he will do for us in the future, and humanity was left waiting in something of an historical vacuum; it was not made clear how the Spirit would help humanity to take up its liberty for flourishing in reciprocal covenantal relations with God. By the time Barth wrote IV/3, however, he had read Oepke's entry for *parousia* in Kittel's dictionary of the New Testament, and this seemed to have had a decisive impact on his understanding of the term.

---

65. Rosato, *The Spirit as Lord*, 116.
66. IV/3, 359.
67. Ibid., 764.
68. See ibid., 281; 286; 305; 321; 488; 525; 757; 763; 874; 899.

Barth now defined *parousia* as "effective presence," and, following Oepke's definition of *parousia* in the fourth Gospel, he insisted that "the coming of the Resurrected, the coming in the Spirit and the coming at the end of the days merge into one another . . . In all these forms [the effective presence of Christ] is one event."[69] To describe Pentecost as effective presence is to signal a commitment to thinking about the noetic side of reconciliation not as the revelation of dogmatic information, but the attraction of human subjects into the truth of an encounter. With the outpouring of the Spirit the presence of Christ in the world "has not only taken place but is still taking place today."[70] Guaranteeing Christ's promise to remain with us, the Spirit's salvation initiative is to order history and the world teleologically in anticipation of Christ's final coming and the consummation of the covenant of freedom on earth, giving human subjects a concrete freedom to work towards this and therefore to enjoy the reciprocity with God that primarily and absolutely belongs to Jesus Christ in His divine-human perfection:

> Within the limits of its creaturely capacity and ability [the community of Christ] is ordained and summoned to co-operate with Him in His work . . . It is sent into the world to play its own part in its own way, not merely knowing it better in its good and evil . . . nor merely hoping and suffering with it, but also waiting with it for its future and with it hastening towards this future.[71]

It is Christ who sows the reconciling seeds, and Christ who, at His final coming, will gather in the harvest; but it is the Spirit who cultivates the historical field here and now.

Barth defines the Pentecostal promise of the Spirit in two ways: first, "the Spirit promises." This is the promise of the Spirit that Christ will remain with His followers throughout history (Matthew 28:20), incorporating them, through the work of the Spirit, into the event of His covenantal freedom, and thus giving them the freedom to co-operate with His ongoing being-in-action. The Spirit promises that the Kingdom of God has already begun to unfold on earth, that it will be consummated, and that Christ's followers are given a share in the historical actualization of the covenant. Barth says that those who are "touched" and "filled" with the power of the Spirit— that is, Christians are determined, guided, comforted, admonished and strengthened to work towards the freedom in which God and humanity exist together.[72] The Spirit "makes them Christians, and arms them to exist

69. Ibid., 292–93.
70. Ibid., 295.
71. Ibid., 777.
72. Ibid., 352.

as such . . . He is their assistance in the Christian knowledge, confession, freedom and actualisation of freedom which they have to achieve daily."[73]

Second, the "Promise of the Spirit" means "that the Spirit is promised" to those who "do not yet have it," that is, non-Christians.[74] These people "miss the freedom given them by [the Spirit], [and] do not know how to make any use of it."[75] That is, they are not yet aware that they have a role to play in the drama of Christ's history, and therefore in the objective, historical consummation of the freedom of God and humanity for one another. Barth insists, however, that despite their unfaith, the Spirit does not abandon non-Christians. The Holy Spirit "is promised to them too." Eschatologically the Spirit will gather up the whole world and bring it into the freedom for participation in God's covenant.[76]

Spirit, Election, and the Trinity Reviewed

Yet if the Spirit is to perform His own salvation-history initiative in service of Christ's mission to consummate the reciprocal freedom of God and humanity for one another, this must also have its ground in the elective desire of the triune Godhead. Given the danger, highlighted by the critics, that the *vinculum* doctrine risked undermining the concrete role the Spirit plays in bringing humanity into active participation in Christ's human obedience, there would need to be an expansion of the Spirit's function within the triune Godhead in line with Barth's Christocentric actualism in II/2. Nimmo has offered a reconstruction of Barth's pneumatology that helps to posit a greater economic interval between the Son and Spirit, and also to secure the import of the Church to the historical consummation of the covenant.

For Nimmo, although Barth fails to offer any "sustained engagement with the pneumatological dimension of election"[77] there is good reason to find that just as Jesus Christ is both electing and elected God in the triune self-determination of God for the covenant of grace, so too we might read the Spirit as electing and elected God in the third mode of God's being. "The purpose of the eternal election of Jesus Christ is . . . in his divine-human unity to fulfil the covenant of God with humanity. In a similar fashion . . . it would be possible to consider parallel pneumatological statements that

---

73. Ibid., 351–53.
74. Ibid., 353.
75. Ibid., 354.
76. Ibid., 355.
77. Nimmo, "Barth and the Election-Trinity Debate," 167.

refer to the role of the Spirit in the fulfilment of the covenant of God with humanity."[78] Here Nimmo quotes Barth in II/2:

> In the beginning it was the resolve of the Holy Spirit that the unity of God, of Father and Son should not be disturbed by this covenant with man, but that it should be made the more glorious.[79]

As electing God, the Spirit glorifies Godself in the determination that the relationship between the Father and Son should be actualized and consummated historically in the Son's taking of the human other into fellowship with God. As elected God, this pneumatological glorification of Godself would then have to be actualized historically in the work of the Spirit as guarantor of Christ's efficacy in human history. The Spirit is the one elected in the Godhead to ensure that what takes place vicariously between God and humanity in the Son will become a living reality actively participated in by the community of Christ as His resurrected body. It is the Spirit's elected purpose to mediate Christ's covenantal truth in the life of the Church in the time between times. On this reading, "the mediating activity of the Spirit in the time between Jesus Christ and the community of God is part of the eternal determination of the Spirit."[80] In other words, it belongs to the Spirit's electing and elected mode of divine self-glorification that what takes place in the particular divine-human act of Jesus Christ will also become a lived reality between the members of the community of God and Jesus Christ. It is the freedom of the Spirit to give to the Church a history for its own covenantal freedom, for the sake of bringing glory to God not only in the earthly history of Jesus Christ, but also, by the spiritual appropriation of this particular life-act, in the history of other human beings as they live the risen drama of Christ's resurrected body. This coheres with Barth's pneumatological statement in IV/3 that the purpose of God's giving us this time between the first and last *parousia* is not only in order that we might enjoy the freedom to take part in the covenant's truth, but that in so doing God might make use of us to glorify Godself in this particular pneumatico-ecclesiological form:

> Why must there be, between Easter time and the definitive end time, this intervening time, the time of the promise of the Holy Spirit, the time of Jesus as our hope? . . . [I]t was and is the goodness of God that to His own glory and the salvation of the

---

78. Ibid., 168.
79. II/2, 102.
80. Nimmo, "Barth and the Election-Trinity Debate," 175.

creature He does not overlook the latter, but wills to give and gives it time and space and opportunity for the expression of its freedom within the context of His work . . . [T]he reconciliation of the world to God as it is not yet concluded as revelation but still moves forwards to its goal, has its own specific glory.[81]

Nimmo therefore finds that just as Barth insists there can be no *logos asarkos* that is not also the *Verbum incarnandum*,[82] so too we ought to insist that

> there is simply no third person of the Trinity *in abstracto*, no Spirit to be considered either in time or in eternity without the mediating activity between Jesus Christ and the community of God in view. In turn, this would mean that the idea of a *pneuma anecclesion* . . . can only ever be a conceptual placeholder and cannot be the subject of independent inquiry . . . . [the *pneuma anecclesion*] is always the *pneuma inecclesiandus*, the Spirit destined to be "enchurched."[83]

Such a trinitarian and pneumatological reconstruction helps to indicate that both the Son and the Spirit have a concrete role to play in bringing creatures into the fullness of reciprocal life with their creative Father, and it would therefore demonstrate that the noetic function of the Spirit is not just the communication of propositions about Christ, but the drawing of human subjects into Christ's being-in-action, which is reciprocally the site of human flourishing and divine glorification. On this reading it would no longer be possible to read the life of the Church and the historical activity of the Spirit as being abstract, overly epistemic and accidental to God's free self-determination. As Nimmo says, "Perhaps the dominant reason for thinking after Barth in this way is to recognise that in the activity of the Spirit in the community of God one has to do with the very essence of God."[84] In contrast to the sense of disjunction between God's essence and God's revelatory historical existence as posited in the earlier works, in IV/3 there is a pneumatological possibility to see the event of the Spirit's prophetic work in the Church as itself belonging to the triune freedom of God to be *this* God,

---

81. IV/3, 360. See also, ibid., 768 on the "sending" of the community by the Spirit, where Barth says that in the New Testament "'sending' means to be invested with δόξα to participate in the dignity, authority and power given to the one commissioned . . . for the discharge of his mission." See also, ibid., 793–94.

82. Ibid., 724.

83. Nimmo, "Barth and the Election-Trinity Debate," 178.

84. Ibid., 179.

namely, the God who wills to be known and glorified in the covenant with humanity.

If the Spirit mediates the liberation of humans by Christ for participation in His ongoing, dramatic consummation of the covenantal truth in world-history, what are the particular marks of the Christian life as Barth sees it? For what exactly does the Spirit—the Lord of freedom (2 Corinthians 3:17)—liberate us? It is to this question that I now turn.

The Call to Freedom, and the Freedom to Call

Barth conducts his reconciliation ethics within the interrelated doctrines of vocation (*Berufung*, IV/3) and invocation (*Anrufung*, the ethical fragments of IV/4 published posthumously as *The Christian Life*). Vocation is defined as the call to enjoy the liberation procured through the justification (IV/1) and sanctification (IV/2) of the ethical agent by Christ; it is the invitation to the human to become a Christian, living in active, subjective correspondence to and affirmation of the objective, Christological determination of humanity as righteous and holy.[85] Again, this subjective side of salvation is not the acquisition of knowledge about a brute fact, but active participation in the covenantal reality, for which humans are liberated and in which they flourish. The doctrine of reconciliation is therefore structured with IV/3 as

---

85. See IV/3, 481ff. There is not space here to treat of the relation between occupational vocation (*Beruf*) and Christian calling (*Berufung*) which are treated respectively in Barth's ethics of freedom (III/4) and the soteriology of liberation (IV/3) (On this distinction, see Kuzmic, "*Beruf* and *Berufung* in Karl Barth's *Church Dogmatics*," 262-78. On the relation between the two types of vocation in the Protestant tradition, complicated in no small part by Luther, see, for example, Volf, *Work in the Spirit: Toward a Theology of Work*, 105ff.; Calhoun, "Work and Vocation in Christian History," 106ff.; Preece, "Barth's Theology of Work and Vocation for a Postmodern World," 147-70). It must suffice to point out in passing that Barth's distinction between the two types of vocation subverts the idea that our spiritual vocation is to be measured primarily or exhaustively by the kinds of professional occupation we pursue, downplaying the modern western employment ethos (see Preece, "Barth's Theology of Work and Vocation for a Postmodern World," 152ff.). Secular occupation and historical situatedness (*Beruf*) is important to the Christian life, in Barth's view, but is relativized by our primary spiritual calling (*Berufung*) to service of God's kingdom (Preece, "Barth's Theology of Work and Vocation for a Postmodern World," 153, 159). That said, Barth allows no simple bifurcation between *Beruf* and *Berufung*; the former falls under the canopy of the latter (see Kuzmic, "*Beruf* and *Berufung*," 268). Occupation is an integral part of our engagement with creation as the *theatrum gloriae Dei* (the theatre of God's glory) and as the external basis of the covenant, but this service must always be delimited as forming the mere circumference of election, which is the internal basis of creation and the primary locus of the call to a discipleship that transcends professional labor. (See also, Preece, "Barth's Theology of Work and Vocation," 154-55; III/1 §§41.2-3.)

the apex or unification of the treatment of the human agent in IV/1 and IV/2: "justification and sanctification are the foundation and presupposition of liberation; liberation is the goal of justification and sanctification."[86] Having delineated the nature of the call to live one's justified and sanctified liberation by and for Jesus, Barth traces the special ethics of reconciliation primarily in terms of the pattern of invocation, wherein human agents exercise their subjective correspondence to the objective actualization of covenantal restoration primarily by participating in Christ's calling upon the Father in the Lord's Prayer. The question addressed in this section is what this subjective acceptance of one's vocation entails. How does the subjective activity of the human agent (*de facto*) relate to the objective reconciliation of Jesus Christ (*de jure*)? To what extent does Barth take the human agent seriously as a powerful and free agent of the covenant? And what is the particular purpose and value of accepting one's vocation and liberation to become a Christian? In view of typical charges of Christomonism, I shall ask whether human subjects are genuinely free to participate in asymmetrical, covenantal reciprocity with God, or whether human freedom is shut down by Barth's soteriological objectivism.

Defining the Moral Field

First it is necessary to re-iterate the point made in Chapter 2 that Barth's reconciliation ethics shift the terms in which ethical investigation is typically pursued. The ethical question "what ought we to do?" is not, for Barth, to be answered in light of the modern need to defend the absolute autonomy and self-determination of the human subject over against opposing objects (whether this be God, nature, or other human beings). Often, modern incompatibilist anxieties about whether freedom is a genuine human capacity emerge because of an assumed link between indeterminacy and moral accountability: if the former is thought to have been disproved—either metaphysically via hard determinism; or theologically by de-historicizing the concept of God, and thereby construing God as an omniscient monad whose foreknowledge necessitates the corroboration of human actions—any meaningful idea of human responsibility is obliterated, it is claimed.[87] But Webster contrasts Barth's account of freedom with that of certain modern treatises: "Above all, freedom is not some inner recess of subjectivity

---

86. Gorringe, *Karl Barth against Hegemony*, 224.

87. As Biggar notes, the meaning of the word freedom in modern history tends to assume that "God and humanity are essentially at odds with one another" (Biggar, *The Hastening that Waits*, 5).

over against 'nature.'"[88] As I argued in Chapter 2, Barth repeatedly insists that freedom is not choice. Rather, for Barth freedom means flourishing or fulfilment; it is the liberty to become most fully oneself "according to the orders of creation, which is realised by acknowledgement of God's gracious act of reconciliation in Christ . . . What Barth means is something akin to *eudaimonia*, the happiness or joy of living the kind of life for which one is specifically fitted."[89] Whereas for many modern thinkers our freedom to make certain decisions undergirds our moral accountability, for Barth it is our relationship to God that is normative for any such notion, and it is this prior delimitation of the ethical parameters by the covenantal space that informs Barth's conception of human freedom. As he says, "The source of man's freedom is also its yardstick."[90]

Any criticism of Barth that insists that moral responsibility is attributable solely on the basis of a decision-based ethics of autonomy can therefore be persuasive only if one fundamentally disagrees with Barth's definition of human freedom. Macken accuses Barth of undermining the integrity of human freedom by subsuming the creature under a totalizing "ontology of grace" whereby resistance to God's offer of salvation is ultimately impossible, thus reducing "Creation to an epiphenomenon of Reconciliation."[91] And despite censuring Macken for "failing to distinguish spiritual freedom from the liberal notion of formal freedom of choice" (as Webster puts it), Biggar "curiously"[92] criticizes Barth along the same lines, finding that the "inexorable necessity" of salvation "raises questions about the graciousness of a grace that does not concede to the beloved the freedom to turn away permanently."[93] Biggar describes Barth as a "compatibilist" whose anthropology states "that human beings are *determined* to choose *freely* what is right. This yields a notion of human freedom that is more apparent than real."[94] But for Webster such a critique "persists in characterising moral freedom in a way that is hostile to Barth's extensive reordering of the notion. Lurking within the critique is a notion of freedom as a kind of spiritual neutrality, as some arena in human life or consciousness in which we are able to exist and operate in relative isolation from the formative activity of

---

88. Webster, "Freedom in Limitation," 115.
89. Biggar, *The Hastening that Waits*, 4.
90. Barth, "The Gift of Freedom," 73.
91. Macken, *The Autonomy Theme*, 152–53; 157.
92. Webster, *Barth's Ethics of Reconciliation*, 227 n. 35.
93. Biggar, *The Hastening that Waits*, 5; see also, ibid., 162.
94. Ibid., 5.

God."[95] As I showed in Chapter 2, the language of "compatibilism" derived from the post-Enlightenment philosophical tradition simply does not cohere with Barth's very subversion of this tradition and its lexicon by finding an alternative logic at play in Christian thought and speech. The attempt to read Barth's ethics through a modern philosophical lens is likely only to "exacerbate" the sense of incompatibility between divine and human action, because such an attempt fails to notice that for Barth the relation of divine and human agency can be expounded only on the basis of the normativity of Holy Scripture.[96] Barth, in other words, simply "will not provide what critics believe he is obligated to provide, namely an account of 'contra-causal' freedom,"[97] because this does not do justice to the way the Bible describes God and humanity respectively as commanding and obedient subjects. The biblical description of the interrelation of divine and human agency defies comparison to any general ethical compatibilism because, as Hunsinger says, it is "absolutely unique in kind."[98] The language of compatibilism suggests a decidedly un-Barthian attempt to resolve a tension between antinomies that, for Barth, emerge out of the equally errant presuppositions of causal determinism and contra-causal choice. Barth is unapologetic, then, when he insists that the Christian "has the freedom to be this man who is justified before God, sanctified for him, and called by him. He has only this freedom—everything else called freedom is unfreedom."[99]

As I have argued, however, Barth does not take Christ's objective achievement to obscure the role of the human subject in the covenant's history. Nor does his insistence on the sovereignty of God's covenantal lordship and eternal election obliterate genuine human contingency. Rather, by describing Christ's objective truth as a drama or event, Barth provides an opportunity to reflect theologically on the nature of human attraction into the depths of that story.

The Christian Vocation for Freedom

Barth is not uninterested in giving the creature a concrete agential role in the life of the covenant. But he will do so only within the account of spiritual calling to service of God and grateful invocation of God's name. For Barth the call of Christ to participate in the covenant instituted, upheld

---

95. Webster, *Barth's Ethics of Reconciliation*, 227.
96. Webster, "Freedom in Limitation," 102.
97. Ibid., 111.
98. Hunsinger, *How to Read Karl Barth*, 197.
99. ChrL, 29.

and restored in and through Him is, like justification and sanctification, issued objectively and universally in Him. This means simply that because the election of God and humanity to covenantal relations is true "before the foundation of the world" (Ephesians 1:4), the decision is already made that human beings are called to serve God. Whether they accept this calling or not cannot undo the fact that this call has been issued: "There is no man whose history is not decided in the history of Jesus Christ ... 'The Master is come, and calleth for thee [Jn. 11:28].'"[100] Yet this call will be pursued only by a few who, in acceptance of the illuminating work of the Holy Spirit, "prove worthy of, and act in accordance with, the fact that as the called of God they are His elect, predestined from all eternity for life with Him and for His service."[101] Barth, then, has a doctrine of vocation that is universalist in its eschatological scope, but particularist in its pneumatological and historical delineation.[102] The simple fact of reality is that all humans live, *de jure*, in "co-existence with the existence of the God-man Jesus," but because our pneumatic ordination for this covenantal reciprocity is a matter of freedom and not enforced subjection, not all play the part assigned to them in the drama: we are all "foreordained and predisposed, though naturally not forced, to be a hearer of the Word of God."[103]

If, as Willis notes, the sense of passivity in the doctrines of justification and sanctification makes it slightly unclear how Christians have an analogical share in Christ's vicarious, objective fulfilment of the covenant, the doctrine of vocation makes clearer the agential authenticity of the human as a subject of the covenant.[104] Webster rightly finds that "Corresponding ... to the fundamental passivity articulated in the doctrine of justification, there is a no less fundamental activity in the Christian life."[105] As willing receivers of the Spirit's two-fold promise, Christians are those who are distinguished by their active acceptance of the freedom to flourish in covenantal relations with God. The light of Christ "shines on all men,"[106] but in the power of the resurrection and the sending of the Holy Spirit vocation entails the event by which a particular human is "illuminated" for "a seeing of which man was previously incapable but of which he is now capable ... 'In thy light shall we

---

100. IV/3, 486.
101. Ibid., 485.
102. See Greggs, *Barth, Origen, and Universal Salvation*, 143.
103. IV/3, 491; see also, 529ff.
104. Willis, *The Ethics of Karl Barth*, 258-60.
105. Webster, *Barth's Ethics of Reconciliation*, 97.
106. IV/3, 508.

see light' (Ps. 36:9)."[107] The acceptance of vocation is the entrance into active knowledge of the liberating life-act of Jesus Christ.[108] What is this active participation of the human in the covenant, and how does the subjective freedom of the Christian correspond to the objective liberation of humanity by Christ? Is there a disjunction between what Christ is and does (objectivity), and what Christians know (subjectivity)?

As Wright notes, Barth delineates what it is that denotes the Christian's particular freedom by first ruling out a number of classical definitions of the Christian.[109] First Barth rejects the idea that Christians are ones who are essentially removed from the world on the basis of the receipt of the eschatological *kerygma*.[110] Barth questions whether it suffices to describe the Christian in terms that fix upon the future and therefore upon the results of Christ's work rather than on His person.[111] Barth will reject any claim that the central point of the Gospel is the particular benefits accrued by the individual, rather than the service of God's self-glorification in the universal consummation of the Gospel.

Next, Barth rejects that the particularity of Christian identity is primarily to be described in terms of a distinctive moralistic ethos.[112] It is true that the Christian is required to live in a certain manner, and therefore according to a distinctive ethic, but the "Christian ethos does not allow itself to be understood as an end in itself."[113] It does not do sufficient justice to the particularity of Christian freedom to say that the Christian is liberated to live a moral life, because this relativizes the difference between the Christian and non-Christian, sterilizing the power of the former.[114] After all, Barth admits, the non-Christian very often lives a morality "which is . . . an example to Christians, and puts them to shame."[115]

Finally, Barth rejects the "classic" answer that a Christian is one who is primarily liberated to enjoy the benefits of salvation (*beneficia Christi*).[116] Barth cites multiple reasons for rejecting this as a sufficient answer to the question of Christian freedom, but perhaps the most powerful is that it

---

107. Ibid., 509.
108. Ibid., 526.
109. Wright, "Witnessing Christians from Karl Barth's Perspective," 240.
110. IV/3, 558.
111. See Wright, "Witnessing Christians from Karl Barth's Perspective," 241.
112. IV/3, 558ff.
113. Ibid., 560.
114. Ibid., 559.
115. Ibid.
116. Ibid., 561.

produces an egocentric binary between Christians and non-Christians that Barth's universalist leanings simply will not permit.[117] If a Christian is one who first and foremost enjoys the assurance that she is personally saved and thereby free, then she has in some sense missed the entire gracefulness of the Gospel, which demonstrates God's love for everyone. There is an inherent discontinuity between the view that "on the one side we have the selflessness and self-giving of God and Jesus Christ, and on the other the satisfaction with which Christians accept this."[118] Barth counters this perspective, maintaining that "personal interest means the personal acceptance by the Christian of the function assigned to him rather than the concentration of his will and desire and striving on personal advantages which might accrue. We are not really Christians . . . if we are concerned about ourselves."[119] In the Bible, we are never led to think that the one called by God or by Jesus is particularly concerned with themselves; their concern is always primarily with embarking on a discipleship that glorifies God, and only secondarily with their own "existential" experience of blessedness (note the subversive reference to Bultmannian individualism).[120] Whereas the "classic" position breeds an unhealthy translation of the *pro nobis* into a restrictive "many tongued but monotonous *pro me, pro me*,"[121] an authentic definition of Christian freedom will uphold the unity-in-distinction of the Christian and the non-Christian as an echo of the unity-in-distinction of the graceful God and the sinful creature. "For all the seriousness with which we must distinguish between Christians and non-Christians, we can never think in terms of rigid separation. All that is possible is a genuinely unlimited openness of the called in relation to the uncalled, an unlimited readiness to see in the aliens of to-day the brothers of to-morrow, and to love them as such."[122]

---

117. As Greggs notes, Barth refuses to categorize humans according to a binary differentiation between "saved or lost," because the salvific end of the individual does not constitute the key-stone of Christ's truth, nor does reference to it do justice to the eschatological messiness and particularity of the outworking of God's saving purposes. (Greggs, *Barth, Origen, and Universal Salvation*, 132) Moreover, since creation is the theatre of God's glory (IV/3, 137ff.), God will make use both of Christians and non-Christians in order to reflect and refract the light of His covenantal truth, such that both directly and indirectly the agency of human subjects will become public "parables" *extra muros ecclesiae* (beyond the walls of the Church) of Christ's divine-human truth (see also, IV/3, 110ff.; 152ff.).

118. IV/3, 567.
119. Ibid., 931.
120. Ibid., 572ff.; 566.
121. Ibid., 567; see also, IV/1, 504.
122. Ibid., 494.

Freedom as Witness

With this three-fold rejection, Barth comes to his own definition of the central category for a Christian theology of freedom: witness.[123] Witness and service, as Barth's choice motifs for the Christian life, are sufficiently "modest" to "express the fact that the Christian's acts are not self-creation, but 'free action' in which the Christian 'accompanies his sovereign Lord in His action, assisting, seconding and helping Him.'"[124] Since covenant history is grounded eternally in God and fulfilled in Jesus Christ, the freedom of the creature cannot, for Barth, be anything more than the vocation to witness. It is not as if the human subject is called upon to inaugurate, maintain or complete divine-human relations, since God achieves this once for all in Christ. The call to freedom is not a command to "act or be like" God. "We are to play our part but not try to play his."[125] This limitation of the freedom of the human agent is in fact utterly liberating, since it allows human action to be just that: human and not divine.[126] The "victory already won in Jesus Christ and to be definitively and universally demonstrated in His final revelation, fortunately [does] not depend on your or my personal Christianity."[127] Yet as I demonstrated in Chapter 3, Jesus Christ does not live for Himself, but in order that the whole world may participate in what He is—namely, divine-human covenantal reciprocity. If it is tempting to read Barth's vicarious soteriology as restricting the space for authentic creaturely participation in the covenant's history, one must remember the point identified in Chapter 2 that for Barth "the omnicausality of God must not be construed as His sole causality."[128] As Hunsinger reminds us, "Barth does not deny that human freedom 'cooperates' with divine grace. He denies that this cooperation in any way effects salvation."[129] Bearing in mind, then, that "Election is oriented toward the full agency of the creature as a partner in God's own mission,"[130] the highest liberty accorded to the creature is the call to confess Jesus's name, and thereby to participate in Christ's self-witness. Witness is the role God gives the human to know the truth, to be of the truth, and to

---

123. Ibid., 575.
124. Webster, *Barth's Ethics of Reconciliation*, 97–98; citing IV/3, 602.
125. ChrL, 171.
126. Webster, *Barth's Ethics of Reconciliation*, 108; 212.
127. IV/3, 656.
128. IV/4, 22. See also, Nimmo, *Being in Action*, 128.
129. Hunsinger, *How to Read Karl Barth*, 185.
130. Barter, "A Theology of Liberation in Barth's *Church Dogmatics* IV/3," 156.

share the truth of God and humanity in covenantal harmony.[131] This witness is not the conveyance of dogmatic information about God to the ignorant. It is the public attestation, through the living of an exemplary life in fellowship, that the highest dignity and mode of human flourishing accorded to us is the glorification of God through faithful participation in the covenant.

The freedom of the Christian is therefore rooted irreducibly in the "I am" sayings of Jesus. Barth reminds us of Jesus's testimony in John 18:37: "To this end was I born, and for this cause did I come into the world, that I should bear witness unto the truth."[132] Jesus's "I am the truth" signals therefore that simply by "speaking of Himself, He speaks the truth."[133] Since Christ alone has fulfilled the truth, and has witnessed to it in the eloquence and radiance of His own being, all we are required to do is, like John the Baptist, to become "martyrs"—those who point beyond ourselves in order to point to the heart of the elected covenant of grace.[134] Yet this martyrdom is not arbitrary spectatorship, nor simply "witnessing to knowledge of a fact,"[135] but active co-operation with Christ in the historical consummation of the covenant. Just as Christ's subjective self-witness in the *munus propheticum* is a function of His objective and historical actualization of divine-human partnership, so too our subjectivity as Christian witnesses is gathered up by God as a secondary form of the *ministerium Verbi divini* and commissioned for a share in the cultivation of the covenantal field.[136] For Christ wills "to call certain men to His side, to invite and summon them to participate in what He does."[137]

Vocation, then, has its basis and *telos* in the fact that Christ gives us the same goal as is His own: the fulfilment of the covenant. Those critics who complain that Barth does not do enough to secure creaturely agential freedom tend, once again, to separate the subjective from the objective in a way that Barth does not permit. And this results in a failure to apprehend the depth of fellowship and reciprocal agency that Barth envisages between God and the world within the covenantal narrative. Mangina correctly suggests that although it is a misreading of IV/1 and IV/2 to see the objective actualization of salvation in the incarnation and crucifixion as being

---

131. As Greggs observes, "In this way Barth guards against the over-objectification of his theology" (Greggs, *Barth, Origen, and Universal Salvation*, 129).

132. IV/3, 612.

133. Ibid.

134. Ibid., 611.

135. Nimmo, *Being in Action*, 180.

136. IV/3, 482.

137. Ibid., 598; see also, 608 and II/2, 510.

events that are external to our contemporaneous lives and experience, if the first two parts of *Church Dogmatics* IV at times appear to permit such an interpretation, IV/3 conclusively forbids it.[138] Whilst it is "typical" to see Barth as "advocating a mainly retrospective version of the *theologia crucis*" and an "unyielding stress on the objective enactment of reconciliation"[139] this neglects to take seriously the *munus propheticum* which is not a "mere noetic postscript to the doctrine of reconciliation"[140] but concerns the gift of freedom in which the Christian participates actively and with the ontic significance of a dignified and powerful subject in Jesus's divine-human "I am." As Healy argues, witness does not just "show" the truth, but actually justifies "God's actions in Christ by sanctifying us in the Spirit."[141] In other words, witness is the demonstration by human subjects that they know the truth to the extent that they live by and for it, and is therefore the return made on God's mediatorial guarantee in Christ and the Spirit. It is the consummation *in nobis* of that which is already actual *extra nos* in Christ—namely, the fulfilment of God's eternal desire that just as God elects humanity, so in return humanity will elect God in faith. Whilst, then, "Barth does have a strong cognitivist streak,"[142] the "distinctive spirituality of knowledge" engendered in IV/3 is, as Ford recognizes, "more Hegelian than Kantian: the involvement of men in the historical unfolding of the *ratio* of the immanent Trinity. The spirituality is comprehensively described theocentrically, as participation in God's own ascesis in time and eternity."[143]

Human subjectivity is therefore ingredient in the historical fruition of Christ's objective truth, and belongs to the very essence of God's life in its historical existence. As Barth reminds us, active knowledge of Christ "is no mere noetic apprehension and understanding of God's being and action, nor as such a kind of intuitive contemplation."[144] Rather, it entails the co-ordination of Christ's universal and covenantal history with that of the human's particular history, in order that they "should enter into their

---

138. Mangina, *Karl Barth on the Christian Life*, 77.

139. Ibid.

140. Ibid.

141. Healy, "Karl Barth's Ecclesiology Reconsidered," 293.

142. Mangina, *Karl Barth on the Christian Life*, 81.

143. Ford, *Barth and God's Story*, 169. Hence the inclusion of human witnesses by God's trinitarianally grounded self-glorification therefore demonstrates that "In his free grace God purges himself from the base suspicion that he is an unchangeable, untouchable, and immutable deity whose divine nature condemns him to be the only one at work" (*ChrL*, 102).

144. IV/3, 510.

union with Him, their *unio cum Christo*."[145] After all, "What kind of vocation, illumination and awakening would it be, what kind of knowledge, if they were merely left gaping at the One who discloses Himself to them?"[146] Christian witness therefore entails becoming a "co-worker"[147] with Christ in the completion of a fellowship that is genuinely and not merely apparently "reciprocal."[148] "[A]s this co-operating assistant in the work of Christ he does acquire and take and have his own share, to be responsibly fulfilled."[149] The Holy Spirit's enlightening gift to the community is therefore "to call them to [Christ] and thus to make known to the whole world that the covenant between God and man concluded in Him is the first and final meaning of its history, and that His future manifestation is already here and now its great, effective and living hope."[150]

The freedom of Christian witnesses is an utterly communal and ec-centric freedom. For Barth, *klesis* (calling) leads naturally to *ecclesia* (Church), because Christ wills not that individuals would witness to the truth of the covenant, but that, precisely as members of His unifying and relational body, they would undertake their service in fellowship with each other.[151] There can be no individualistic, self-isolating or self-glorifying freedom to become a Christian, because the gift of the Holy Spirit is liberation for relations with God and with neighbor. "There is no *vocatio*, and therefore no *unio cum Christo*, which does not as such lead directly into the communion of saints, i.e. the *communio vocatorum*."[152] Similarly, the freedom of the Church catholic in its joint apostolic commission cannot be the freedom to enjoy the benefits of salvation for itself.[153] The Church, as the risen body of Christ, does not exist for itself, but for God's sake and for the world.[154] Barth draws on Christ's prayer in John 17 to remind the reader that the Church is not free from the world but free for it: "Christians, as is plainly emphasised in John's Gospel (17:11), are in the world even though they are out of it. Jesus does not pray that they should be taken out of the world

---

145. Ibid., 540.
146. Ibid., 542.
147. Ibid., 598. See also, Wright, "Witnessing Christians," 249.
148. IV/3, 543.
149. Ibid., 602.
150. Ibid., 680.
151. Ibid., 681–682.
152. Ibid., 682; see also, *ChrL*, 82ff.
153. IV/3, 764.
154. Ibid., 831.

(17:15)."[155] The basis of the Church's call to serve the world is founded in the relationship of the Son to the Father (John 20:21).[156] Just as the Father sends the Son into the world to serve humanity and to witness to the truth of the covenant, so too God makes use of the Church and gives it the freedom to glorify God by calling it to "solidarity" with the world.[157] And this solidarity means "full commitment to it, unreserved participation in its situation, in the promise given it by creation, in its responsibility for the arrogance, sloth and falsehood which reign within it, in its suffering under the resultant distress, but primarily and supremely in the free grace of God demonstrated and addressed to it in Jesus Christ, and therefore in its hope."[158] What we see consistently in Barth's use of the concept of freedom, whether predicated of God, of Jesus Christ, of the human individual, or of the Church, is the layering up of multiple series of reciprocal relations. Throughout the orders of reality, both in the Godhead and in creation, freedom means the consummation of one's essence through "ec-centrically"[159] responsible existence and reciprocal being-in-action. "The liberation of the Christian takes place as he is drawn out of solitariness into fellowship."[160]

The freedom of the community of God for solidarity with the world means that "the Christian cannot leave the non-Christian at peace" but must be "a most disturbing fellow-man, effectively reminding him by his existence where he also belongs and what is his own true though not yet grasped and appropriated being as his promised future."[161] Yet this disturbing witness of the Christian is not the "pious egocentricity,"[162] "sacred egoism,"[163] or the "fine occupation" of the "righteous" to "make proselytes."[164] Barth cautions that there is a tendency in modern Evangelical circles to find that "I myself as a Christian am the most proper object of knowledge to myself as a theologian."[165] But a flourishing Christian, and one who is therefore of particular use to God in the revelation of the covenant, is one who refers not to

---

155. *ChrL*, 97; see also, IV/3, 768.

156. IV/3, 768.

157. Ibid., 773; see also ibid., 826.

158. Ibid., 773.

159. See *ChrL*, 94.

160. IV/3, 664. See also, Barter, "A Theology of Liberation in Barth's *Church Dogmatics* IV/3," 162.

161. IV/3, 495–96.

162 Ibid., 570.

163. *ChrL*, 101; see also, IV/3, 767.

164. IV/3, 587.

165. Ibid., 677.

herself, but to the glory of God's Word. The freedom with which we call the non-Christian to the truth will not therefore be the liberty to prattle about our own experiences, nor the more pernicious issuing of threats designed to "convert the heathen." Conversion "is the work of God alone."[166] Witness, by contrast, is simply joyful and exemplary existence in service of others.

"[F]reedom is *being joyful*."[167] The freedom for joy is synonymous with the freedom of the Christian, since a "gloomy, morose and melancholy Christian can obviously attest only a gloomy, morose and melancholy Gospel. But this would contain an inner contradiction which certainly does not correspond to the Word of the living Jesus Christ and which cannot, therefore, serve to attest it."[168] Despite the threefold "affliction" of the Christian (§71.5) by the world, the self and by Christ,[169] which challenges her and causes her to suffer in the call to service, if she is truly a bearer of the *kerygma* of freedom she will accept the command to issue "an address of radiant content" and will do so in a "cheerful manner."[170]

Freedom for Invocation

Two of the specific marks of Christian freedom are the liberation from anxiety to prayer,[171] and the deliverance from indecision to action.[172] Given that our participation in God's life is guaranteed by Christ and the Holy Spirit, we are freed from the "substantial tyranny" of pride, sloth and falsehood, by which we hopelessly arrogate to ourselves the false freedom to command ourselves in rebellion against God.[173] We need no longer worry about and stall over the ethical question, since we do not have to decide for ourselves what we ought to do, nor whether we are powerful enough to do it. For precisely as those who are *simul iustus et peccator*,[174] God wills to make use of us in the mediation of God's own reality.

Barth focuses on prayer and action in *The Christian Life* in his treatment of invocation as the primary pattern of Christian liberation. To answer

166. Ibid., 876.
167. Barth, "The Gift of Freedom," 75.
168. IV/3, 661.
169. Ibid., 620–34.
170. Ibid., 802.
171. Ibid., 671–72.
172. Ibid., 669.
173. Barter, "A Theology of Liberation in Barth's *Church Dogmatics* IV/3," 160; see also, *ChrL*, 234.
174. IV/1, 517; 596; 602–3.

the ethical question "what ought we to do?" with the response "call upon me" (Psalm 50:15)[175] is, as Jüngel notes, "startling";[176] prayer does not, at first sight, satisfy our modern thirst for autonomy, the power to derive for oneself the moral law and thereby rationally to move oneself to concrete action, and Kant infamously denounced it as "superstitious illusion (a fetish-making)" which oversteps the "boundaries of our reason with respect to the supernatural."[177] Yet for Barth it is precisely prayer that constitutes "*good* human action,"[178] and invocation provides not only the ethical answer but also the ethical question itself because the very act of asking "what ought we to do?" is what is commanded.[179] Again, theological ethics can be conducted only within the site of divine-human encounter as the moral space in which the ethical question is posed. To raise the question in abstraction from this event is necessarily to forestall the utility of the answer.

Barth considered structuring the special reconciliation ethics around a number of central concepts, including "freedom, conversion, decision, faith, thanksgiving, and . . . faithfulness,"[180] but finds that all of these elements converge under the canopy of invocation in a "choreography" of prayerful action or active prayerfulness.[181] The freedom to call upon God, "in all the richness of the action included in it" is "the one thing in the many that the God who has reconciled the world to himself in Jesus Christ demands of man as he permits him to it."[182] By joining Christ in calling upon the Father,[183] hallowing His name,[184] and prayerfully working towards the coming of God's kingdom on earth,[185] the Christian takes up her freedom to participate in the drama of the covenant, and therefore in the life of God. This, and nothing else, is the true site of human flourishing for Barth.

In his reflections on invocation, Barth is able to emphasize the genuine, though asymmetrical, reciprocity that exists between God and the creature. This in part is because, as Drewes and Jüngel observe, the ethics of

---

175. *ChrL*, 44.

176. Jüngel, "Invocation of God as the Ethical Ground of Christian Action," 164.

177. Kant, *Religion Within the Boundaries of Mere Reason*, 185–86.

178. *ChrL*, 3.

179. Ibid., 3; see also, Jüngel, "Invocation of God," 165.

180. *ChrL*, 42.

181. See Boulton, *God Against Religion*, 100; see also, Cocksworth, *Karl Barth on Prayer*, 103.

182. *ChrL*, 43.

183. Ibid., 64.

184. Ibid., 153.

185. Ibid., 234.

reconciliation "bring out more sharply the eschatological orientation of the doctrine of reconciliation than do the corresponding discussions in IV/3."[186] That is, it becomes clearer how the "good action" of the liberated Christian is appropriated by God for the prophetic mission of the risen Christ in consummating the covenant on earth as in heaven. In the time of the Spirit, God commissions the Christian's "whole life" to be an act of invocation. Everything we do must be in glorification of, service to, and dependence upon God. That we cry, "Thy Kingdom come" and "Come Holy Spirit" indicates that we may not "simply sit around for God's action to transform the world."[187] Rather, the prayer reveals a zeal for God's honor (§77), such that whilst the Christian herself participates in the lordless powers of "Leviathan" (the political realm),[188] "Mammon" (the economic sphere)[189] and the "*Cthonic* forces" (the conceptual, artistic and technological site of human rebellion),[190] yet she has allowed her vocation to ready her for active non-participation and subversive activity in the world.[191] Although the lordless powers pretend to develop and safeguard freedom, in fact they disrupt authentic life,[192] and liberation from their grasp occurs through faithful obedience to God in the hallowing of the Father's name. Hence this continual, multi-faceted and active calling upon God in absolute dependence is by no means arbitrary or ethically indolent. But invocation does not simply precede or prepare one for political and social responsibility, as if prayer is separate from ethical practice; it is itself a part of that responsibility.[193] Dedication to a life of prayer is the most direct form of co-operation with God's will, and therefore the most radically disruptive and genuinely political activity that humans can pursue in their conflict with the world.[194]

That we ought to pray is revealed primarily by the fact that this is what Jesus did in His supreme and restorative human dignity, thus setting "a prior example of what he demanded" of the ethical creature.[195] All that is required of us in order to become dignified, flourishing and peaceful creatures, is that

---

186. Ibid., xii.
187. Cocksworth, *Karl Barth on Prayer*, 153.
188. ChrL, 219–22.
189. Ibid., 222–27.
190. Ibid., 227–32.
191. Ibid., 206.
192. Ibid., 233.
193. See Cocksworth, *Karl Barth on Prayer*, 113.
194. See ibid., 151ff.
195. ChrL, 64.

we join Christ in the cry "Abba, Father,"[196] allowing Him to take us "up into the movement of his own prayer."[197] But this is demanded, and in all seriousness. It is the human subjective that God allows to participate in God's own objective becoming. For God "does not just establish" the covenant between God and humanity but calls and impels humanity "to play [its] own free and active part";[198] "What God the Father wills with and for us to his own glory and our own salvation is more than a solid but stationary relation or a firm but passive connection. He is the living Father of his living children . . . They have to actualise the partnership in this history."[199] There can be no abstraction of God's Fatherly being-in-action from human existence, and so there can be no obfuscation of the integrity of human obedience to God's very essence. "In the covenant of grace they are distinct partners, but precisely in their distinction they are partners who are inseparably bound to one another."[200]

This means that human subjectivity cannot be considered an arbitrary noetic, nor prayer as being bereft of ontic significance. Rather, human subjectivity must be viewed as being liberated for authentic participation in the covenantal space of God's own being-in-becoming. God does not come to Godself outside of the sphere in which God comes to humanity, calling humanity to obedience and faithfulness. The very objectivity of God's life consists in the fact that "He is not anonymous. He has a name."[201] God the Father *is* precisely in the act of the sending of the Son in order that humanity would sound the vocative "our Father" (John 14:7ff.; 17:26). And so, the human "invocation of God as their Father, as a free and responsible human action, belongs inseparably, as a kind of lower pole, to the objective or, more accurately, the divinely subjective element in the dealings."[202] Barth continues,

> The divinely subjective element in these dealings, which not only corresponds to the humanly subjective element of their invocation but is indissolubly related and united with it, consists of the hearing which God grants to those who call upon him

---

196. Ibid., 102.
197. Ibid., 64.
198. Ibid., 74.
199. Ibid., 85.
200. Ibid., 27–29.
201. Ibid., 115; see also, ibid., 52–53: "he is an object only to the extent that a person, an independent subject, can also be object—that is, by making itself an object to others without ceasing to be a subject . . . Here Kierkegaard is right: subjectivity is truth."
202. Ibid., 102.

... This is the upper pole, the divinely subjective element in the dealings, intercourse, and exchange without which the humanly subjective element that may also be at work ... could not be understood.[203]

Since, for Barth, God's being is in action, it is not insignificant that he now concludes "It is very proper for [God], then, to let his action be codetermined by his children who have been freed for obedience to him."[204] This does not mean that humanity has any ontological control over the being of God; God's being is in becoming, but God does not *become*. It simply means that in the self-determination to be our Father, God permits the asymmetrical reciprocity of human invocation and divine hearing to form the covenantal shape of God's own life. This happens primarily in Jesus's obedience to the Father, in vicarious fulfilment of human subjectivity;[205] but by the liberating power of the Spirit, it also occurs contemporaneously in the Church. Despite his anti-Pelagianism, then, invocation "is Barth's 'synergism' ... The notion of a *co-operatio* (co-operation) between God and the human person in their mutual dealings with one another has here found a genuine Protestant, 'evangelical' formulation."[206]

Once again, the unity of the objective and subjective categories in soteriological and ethical investigation allows Barth to resist competitive or oppositional modes of thinking about the divine-human relation in favor of a deeply participative model of unity-in-distinction, where "God's glory and man's salvation, while they are so different, are not two things but one."[207] Barth does not conceive of divine being and human knowing as being separate from one another, but takes them to be mutually implicated in the historical actualization of truth. Jüngel observes, with typically intense acuity, that understanding invocation as good action is possible only when one begins to operate with an alternative, non-propositional object-subject schema in pursuit of questions of truth.[208] When truth is taken to be the "correspondence of mind and thing ... then only propositions which count as expressions of the intellect ... can make a claim to be true, and subsequently verified or falsified."[209] On this account, truth is taken to be existing "over there" and propositions are valid to the extent that they exhibit "what

203. Ibid., 102–3.
204. Ibid., 104.
205. Ibid., 123.
206. Jüngel, "Invocation of God," 161.
207. *ChrL*, 30.
208. Jüngel, "Invocation of God," 170ff.
209. Ibid., 171.

is the case,"[210] that is, where the subjective corresponds appropriately to the objective (with a disjunction between the two assumed *a priori*). Hence "the statement of Mt. 4:17 'The Kingdom of Heaven is at hand,' can be true or false. But the statement of Mt. 6:10, 'Thy Kingdom come,' can be neither true nor false."[211] On such a model prayer cannot be taken to be meaningful ethical action. But for Barth and Jüngel, in reminiscence of Hegel more than Kant, Christian thinking requires an alternative approach to truth, where what is true is not the authentication of what there is, but rather an event that is "occurring";[212] here truth is understood "much more primordially as that interruption of the ontological cohesion of the (created) world . . . through which we attain to the position of being over against our world."[213] Such an approach to truth views the object-subject relation holistically, so that what is real and what we know are mutually implicated in a pattern of "primordial correspondence and unconditional trustworthiness."[214] We ask because we know we are *of* the truth, and that as such our moral conduct is eschatologically bracketed by the "certainty of the Coming One."[215] Invocation is the human or subjective element in the historical actualization of God's desire to be known and glorified by humanity; but this is "an integral part of the history of the covenant,"[216] and the exercise of human freedom is therefore proper to God's own freedom, just as human flourishing is ingredient in divine reality.

Human Freedom and the Charge of Ethical Abstraction

I have been assessing whether Barth's discussion of human freedom, as the vocation to call upon God in public gratitude for our life in Christ, convinces as a Christian ethic. This is the question put to readers of the *Church Dogmatics* by some ethicists who have complained that by subsuming the freedom of the Christian under the meta-narrative of Christ's graceful triumph, Barth fails to do justice to the empirical situation of the ethical agent, to her concrete trials within the ethical situation, and therefore to the particularity of her freedom and moral responsibility to God and neighbor.[217] This, it is

210. Ibid.
211. Ibid.
212. Ibid., 172.
213. Ibid., 171.
214. Ibid.
215. Ibid., 172.
216. *ChrL*, 102.
217. Willis, *The Ethics of Karl Barth*, 199; West, *Communism and the Theologians*,

said, lends "a peculiar 'abstractness' to Barth's ethics that gives his account of the moral life an aura of unreality."[218] Whilst, as Mangina notes, there is a "grain of truth" in this charge, such concerns are largely "misplaced."[219] It is true that Barth does not, on the whole, "labour to sketch out the discrete political, economic, sociological, or psychological circumstances in which the command of God might be received."[220] This does not, however, mean that Barth neglects the importance of such factors for human freedom. If Barth refuses to offer "detailed empirical analysis" it is simply because, as Nimmo correctly asserts, Barth is a systematic theologian, and his task is to expound the command of God and the requisite obedience of the creature as it is issued universally in Christ. His concern is with the over-arching theological ontology that enables the Christian to respond to the ethical question, "what ought we to do?" in the particularity of her own life-act and in the mobilization of her uniquely gifted Spiritual wisdom. As Nimmo says, "It is arguably a sign of how seriously Barth takes the actual complexity of the situation of the ethical agent that he does not attempt to trivialise it in the *Church Dogmatics*—a work of systematic theology—by perfunctory descriptive analysis."[221] For Jüngel it is one of Barth's greatest assets that his ethics "does not seize in advance or ideologically anticipate concrete human action but rather sets it free as concrete action which in its concreteness is obedient through and through."[222]

Moreover, such criticisms also tend to miss the moments where Barth does emphasize the uniqueness of each ethical agent's situation, vocation, and gifts. Barth reminds us that the "Holy Spirit does not enforce flat uniformity,"[223] but makes use of each Christian witness in the multiplicity of ministries.[224] Barth builds on the Pauline understanding of the spiritual gifts (1 Corinthians 12:4–5, Romans 12:3–4, Ephesians 4:1–2) in order to explicate the corporate nature of freedom in Christ's risen body, providing commentary on the several callings of individuals to the praise of God, preaching, instruction, evangelization, mission, theology, prayer, the cure of souls, the living of an exemplary Christian life, the diaconate, prophetic

---

313; see also, Nimmo, *Being in Action*, 74ff. for more on this line of critique.
218. Hauerwas, "On Honour," 149.
219. Mangina, *Karl Barth on the Christian Life*, 190.
220. Nimmo, *Being in Action*, 75.
221. Ibid., 76.
222. Jüngel, "Invocation of God," 157.
223. IV/3, 855.
224. Ibid.

action and fellowship.²²⁵ And with the pneumatic plurality of the community will doubtless come a multiplicity of vocational afflictions. Rather than anticipate possible examples of ethical trial, Barth encourages openness to God's Word through the reading of Scripture, performance in worship, the practice of prayer, concrete and enthusiastic participation in secular society, and absolutely joyful confidence in the ultimate insignificance of one's sinful pride, sloth, and falsehood. And the apocryphal anecdote that Barth began each day with the Bible in one hand and the newspaper in the other suggests that he himself understood the importance of ethical particularity and empirical situatedness in the discernment of the divine command.

A more difficult charge to resist is that Barth is "too reticent about the more durable aspects of moral selfhood,"²²⁶ allowing almost no place for human spiritual growth and progress in his theology of freedom, so that the pattern of flourishing is not the gradual improvement of the disciple's character, but that of a radically new gift which must be received afresh each day.²²⁷ Hunsinger's critique of Barth is the most sophisticated of this kind, and he finds that Barth tends to emphasize the "again and again" aspects of the Christian life, without also doing justice to the "more and more";²²⁸ Barth combines the Lutheran *simul iusts et peccator* and Calvin's *simul* of justification and sanctification²²⁹ in order to emphasize the provisionality of our participation in Christ,²³⁰ and consequently obscures the attention both paid to spiritual growth.²³¹ As already mentioned, Barth's primary theological interest is in the "large-scale narrative of the acts of God," and he consistently allows this to relativize ontologically the individual's life-act, so that "life under the call of God is not presented as a sequence of evolving stages or a biographical progression, but more episodically."²³² Yet it is not necessary, as Hunsinger and Nimmo both maintain, to read Barth as ruling out a theology of spiritual progress altogether.²³³ At certain key moments Barth allows that sanctification entails "living in conversion with growing

---

225. Ibid., 865–901.
226. Webster, *Barth's Ethics of Reconciliation*, 74.
227. IV/2, 328.
228. Hunsinger, "A Tale of Two Simultaneities," 87.
229. Ibid., 76.
230. Ibid., 84.
231. Ibid., 86.
232. Webster, *Barth's Ethics of Reconciliation*, 74–75.
233. Hunsinger, "A Tale of Two Simultaneities," 86–87; Nimmo, *Being in Action*, 165.

sincerity, depth and precision."[234] Moreover, Hunsinger focuses his critique entirely on Barth's doctrine of justification and sanctification, and hence on the more objective moments in Barth's theology of reconciliation, without paying attention to the way in which vocation entails the subjective participation of the individual within the covenantal space opened up for all human beings by Christ. The eschatological configuration of the third-part volume of Barth's soteriology indicates that the provisionality of the time in the Spirit permits the opportunity for the growth and expansion not just of the individual witness but of the community of witnesses. The two-fold promise of the Spirit may be read as the guarantee that by answering the call to discipleship, both the individual and the community of God will journey deeper and deeper into the elective desire of God for genuinely reciprocal covenantal harmony. "For Barth, then, as a call to ongoing discipleship, vocation is 'not merely *vocatio unica* but also *vocatio continua*.'"[235] There is "a progressive building on that which is already built,"[236] whereby "Every step forward includes a repetition of those already taken."[237] These qualifications aside, however, one is ultimately left with the feeling that Hunsinger is right to conclude that "Barth left a large logical space at this point that remains to be more adequately filled."[238]

Conclusion

In this chapter I have examined Barth's mature theology of human freedom, and found, in line with the main argument of Part B of this book, that a sensitive appraisal of the object-subject relation in Barth's works provides some resistance to scholarly cries of pneumatological neglect, Christomonism, and ethical abstraction. Where the objective is taken simply to be "what there is" and "what has been achieved," outside of the thinking subject, and where the subjective is taken to be the presentation of cognitive propositions which correspond to the truth, it is inevitable that scholars will charge Barth with pneumatological and ecclesial neglect; and this in turn will perpetuate the idea that Barth draws an unnecessarily sharp distinction between divine and human being and action. Where, however, we begin to see that for the mature Barth the objective actualization of the covenant and its subjective mediation are mutually implicated, it becomes evident that while there is

---

234. IV/2, 566.
235. Nimmo, *Being in Action*, 167; citing IV/3, 536.
236. Nimmo, *Being in Action*, 166.
237. IV/2, 631.
238. Hunsinger, "A Tale of Two Simultaneities," 87

a clear distinction between "the truth" and those who are "of the truth" there can be no false opposition between them. Rather, the truth occurs where spiritually awakened subjects are drawn into active encounter with God. This is the entire purpose of Jesus Christ's "I am," as Barth sees it. And Barth's historicized actualistic ontology allows him to integrate divine and human agency, so that, whilst they are not the same, they are indissolubly related. Hence in contrast to Barth's earlier *aprioristic* and competitive intellectual tendencies, by the end of his career he had, to a large extent, come to think in deeply participative terms. Despite the typical criticisms which argue to the contrary, it has been my contention throughout this book that in IV/3 and beyond Barth views human flourishing as ingredient in God's triune reality, and that the freedom of God and the freedom of humanity are reciprocally established in God's double election of Jesus Christ.

CONCLUSION

Freedom is being joyful.

—Karl Barth[1]

No morose theologians! No boring theology! . . . In my life I have spoken many words. But now they are spoken. Now it is your turn.

—Karl Barth[2]

Summary of Work

Barth was not interested in conducting explicit investigation into the logical structures of his own thought, and he tended not to advert to important shifts in his use of theological categories such as the objective and subjective, or pairs of terms such as being and act, and being and knowing. That is a consequence of his theological method which is alive to the contemporaneous voice of God in Scripture, prayer and the Church; he was concerned with finding a theology that served the community in its day, not in providing a timeless system or locating the precise moments when he had changed his mind or tried something new. Yet that desire to

1. Barth, "The Gift of Freedom," 75.
2. Barth, "No Boring Theology!," 3.

do living theology stands somewhat in tension with the fact that he built perhaps the grandest theological system since Aquinas's *Summa*. As a result, it can be difficult for the reader of the *Church Dogmatics* to make sense of certain highly complex concepts elevated to a central position—such as freedom—and the manner of their function within Barth's architectonic. Often, central concepts such as freedom are neither mobilized consistently nor in a technically precise manner. It has been the task of this book to grapple with a theme which is at once basic to the *Church Dogmatics* and utterly diverse in its various guises. The aim has been to provide clarity on some of the most challenging, debated, and complex moments in Barth's thought—particularly the soteriological epistemology of IV/3, which has yet to win a satisfactory scholarly appraisal.

The study demonstrated how Barth's references to divine and human freedom develop in line with his increasing Christocentric and actualistic desire to promulgate an utterly participative theology of divine and human agency by portraying their deeply reciprocal relationship in the name Jesus Christ. Since the concept of freedom is not commonly used in the Bible, our investigation into Barth's fascination by it, along with the centrality of the object-subject schema that governs its use, drew on an analysis of resources available within Barth's German-language intellectual heritage. By placing Barth first in the context of his post-Kantian liberal background, and later in conversation with Hegel, the study engaged with a conceptual tradition native to Barth so as to bring into sharper focus the technical moves underlying his vision of the divine-human relationship. It was found (Chapter 1) that the early Barth betrayed a quasi-Kantian desire to protect the lordship of an utterly transcendent and somewhat abstract God, emphasizing God's freedom *from* at the expense of the freedom *for* aspects of his theology. By contrast (Chapter 2), the *Church Dogmatics* reveal Barth's increasing readiness to integrate terms such as being and acting, and being and knowing, within a Christocentric and historicized framework. This in turn underwrites Barth's mature understanding (explored in Chapter 3 through a close reading of IV/3) of God and humanity as being ordered in asymmetrical reciprocity, where the emphasis is on the freedom of God and humanity *for* each other, mediated by Jesus Christ's covenantal and prophetic life-act. Turning to Hegel's logical investigation into various forms of Christian thinking helped to demonstrate (Chapter 4) that by IV/3 Barth no longer conceives the being of God and the acquisition of theological knowledge in separation, but takes being and knowing to form an inseparable unity in distinction. And by thinking triadically of being and knowing as a pair (which is to recognize that each individual term in the pair can be understood only in terms of its mutual relation to the other), it became possible to take the objective and subjective sides of reconciliation in Barth's soteriology not as two disjunct moments in a basically non-participatory theology, but as being mutually implicated in the drama of the covenant, as two sides of one eschatological coin. This created the possibility (Chapter 5) to retrieve Barth's understanding of the subjective and noetic, associated largely with the pneumatological and ecclesiological strands of his thought, which are often construed in unduly externalistic and abstract terms (everything, it is often complained, is done for humans and outside of their lives, with no real place for the Spirit and Church in the doctrine of reconciliation). It was seen that the pneumatological mediation and appropriation of salvation for Christians gives them the tangible, not abstract, freedom to participate in Jesus Christ's covenantal life-act—to invoke his name—and therefore to flourish at the heart of God's self-glorifying reality, fulfilling their identity as creatures of God simply by calling on the Father.

Freedom from Fear:
The Freedom of the Theologian

If this book has succeeded in giving a generous reading of Karl Barth, and of a text (IV/3) that has so often been the recipient of theological disinterest and suspicion, then it should also be possible, on the basis of that reading, to think ahead to the future of theology, invigorated by the promise of the Spirit that Barth so joyfully envisaged in his last completed work and in the lecture fragments of IV/4.

At the start of this book I established that, for all the technical depth and intellectual breadth of his work, Barth's writings can be summed up and interpreted by the very simple idea that "Jesus means freedom!" Barth attempted not only to convey this materially in his doctrine, but also formally in and through his theological method. In some respects, Barth was a traditionalist and a conservative—he serves the Reformed tradition, assumes many of the classic Christian dogmatic *loci*, and insists that faith and the authority of the Bible are foundational for theology. But Barth was also extraordinarily daring. He took nothing in intellectual history (whether Christian or secular) for granted (just think, for example, of how he tried to remain faithful to his Reformed heritage precisely by revolutionizing the way theology protects God's grace in the doctrines of election and predestination). He refused to rule out any mode of thinking or concept if it could be used in service of the naming of Jesus, or to re-vitalize the Church (hence he and Charlotte von Kirschbaum read voraciously, experimenting with and conversing about historical and contemporary literature. Even a cursory glance at the index of names in the *Registerband* (separate index volume) of the *Church Dogmatics* reveals Barth made critical use of a range of non-Christian thinkers as diverse as Aristotle, Gandhi, Heidegger, Nietzsche, Plato, Weber, and Zola). And Barth refused to say anything simply because it was expected of him, or because it sounded right (one is mindful of his contributions towards Christian responses to politics such as his prominent role in drafting the Barmen declaration of 1934, and his refusal to condemn communism because he felt the burgeoning mood of capitalist self-proclamation within Western anti-communism was equally as pernicious and antithetical to the Gospel as communism itself).[3]

Perhaps one of the reasons Barth's work continues to inspire so much conversation, and why his *Church Dogmatics* remains central to many undergraduate reading lists and postgraduate programs, is because his writing is exciting, joyful and vitalizing. Just when one thinks that one has mastered Barth, or that there is nothing left to say on his work, one realizes that there are new directions in which to go with him, or subtleties in his texts that had been missed or obscured before. It may be that, like many of his great theological forebears, the most important and original work on Barth will not emerge until centuries after his death. Why is his thought so provocative and generative? How is it that his texts can provide such a good theological education for students of theology, half a century after his death?

To my mind, it is because Barth writes with the confidence of a theologian who knows that "Jesus means freedom." Those who complain of Barth that Jesus achieves everything in his theology, annihilating the creature,[4] simply have not recognized *who* Barth's Jesus is. For Barth, Jesus allows genuine contingency, experimentation, hope, creativity, reflection, and risk, because while—historically—God's story and the Church's mission is not yet at an end, from an eschatological perspective Jesus in His prophetic office declares that there is nothing we can do to jeopardize our relationship with God. Barth's Jesus—the Jesus of the Gospels, who walks the land of first century Israel, encountering and liberating those whom He loves—is the model of human freedom not as some Platonic archetype, but because He has true confidence in the Father's freedom and love, and acts freely in the knowledge of it. Barth's own theological confidence, and his message for

---

3. On Barth's contribution to the drafting of the Barmen declaration, see Jehle, *Ever Against the Stream*, 13–14 and 55–56. On Barth's position in relation to Western anti-communism, see Gorringe, *Karl Barth against Hegemony*, 220, and Werpehowski, "Karl Barth and Politics," 231.

4. Macken, and the critics of Barth he draws on, produced probably the best example of a sustained critique of Barth in this vein. See, for example, *The Autonomy Theme*, 181.

students of theology, stems from the liberty for witness that he sees Christians as being called to: we ought simply to intensify and extend God's light, life and love, and to do it with the total confidence that there is nothing we can do to diminish that light, life and love (John 1:5).

We may have confidence to speak up because we know that all our words are human and not divine, historical and relative beliefs, not eternal truths; they are therefore ultimately of limited significance—regardless of how profound or eloquent any one person or group may appear. This confidence through humility, in Barth's view, ought to extend to the theologian, who is called to share in the prophetic action of Jesus.[5] We may make doctrinal mistakes, but these could never actually change the state of affairs between God and humanity (though of course the Church and its theologians should strive to investigate and repair their speech about God critically and accurately). Hence the "free theologian" believes in the forgiveness of theological sins.[6] Barth wondered whether—if we really had confidence in the divine and human freedom in store for us—theologians might develop the kind of forbearance necessary to "dispense with the hard, bitter, and contemptuous thoughts and statements about each other, with the bitter-sweet book reviews and the mischievous footnotes we throw at each other, and with whatever works of darkness there are!"[7]

To talk of the theological confidence Barth drew from the idea that Jesus means freedom is to say that Christians have the freedom from fear. Barth insisted that in the New Testament it is quite impossible to separate Gospel and Law when, time and time again, the central characters in its stories are commanded "Be not anxious!—Be not afraid!"[8] Putting it in Pauline terms, Barth claims that to be a slave to Christ, or to pursue discipleship, means that to take courage from Jesus is not a mere possibility or privilege but an instruction which must be taken seriously and obeyed.[9] There can be no space for anxiety and fear in the face of trial, suffering and evil, as if the threats that confront us here and now could actually result in catastrophe. If the name Jesus Christ truly means that there is nothing that can separate humanity from the love of God, then no matter what happens to me as an individual in the immediate future, I am permitted the confidence to know that through Christ's victory over death all shall be well.

5. By "theologian" Barth does not only mean professional academics, ministers, and students, but "every Christian who is mindful of the theological task entrusted to the whole congregation" (Barth, "The Gift of Freedom," 87).

6. Ibid., 93.

7. Ibid., 94.

8. II/2, 597–99.

9. Ibid., 598.

"Anxiety," Barth says "has to do expressly with penultimate things." And "Fear is the anticipation of a supposedly certain defeat."[10]

Barth shared this theological confidence in the face of fear with Bonhoeffer, whose letters from prison are a testament to the resilience he felt Jesus ought to inspire under conditions of appalling suffering.[11] Bonhoeffer asked for an Archimedean point from which he could begin theology, a place to stand from which he would move the earth, and he found that this was the resurrection.[12] Barth's own Archimedean point was the name Jesus Christ (note the radically ec-centric departure of these from the self-assured location of identity provided by Descartes's foundational *cogito*). For both Bonhoeffer and Barth, the Christian must strive to overcome their anxieties, gloom and neuroses because, in the last resort, Jesus means freedom from the inhibitions, paralysis, and suppression caused by worry.

Consequently, the message of Barth and Bonhoeffer to twenty-first century theologians would be: we must be free from the fear of trying new things in theology which might serve the Church in its age, and which could potentially help to radiate the glory of the name Jesus, bringing liberty and respite to the vulnerable, oppressed, and poor in spirit. To do theology without a sense of daring—to play it safe simply by regurgitating what others have done—would be quite inappropriate, for Bonhoeffer and Barth. But this freedom of the theologian isn't merely an experimental liberty (although it can be a call to improvise on classic themes and methods), but the freedom of a command to do theology in the spirit of joy that characterizes Barth's later works. As Gorringe points out,

10. Ibid., 598.

11. Bonhoeffer complained, in those letters, of the hypocrisy of certain fellow prisoners who—perhaps understandably—were terrified as allied bombs dropped all around the prison, and who made little effort to conceal their dread. Bonhoeffer's dissatisfaction was not with their fear *per se*—"I don't believe I find it easy to despise anyone in real trouble" (Bonhoeffer, *Letters and Papers from Prison*, 70–71)—but with their arrogant professions to others, when things were calm, about living dangerously, and their subsequent readiness to "crumple up themselves under the slightest test of endurance" (ibid., 70). "There's a kind of weakness," he adds "Christianity will not stand for" (ibid., 71). For Bonhoeffer, Jesus gives us the confidence that there are worse things that can happen to us than dying, because death and evil cannot undo what Jesus has done for humanity; it cannot be the end of the story for human beings; it cannot separate us from God's light, love and life; and it cannot have any ultimate victory, or power to determine how things will end up. It was, perhaps, for this reason that Barth insisted that when it came to writing on the theme of discipleship there was nothing better he could say on the subject than Bonhoeffer had, since Bonhoeffer had lived the freedom from fear of confident discipleship even to the point of death (IV/2, 533–34).

12. See Bonhoeffer, *Letters and Papers from Prison*, 85. Barth took a similar line, stating that the "free theologian" starts with "the recognition of the resurrection of Jesus Christ as the directive for [their] reasoning" (Barth, "The Gift of Freedom," 87).

Conclusion

> Theology which stands in the service of the fullness of life will also be generous, affirmative, radiant with the Gospel (the word "radiant" occurs with increasing frequency in Barth's later theology). It will, in short, be a theology of grace, and it is no accident that Barth's two greatest forerunners as theologians of freedom are Augustine and Luther . . . All three at some stage in their careers spoke sharp, angry, and quite unjustified "No's" to their opponents, but "Yes" was the overwhelming content of their gospel.[13]

To be a "Barthian" (a term that itself made Barth theologically uncomfortable)[14] therefore does not necessarily mean simply to repeat what Barth said (although attentive secondary and tertiary Barth scholarship continues to be instructive and fruitful), or to assume his style, but to find new, enduring, and relevant ways of affirming Jesus's "Yes." Katherine Sonderegger laments those lengthy treatments of Barth's method which "march on, correctly but rather mercilessly, revealing so little of the joyful delight and freedom of movement Barth shows at every turn."[15] It is therefore precisely in keeping with the spirit of Barth's work and approach if a new generation of theologians sets a fresh theological agenda for the twenty-first century, with fresh enthusiasm, voice, and vision; even if this were to mean opposing some or much of what Barth says, and how he says it. Barth would insist that his texts are designed to serve his Church in his age, and to inspire other theologians to serve their own communities and tackle the issues pertinent to their times, in the freedom and confidence that Jesus has invited us to be a part of His living, covenantal truth. It would be fitting, then, to conclude a book on freedom and flourishing by asking: what avenues in theology have some of the most sensitive and insightful commentators on Barth been compelled to explore after Barth? Who are some of the most joyful and generous theologians who have conversed affirmatively with Barth while moving beyond him? And what have they suggested as the areas deserving of theological attention in the twenty-first century, in service of God's loving freedom and human flourishing in Jesus?

There is, of course, no way here to offer an exhaustive survey of contemporary theological responses to Barth. What is offered in conclusion is intended merely to illustrate what I mean by the Barthian freedom of the theologian from fear. Daniel Hardy observed (in 2004) that there are,

---

13. Gorringe, *Karl Barth against Hegemony*, 279.

14. See Barth, "No Boring Theology!," 3, where he says one really does not need to be a "Barthian" to be a good theologian.

15. Sonderegger, "On Style in Karl Barth," 65.

roughly speaking, three broad ways in which Barth has inspired theologians. There are those who do their theology by staying almost entirely within Barth's frame of reference, tracing, interpreting and confirming its importance (e.g., Bruce McCormack and George Hunsinger).[16] There are those who disagree radically with Barth and use his work as a critical springboard for alternative approaches to theology (e.g., Wolfhart Pannenberg, Jürgen Moltmann, Hans Küng, Hans Urs von Balthasar, and Graham Ward).[17] And there are those who broadly agree with Barth and do justice to him by moving beyond his frame of reference to enlarge the significance of what he achieved in theology (e.g., Dietrich Bonhoeffer, Donald Mackinnon, Hans Frei, Eberhard Jüngel, Robert Jenson, Stephen Sykes, Oliver O'Donovan, Colin Gunton, David Ford, Rowan Williams, and Stanley Hauerwas).[18] It is worth sketching some of the avenues explored by theologians who would fall into the last category, to see how Barth's work might be of continuing value to theologians who wish to go in quite different directions to him, precisely in order to remain faithful to his vision for theological freedom. To what kinds of daring theological improvisations has Barth helped (directly and indirectly) to inspire those contemporary theologians who are sensitive to his hope for fresh waves of contextualized, Christocentric, and scripture-based Christian theology?[19]

Many have turned their attention to theology and the arts. Karl Barth loved Mozart. In fact his book on Mozart could itself serve as an introduction to Barth on freedom and joy.[20] And yet he was suspicious of the place of much art and music in church worship (albeit for good reasons).[21] Some

16. Hardy, "Karl Barth," 39.

17. Ibid., 40.

18. Ibid., 39–40.

19. In "The Gift of Freedom" Barth outlined the five marks of a "free theologian": 1) they take up theology with a joyfulness inspired by belief in the resurrection (ibid., 87–88). 2) They root all theology in the Bible, through imaginative exegesis and dogmatics (without neglecting the newspapers!) (ibid., 88–90). 3) The "free theologian" is critically aware of their intellectual pre-suppositions and accepts their indebtedness to certain ways of thinking, while constantly challenging them (ibid., 90–91). 4) They do theology in order to serve the Church (ibid., 92–93). 5) "Free theologians" work in conversation with other theologians, and are affirming of, and generous to, them even (or especially) when they disagree with others and are forced to oppose or even sharply contradict them (94–95). To the extent that the theologians surveyed below exhibit these marks, they are "Barthians," even though in many cases their own works bear little sign of replication of Barth's thought, style, or method.

20. See Barth, *Wolfgang Amadeus Mozart*.

21. Barth insists there should be no organ solos in church, and that it is hard to justify the accompaniment of human voices with an organ at all, since it tends to be used simply to conceal the feebleness of the *vox humana* (IV/3, 867). He also found the

theologians such as Jeremy Begbie, Ben Quash, David Ford, and Rowan Williams have attempted daring expressions of the central importance of music, art, theatre, and literature for celebrating the glory of God; reflecting imaginatively on the human condition, culture, and creativity; facilitating spiritual growth, embedding patterns of meditation, and inspiring wise Christian living; and enacting fresh performances of the covenant in worship, liturgy, and praise.[22]

There have also been highly original engagements both with ecclesiology and Christian doctrine from authors deeply respectful of Barth's own in the *Church Dogmatics*. Throughout this book Eberhard Jüngel has been a key interlocutor precisely because he did not simply repeat Barth's work, but signals how readers of the *Church Dogmatics* may intelligently harness the resources native to their own traditions in order to capture the Spirit of Barth's "Jesus means freedom!" Jüngel's Lutheran approach to a Christian theology of freedom improvises on Scripture, revelation, crucifixion, resurrection, pneumatology, ecclesiology, history, and philosophy in ways that emphasize the significance of theological themes, texts, and practices that the Reformed Barth did not explicitly draw out in his own work. One consequence of Jüngel's distinctive doctrinal voice and vision — and why perhaps he has been so helpful to me in providing a fresh reading Barth — is that he is more explicitly interested than Barth was in diagnosing and repairing patterns of Christian thinking in response to classical and modern intellectual, cultural, and political history.[23]

---

presence of artistic representations of Jesus in places of assembly problematic since they would distract one's attention from the preacher, would unduly bind the congregation to a particular image of Jesus, and would almost certainly fail to display the truth of Jesus Christ (IV/3, 867-68). One is inclined to see Barth's views on the place of art in worship as rather patronizing, dismissive of the intelligence and self-awareness of the community, and somewhat unimaginative and uncharacteristically joyless in celebrating the glory of God. There is a fear of certain kinds of mediation here that Barth does not betray when reflecting on the spoken or written word, and this does not seem in keeping with his views on theological freedom and the relativization of all human endeavours by the truth of Jesus Christ.

22. See, for example, Begbie, *Resounding Truth*. Of particular interest is Begbie on Barth and music, 152-56. See also Begbie, *Sounding the Depths*, to which Ben Quash, David Ford, and Rowan Williams all make contributions. See also, Quash, *Found Theology*; and Quash, *Theology and the Drama of History*. See also, Ford *The Shape of Living* and *The Drama of Living* in which the author interweaves reflections on Scripture, poetry, fiction, jazz, and a range of other media in developing a Christian spirituality for daily life.

23. Jüngel's *magnum opus*, *God as the Mystery of the World*, is perhaps the best example of this. In that text Jüngel develops a Lutheran and Pauline theology of freedom focused on the cross to diagnose and repair a great deal of erroneous metaphysical speculation perpetuated on both sides of the debate between theists and atheists. That

In *Wording a Radiance*, Daniel Hardy brings to fruition a life-time's reflections on the Church, pilgrimage, sacrament, worship, and prayer in an extraordinary and prophetic vision for the Church and the world, rooted in his deep appreciation of the energizing attractiveness of a triune God who creates and heals through the infinitely intensifying dynamics of light and love. One detects, in Hardy's writing, an ease about the relationship between nature and grace that is, in many ways, more liberating than Barth's occasionally more cautionary tone—and yet Hardy's work is highly appreciative of, and influenced by, Barth's instinct for the integrity and reciprocity of relationship between God and creation as realized in and through Jesus Christ and the Holy Spirit.[24]

Kathryn Tanner and Katherine Sonderegger have engaged in constructive, Christocentric systematic theology in ways that re-capitulate and re-vitalize many of the classical doctrinal *loci* in a manner at once reminiscent of, and divergent from, Barth. One of the features of their work that marks their departure from Barth is their sensitivity towards, and championing of, women's voices.[25] Yet, as Sonderegger notes, if at first sight the relationship between Barth's work and feminist theology makes for uncomfortable reading, there are resources in Barth's trinitarian thought, Christology, doctrine of creation, and anthropology which facilitate a re-ordering of Christian thought about gender, sex, and sexuality, that have not yet been adequately mined.[26]

Barth's eschatology of hope also paves the way for imaginative engagement in inter-faith relations. Confident that God is already utterly related to Jews, Muslims, those of other faiths, and those of none, making use of all sorts of people and communities in service of God's glory, we may dare to hope for the best for all humans, without the false oppositions and binaries that so often dominate Christian approaches to other faiths, mission, and evangelism. Tom Greggs has located in Barth the doctrinal resources internal to Christianity for compelling Christians to grow in love for their Abrahamic neighbors, and one can see that these resources could be extended and developed in all sorts of ways.[27] Barth's Christocentrism,

---

debate, Jüngel shows, has been fuelled historically by the inadmissible abstraction of the concept of God from the idea of God's historical revelation. See Małysz, *Trinity, Freedom, and Love*, 7–10, for a good introduction on this.

24. See Hardy, *Wording A Radiance*.

25. See, for example, Tanner, *Jesus, Humanity and the Trinity* and Tanner, *Christ the Key*. See also, Sonderegger, *Systematic Theology*.

26. Sonderegger, "Barth and Feminism," 258–60.

27. See for example, Greggs, *Barth, Origen, and Universal Salvation*, 213–15, and Greggs, "Bringing Barth's Critique of Religion to the Inter-Faith Table."

trinitarianism, and prioritization of the Christian Scriptures in the search for meaning lends itself well to those Christian inter-faith approaches which insist on safeguarding the particularity and uniqueness of Christian identity, and which attempt compassionate engagement with other traditions not by coordinating or mediating traditions between faiths, but by drawing on the resources particular to the Christian community's identity, texts, and practices. Barth's Christian theology of freedom urges inter-faith practitioners to resist the surrender of traditions' particularities—operative in so many assimilative inter-faith models which ignore the generativity of otherness and sanctity of difference—and which therefore jettison the integrity of all faiths, and dispense with the possibility for authentic neighborliness, by seeking mere homogenization. This insistence on the particularity of Christian identity in responses to other faiths rings true in Rowan Williams's response to "A Common Word Between Us and You" (a peace initiative between Muslims and Christians led by senior Muslim scholars, clerics, and leaders),[28] and in the practice of Scriptural Reasoning (in which religious communities become guest and host at each other's sacred texts, and thereby go deeper into their own faiths through penetrating exploration and improvisation with their own texts and those of others), developed, amongst others, by Peter Ochs, Laurie Zoloth, Randi Rashkover, Daniel Hardy, David Ford, Aref Nayed, and other Abrahamic scholars appreciative of Barth's theological method.[29]

Finally, there are those theologians who—sharing in Barth's insistence that there is no place for ethical indolence or inactivity in the face of secular aggressions—have explored the intersection of faith, politics, culture, and the public square. Rowan Williams has written widely on Christianity and science, scientism and the so-called New Atheism, politics, economics,

28. See Williams "A Common Word for the Common Good."

29. It is worth noting that Ochs has offered a Jewish tribute to the significance of Barth's *Christian* theology in affirming Israel's enduring covenant. Although critical of Barth's views on Judaism in many respects, Ochs recognizes that it is a function of Barth's Christocentrism and hermeneutics that he provides students of the *Church Dogmatics* with the resources for a "Barthian-post-Barthian" doctrine of non-supersessionism. (Ochs, "Judaism and Christian Theology," 648–49) Readers of Barth in the "postliberal" theological tradition (such as Frei, Lindbeck, Ford, and Hardy) might find in Barth's hermeneutics a "return to Scripture" that undermines supersessionism, rather than the liberal identification of "Barthianism" with "'dogmatic' and supersessionist uses of Scripture" (ibid., 658). This is because for Barth one can only do justice to the freedom of Jesus promised in the Scriptures by "acknowledging the enduring election of Israel" (ibid., 648). In other words, it is a Christian reading of its own Scriptures that compels healthy Christian-Jewish relationships, because as Barth says "A church that becomes anti-Semitic or even only asemitic sooner or later suffers the loss of its faith by losing the object of it" (II/2, 343).

community, and sociology, arguing constructively and generously for the prophetic role of the Christian community in contemporary society, and championing Christian voices and resources in the face of multiple programmatic secularist hostilities.[30] And Timothy Gorringe has developed passionate theological responses to the threats posed by secularism, capitalism, globalization, and cultural imperialism in relation to fields such as environmental ethics, economics, and technology.[31]

Do these lines of theological exploration have anything in common? In their own way, each of them seems to be concerned with forming a wise, compassionate, Christian *hospitality* in response to the fear of the other, increased social allergies to, and intolerance of, those who are weakest and most vulnerable, and a consumerist and isolationist concern for the self. They propose a theology of hospitality modelled on, and drawing strength from, the Bible's witness to the hospitality of Jesus, in response to the secular and religious politics of fear. In the years since Barth's death, the globalization of communities through the transformation of travel, markets, and communication technologies, and the resulting fractures and vulnerabilities that have opened up within those communities, means that there is today a visceral public thirst for the renewal of identity, meaning, and purpose. We see this manifested in the unpredictability of contemporary Western politics; in the apathy and inaction towards the worst humanitarian and refugee crises to have emerged since the Second World War; in the popular distrust of traditional organizations (including religion, political parties and systems, and mainstream media); and in the emergence of new types of asymmetric and unconventional threats to states and communities, including cyber-warfare, cyber-attacks, online abuse, religious extremism and terrorism, and a proclivity for violent protest.

If Jesus means freedom, then perhaps the Holy Spirit means hospitality! Jesus offers a theology of hospitality while at a dinner at a Pharisee's house (Luke 14:7–14) in which He shares a counter-cultural message envisioning the kind of honor and flourishing that a person can enjoy by practicing a life of humility, service, and love for its own sake. One of the images that Jesus employed, at that meal, to describe the Kingdom of God is the vision of a banquet, in which the most unlikely guests are drawn together and healed, where the *status quo* is overturned, and the dynamics of power are interrupted (Luke 14: 15–24). The theologians I have named in this conclusion capture the spirit of Barth because, without merely repeating his work, they

---

30. See, e.g., Williams, "Faith and Science"; Williams, *Lost Icons*; and Williams, *Faith in the Public Square*.

31. See, e.g., Gorringe, *Furthering Humanity*; and Gorringe, "Economics and the Priority of Ethics."

have celebrated and exercised the freedom Barth insists is offered to them by Jesus to capture the provocative message of the Holy Spirit. This message is that, as history unfolds towards the *eschaton*, God will call many unexpected guests to God's table, to do God's work, and to extend and intensify the divine hospitality which is at the heart of the covenant and at the heart of God's own triune life.

Another way to think about what Barth's theology of freedom inspires for future generations of theologians is to ask: what would the intended (but unwritten) volume five of the *Church Dogmatics* have looked like? This would have been Barth's doctrine of redemption, and whereas the doctrine of reconciliation was written from the perspective of Jesus Christ and His history, volume five of the *Dogmatics* would have been written from the perspective of the Holy Spirit and eschatology.[32] One wonders how Barth's radically non-oppositional and more Hegelian lines of thought would have crystallized in his doctrine of redemption, building on the trajectory initiated in *Church Dogmatics* IV/3. Without speculating on what Barth might have said, perhaps one could do worse than to imagine that this volume would have been his theology of hospitality.

Within this theology of hospitality one suspects Barth would have gone to great lengths to consolidate the work done in IV/3 and in the lecture fragments of IV/4 to overcome the false opposition or binary between fundamentally triadic pairs of terms such as Christ and the Spirit, nature and grace, time and eternity, truth and witness, faith and ministry, reconciliation and revelation, recognition and participation, and divine freedom and human flourishing. In that sense, *Church Dogmatics* V would have marked the culmination of a gradual shift away from the theological method employed in the younger Barth's work on the critique of religion. There would have been a pneumatological freedom for doctrinal expression in which the participation of the Church in the heart of the life of God would have been expressed in a way that the revolutionary and admonitory Barth of *Romans* II could not yet envisage. There would have been no nervousness or fear about the Church participating in God's truth, because by IV/3—without wishing to underestimate the perseverance of Barth's anti-synergism—the idea of a God who does not actually *require* the Christian community in some sense is quite inconceivable. It is inconceivable not because God is somehow incomplete "until" God creates (as if God were passed panentheistically into God's creation), or because humanity is in any way called to fulfil God's works of its own authority, but because God's revelation in Jesus and the Spirit shows that God is alive in the Church and the world. Hence,

---

32. See Hunsinger, "The Mediator of Communion," 178.

we are not permitted to imagine a God outside, above or beyond that revelatory actuality. And above all, the sense of supreme joy that pervaded IV/3 would have come through from the perspective of the Spirit's hospitality. After all, freedom means joy. God joyfully comes to Godself eternally by taking our story into His own. For our part, we are called to shout for joy that our liberation for full flourishing is grounded in the very structure of God's inner life.

Whereas Christology was the dominant doctrine of the twentieth century, it may well prove that the best way for theologians to bring Barth into the twenty-first century will be to develop a response to the question he was finally unable to answer: how it is that God the Holy Spirit will make use of all sorts of individuals and communities as witnesses to the unfolding of God's future on earth, as participants in the final consummation of Jesus Christ's covenantal name, and as guests at God's banquet table. This would be in keeping with Barth's own wishes, who wondered whether "someone, and perhaps a whole age, might be allowed to develop a 'theology of the Holy Spirit,' a 'theology which now I can only envisage from afar, as Moses once looked on the promised land.'"[33]

---

33. Busch, *Karl Barth*, 494; see Barth, "Nachwort," 310–11.

BIBLIOGRAPHY

Adams, Nicholas. "Kant." In *The Blackwell Companion to Nineteenth-Century Theology*, edited by David Fergusson, 3–30. Blackwell Companions to Religion. Oxford: Wiley-Blackwell, 2010.

———. *Eclipse of Grace: Divine and Human Action in Hegel*. Oxford: Wiley-Blackwell, 2013.

Allison, Henry E. *Kant's Theory of Freedom*. Cambridge: Cambridge University Press, 1990.

———. *Kant's Transcendental Idealism: An Interpretation and Defense*. New Haven: Yale University Press, 2004.

Althaus, Paul. *Die Christliche Wahrheit: Lehrbuch der Dogmatik*. Gütersloh: Mohn, 1966.

Axt-Piscalar, Christine. "Liberal Theology in Germany." In *The Blackwell Companion to Nineteenth Century Theology*, edited by David Fergusson, 468–85. Blackwell Companions to Religion. Oxford: Wiley-Blackwell, 2010.

Barter, Jane A. "A Theology of Liberation in Barth's *Church Dogmatics* IV/3." *Scottish Journal of Theology* 53.2 (2000) 154–76.

Barth, Karl. *Anselm, Fides Quaerens Intellectum: Anselm's Proof of the Existence of God in the Context of His Theological Scheme*. 1960. Reprint, Pittsburgh Reprint Series. Pittsburgh: Pickwick Publications, 1975.

———. *The Christian Life: Church Dogmatics*. IV/4, *Lecture Fragments*. Translated by Geoffrey W. Bromiley. Edinburgh: T. & T. Clark, 1981.

———. "The Christian's Place in Society." In *The Word of God and The Word of Man*, 272–327. Translated by Douglas Horton. New York: Harper & Row, 1957.

———. *Die christliche Dogmatik im Entwurf*. Edited by Gerhard Sauter. Zurich: TVZ, 1982.

———. *Church Dogmatics*. 4 vols. in 13 parts. Edited by Geoffrey W. Bromiley and Thomas F. Torrance. Edinburgh: T. & T. Clark, 1956–75.

———. *Dogmatics in Outline*. Translated by G. T. Thomson. London: SCM, 1949.

———. *The Epistle to the Romans*. Translated from the 6th ed. by Edwin C. Hoskyns. London: Oxford University Press, 1933.

———. *Ethics*. Edited by Dietrich Braun. Translated by Geoffrey W. Bromiley. Edinburgh: T. & T. Clark, 1981.

———. "Evangelical Theology in the Nineteenth Century." In *The Humanity of God*, 9–32. Translated by John Newton Thomas and Thomas Wieser. London: Collins, 1967.

———. "Fate and Idea in Theology." In *The Way of Theology in Karl Barth: Essays and Comments*, edited by H. Martin Rumscheidt, 25–61. Princeton Theological Monograph Series 8. Allison Park, PA: Pickwick Publications, 1986.

———. "The Gift of Freedom: Foundation of Evangelical Ethics." In *The Humanity of God*, 65–95. Translated by John Newton Thomas and Thomas Wieser. London: Collins, 1967.

———. *The Göttingen Dogmatics: Instruction in the Christian Religion*. Vol. I. Translated by Geoffrey W. Bromiley. Grand Rapids: Eerdmans, 1991.

———. *How I Changed My Mind*. Introduction and epilogue by John D. Godsey. Edinburgh: Saint Andrew, 1969.

———. "The Humanity of God." In *The Humanity of God*, 33–64. Translated by John Newton Thomas and Thomas Wieser. London: Collins, 1967.

———. *Die Kirchliche Dogmatik*. 4 volumes in 13 parts. Zürich: Evangelischer Verlag, 1947–1967.

———. *Letters 1961–1968*. Edited by Jürgen Fangmeier and Hinrich Stoevesandt. Translated by Geoffrey W. Bromiley. Edinburgh: T. & T. Clark, 1981.

———. "Liberal Theology: Some Alternatives." *Hibbert Journal* 59 (1961) 213–19.

———. "Nachwort." In *Schleiermacher-Auswahl, Mit Einem Nachwort von Karl Barth*, edited by. Heinz Bolli, 290–312. Munich: Siebenstern Taschenbuch, 1968.

———."No Boring Theology! A Letter from Karl Barth." *South East Asian Journal of Theology* 2 (1969) 3–5.

———. "An Outing to the Bruderholz." In *Fragments Grave and Gay*, edited by Martin Rumscheidt. Translated by Eric Mosbacher, 71–94. London: Collins, 1971.

———. *Protestant Theology in the Nineteenth Century: Its Background and History*. Translated by Brian Cozens and John Bowden. London: SCM, 2001.

———. "Schicksal und Idee in der Theologie." In *Gesammelte Vorträge*, Vol. 3: *Theologische Fragen und Antworten*, 54–92. Zürich: Evangelischer Verlag, 1957.

———. "The Strange New World within the Bible." In *The Word of God and The Word of Man*, 28–50. Translated by Douglas Horton. New York: Harper & Row, 1957.

———. *Wolfgang Amadeus Mozart*. Grand Rapids: Eerdmans, 1986.

———. "The Word of God and the Task of the Ministry." In *The Word of God and The Word of Man*, 183–217. Translated by Douglas Horton. New York: Harper & Row, 1957.

Barth, Karl, and Rudolf Bultmann. *Karl Barth/Rudolf Bultmann Letters, 1922–1966*. Edited by Bernd Jaspert. Translated by Geoffrey W. Bromiley. Edinburgh: T. & T. Clark, 1982.

Begbie, Jeremy. *Resounding Truth: Christian Wisdom in the World of Music*. London: SPCK, 2007.

———, ed. *Sounding the Depths: Theology through the Arts*. London: SCM, 2002.

Beiser, Frederick C., ed. *German Idealism: The Struggle Against Subjectivism, 1781–1801*. Cambridge: Harvard University Press, 2002.

———. *Hegel*. Routledge Philosophers. Abingdon: Routledge, 2005.

———. "Introduction: Hegel and the Problem of Metaphysics." In *The Cambridge Companion to Hegel*, edited by Frederick C. Beiser, 1–25. Cambridge: Cambridge University Press, 1993.

Berkouwer, G. C. *The Triumph of Grace in the Theology of Karl Barth*. Translated by Harry R. Boer. London: Paternoster, 1956.

Bloesch, Donald G. *Jesus Is Victor! Karl Barth's Doctrine of Salvation*. 1976. Reprint, Eugene, OR: Wipf & Stock, 2001.

Bonhoeffer, Dietrich. *Act and Being: Transcendental Philosophy and Ontology in Systematic Theology*. Edited by Hans-Richard Reuter and Wayne Whitson Floyd Jr. Translated by H. Martin Rumscheidt. Dietrich Bonhoeffer Works 2. Minneapolis: Fortress, 2009.

Boulton, Matthew Myer. *God against Religion: Rethinking Christian Theology through Worship*. Grand Rapids: Eerdmans, 2008.

Bowie, Andrew. *Introduction to German Philosophy: From Kant to Habermas*. Cambridge: Polity, 2003.

Bromiley, Geoffrey W. *Introduction to the Theology of Karl Barth*. Grand Rapids: Eerdmans, 1979.

Brunner, Emil. *Dogmatics*. Vol. 1, *The Christian Doctrine of God*. Translated by Olive Wyon. London: Lutterworth, 1949.

Bultmann, Rudolf. *The Gospel of John: A Commentary*. Translated by G. R. Beasley-Murray. 1971. Reprint, Johannine Monograph Series. Eugene, OR: Wipf & Stock, 2014.

Busch, Eberhard. *Karl Barth: His Life from Letters and Autobiographical Texts*. Translated by John Bowden. Grand Rapids: Eerdmans, 1994.

———. "God Is God: The Meaning of a Controversial Formula and the Fundamental Problem of Speaking about God." *Princeton Seminary Bulletin* 7.2 (1986) 101–13.

———. *The Great Passion: An Introduction to Karl Barth's Theology*. Translated by Geoffrey W. Bromiley. Grand Rapids: Eerdmans, 2004.

Burbidge, John W. "Hegel's Conception of Logic." In *The Cambridge Companion to Hegel*, edited by Frederick C. Beiser, 86–101. Cambridge: Cambridge University Press, 1993.

Butin, Phil. "Two Early Reformed Catechisms, the Threefold Office, and the Shape of Karl Barth's Christology." *Scottish Journal of Theology* 44 (1991) 195–214.

Calhoun, Robert L. "Work and Vocation in Christian History." In *Work and Vocation: A Christian Discussion*, edited by John Oliver Nelson, 82–115. New York: Harper, 1954.

Calvin, John. *Institutes of the Christian Religion*. Edited by J. T. McNeill. Philadelphia: Westminster, 1960.

Cocksworth, Ashley. "Attending to the Sabbath: An Alternative Direction in Karl Barth's Theology of Prayer." *International Journal of Systematic Theology* 13.3 (2011) 251–71.

———. *Karl Barth on Prayer*. T. & T. Clark Studies in Systematic Theology 26. London: Bloomsbury T. & T. Clark, 2015.

Colwell, John. *Actuality and Provisionality: Eternity and Election in the Theology of Karl Barth*. Edinburgh: Rutherford House, 1989.

Come, Arnold B. *An Introduction to Barth's "Dogmatics" for Preachers*. London: SCM, 1963.

Couenhoven, Jesse. "Karl Barth's Conception(s) of Human and Divine Freedom(s)." In *Commanding Grace: Studies in Karl Barth's Ethics*, edited by Daniel L. Migliore, 239–55. Grand Rapids: Eerdmans, 2010.

Dempsey, Michael T. Introduction to *Trinity and Election in Contemporary Theology*, edited by Michael T. Dempsey, 1–25. Grand Rapids: Eerdmans, 2011.
Desmond, William. *Hegel's God: A Counterfeit Double?* Ashgate Studies in the History of Philosophical Theology. Aldershot, UK: Ashgate, 2003.
Dews, Peter. *The Idea of Evil*. Oxford: Blackwell, 2008.
Diller, Kevin. "Karl Barth and the Relationship between Philosophy and Theology." *Heythrop Journal* 48 (2009) 1–18.
Dorrien, Gary. *The Barthian Revolt in Modern Theology: Theology without Weapons*. Louisville: Westminster John Knox, 1989.
Driel, Edwin Chr. van. "Karl Barth on the Eternal Existence of Jesus Christ." *Scottish Journal of Theology* 60.1 (2007) 45–61.
Eyeons, Keith. "Retreat and Restructuring: Karl Barth's Strategic Use of John's Gospel in the *Church Dogmatics*." PhD diss., University of Cambridge, 2009.
Fergusson, David. "Hegel." In *The Blackwell Companion to Nineteenth-Century Theology*, edited by David Fergusson, 58–75. Blackwell Companions to Religion. Oxford: Wiley-Blackwell, 2010.
Floyd, Wayne Whitson Jr. Introduction to Bonhoeffer, *Act and Being: Transcendental Philosophy and Ontology in Systematic Theology*, edited by Hans-Richard Reuter and Wayne Whitson Floyd Jr., translated by H. Martin Rumscheidt, 1–24. Dietrich Bonhoeffer Works 2. Minneapolis: Fortress, 2009.
Ford, David F. *Barth and God's Story: Biblical Narrative and the Theological Method of Karl Barth in the "Church Dogmatics."* Studien zur interkulturellen Geschichte des Christentums 27. 1981. Reprint, Eugene, OR: Wipf & Stock, 2008.
———. *The Drama of Living: Becoming Wise in the Spirit*. London: Canterbury, 2014.
———. *The Shape of Living: Spiritual Directions for Everyday Life*. London: Canterbury, 2012.
Frei, Hans. *Types of Christian Theology*. Edited by George Hunsinger and William C. Placher. New Haven: Yale University Press, 1992.
Godsey, John D., ed. *Karl Barth's Table Talk*. Edinburgh: Oliver & Boyd, 1963.
Gorringe, Timothy. "Economics and the Priority of Ethics." *Studies in Christian Ethics* 28.4 (2015) 419–30.
———. *Furthering Humanity: A Theology of Culture*. Aldershot, UK: Ashgate, 2004.
———. *Karl Barth against Hegemony*. Oxford: Oxford University Press, 1999.
Greggs, Tom. *Barth, Origen, and Universal Salvation: Restoring Particularity*. Oxford: Oxford University Press, 2009.
———. "Bringing Barth's Critique of Religion to the Inter-Faith Table." *Journal of Religion* 88.1 (2008) 75–94.
———. "The Order and Movement of Eternity: Karl Barth on the Eternity of God and Creaturely Time." In *Eternal God, Eternal Life: Theological Investigations into the Concept of Immortality*, edited by Philip G. Ziegler, 1–23. London: Bloomsbury T. & T. Clark, 2016.
Gunton, Colin E. *The Barth Lectures*. Edited by P. H. Brazier. London: T. & T. Clark, 2007.
———. "Barth, the Trinity, and Human Freedom." *Theology Today* 43.3 (1986) 316–30.
———. *Becoming and Being: The Doctrine of God in Charles Hartshorne and Karl Barth*. Oxford: Oxford University Press, 1978.
———. "God the Holy Spirit: Augustine and His Successors." In *Theology through the Theologians: Selected Essays 1972–1995*, 105–28. Edinburgh: T. & T. Clark, 1996.

———. "No Other Foundation: One Englishman's Reading of *Church Dogmatics*." In *Reckoning with Barth: Essays in Commemoration of the Centenary of Karl Barth's Birth*, edited by Nigel Biggar, 61–79. London: Mowbray, 1988.

———. "Salvation." In *The Cambridge Companion to Karl Barth*, edited by John Webster, 143–58. Cambridge Companions to Religion. Cambridge: Cambridge University Press, 2000.

Guyer, Paul. "Thought and Being: Hegel's Critique of Kant's Theoretical Philosophy." In *The Cambridge Companion to Hegel*, edited by Frederick C. Beiser, 171–210. Cambridge: Cambridge University Press, 1993.

Hardy, Daniel W. "Karl Barth," In *The Modern Theologians: An Introduction to Christian Theology since 1918*, 3rd ed., edited by David F. Ford with Rachel Muers, 21–42. Oxford: Blackwell, 2005.

———. "The Reception of Schleiermacher and Barth in England." In *Barth and Schleiermacher: Beyond the Impasse?*, edited by James O. Duke and Robert F. Streetman, 138–62. Philadelphia: Fortress, 1988.

Hardy, Daniel W, et al. *Wording A Radiance: Parting Conversations on God and the Church*. London: SCM, 2010.

Hart, Trevor. "Revelation." In *The Cambridge Companion to Karl Barth*, edited by John Webster, 37–56. Cambridge Companions to Religion. Cambridge: Cambridge University Press, 2000.

Hauerwas, Stanley. "On Honour: By Way of a Comparison of Barth and Trollope." In *Reckoning with Barth: Essays in Commemoration of the Centenary of Karl Barth's Birth*, edited by Nigel Biggar, 145–69. London: Mowbray, 1988.

Healy, Nicholas. "Karl Barth's Ecclesiology Reconsidered." *Scottish Journal of Theology* 57.3 (2004) 287–99.

Hector, Kevin W. "God's Triunity and Self-Determination: A Conversation with Karl Barth, Bruce McCormack, and Paul Molnar." *International Journal of Systematic Theology* 7.3 (2005) 246–61.

Hegel, G. W. F. *Faith and Knowledge*. Translated by Walter Cerf and H. S. Harris. Albany: State University of New York Press, 1977.

———. *Hegel's Logic: Being Part One of the Encyclopaedia of the Philosophical Sciences (1830)*. Translated by William Wallace. Oxford: Clarendon, 1975.

———. *Hegel's Philosophy of Mind: Being Part Three of the Encyclopaedia of the Philosophical Sciences (1830)*. Translated by William Wallace. Oxford: Clarendon, 1971.

———. *Lectures on the History of Philosophy*. Volume 3, *Medieval and Modern Philosophy*. Translated by E. S. Haldane and Frances H. Simson. Lincoln: University of Nebraska Press, 1995.

———. *Lectures on the Philosophy of Religion*. Vol. III. Edited by Peter C. Hodgson. Translated by R. F. Brown et al. Oxford: Oxford University Press, 2007.

———. *Phenomenology of Spirit*. Translated by A. V. Miller. Oxford: Oxford University Press, 1977.

———. *The Science of Logic*. Translated and edited by George di Giovanni. Cambridge Hegel Translations. Cambridge: Cambridge University Press, 2010.

Hendry, George S. "The Freedom of God in the Theology of Karl Barth." *Scottish Journal of Theology* 31.3 (1978) 229–44.

Hodgson, Peter C. *Hegel and Christian Theology: A Reading of the "Lectures on the Philosophy of Religion."* Oxford: Oxford University Press, 2005.

Houlgate, Stephen. *Freedom, Truth and History: An Introduction to Hegel's Philosophy.* Ideas. London: Routledge, 1991.

———, ed. *The Hegel Reader.* Blackwell Readers. Oxford: Blackwell, 1998.

Hunsinger, George. "Election and the Trinity: Twenty-Five Theses on the Theology of Karl Barth." *Modern Theology* 24.2 (2008) 179–98.

———. *How to Read Karl Barth: The Shape of His Theology.* Oxford: Oxford University Press, 1991.

———. "Karl Barth's Christology: Its Basic Chalcedonian Character." In *The Cambridge Companion to Karl Barth*, edited by John Webster, 127–42. Cambridge Companions to Religion. Cambridge: Cambridge University Press, 2000.

———. "The Mediator of Communion: Karl Barth's Doctrine of the Holy Spirit." In *The Cambridge Companion to Karl Barth*, edited by John Webster, 177–94. Cambridge Companions to Religion. Cambridge: Cambridge University Press, 2000.

———. "A Tale of Two Simultaneities: Justification and Sanctification in Calvin and Barth." In *Conversing with Barth*, edited by John C. McDowell and Mike Higton, 68–89. Barth Studies. Aldershot, UK: Ashgate, 2004.

———. "Truth as Self-Involving: Barth and Lindbeck on the Cognitive and Performative Aspects of Truth in Theological Discourse." *Journal of the American Academy of Religion* 61.1 (1993) 41–56.

Jehle, Frank. *Ever Against the Stream: The Politics of Karl Barth, 1906–1968.* Translated by Richard Burnett and Martha Burnett. Grand Rapids: Eerdmans, 2002.

Jenson, Robert W. *Alpha and Omega: A Study in the Theology of Karl Barth.* New York: Nelson, 1963.

———. *God after God: The God of the Past and the God of the Future, Seen in the Work of Karl Barth.* Indianapolis: Bobbs-Merrill, 1969.

———. "Karl Barth." In *The Modern Theologians: An Introduction to Christian Theology in the Twentieth Century*, edited by David. F. Ford, 21–36. 2nd ed. Oxford: Blackwell, 1997.

———. "You Wonder Where the Spirit Went." *Pro Ecclesia* 2.3 (1993) 296–304.

Jones, Paul Dafydd. *The Humanity of Christ: Christology in Karl Barth's Church Dogmatics.* T & T Clark Theology. London: T. & T. Clark, 2011.

———. "Karl Barth on Gethsemane." *International Journal of Systematic Theology* 9.2 (2007) 148–71.

———. "Obedience, Trinity, and Election: Thinking With and Beyond the *Church Dogmatics*." In *Trinity and Election in Contemporary Theology*, edited by Michael T. Dempsey, 138–61. Grand Rapids: Eerdmans, 2011.

Jüngel, Eberhard. "Einführung in Leben und Werk Karl Barths." In *Barth-Studien*, 22–60. Gütersloh: Gerd Mohn, 1982.

———. *God as the Mystery of the World: On the Foundation of the Theology of the Crucified One in the Dispute between Theism and Atheism.* Translated by Darrell L. Gruder. Grand Rapids: Eerdmans, 1983.

———. *God's Being Is in Becoming: The Trinitarian Being of God in the Theology of Karl Barth. A Paraphrase.* Translated by John Webster. Edinburgh: T. & T. Clark, 2001.

———. *Gott als Geheimnis der Welt: Zur Begründung der Theologie des Gekreuzigten im Streit zwischen Theismus und Atheismus.* Tübingen: Mohr/Siebeck, 2010.

———. *Gottes Sein ist im Werden: Verantwortliche Rede vom Sein Gottes bei Karl Barth. Eine Paraphrase.* Tübingen: Mohr/Siebeck, 1986.

———. "Invocation of God as the Ethical Ground of Christian Action: Introductory Remarks on the Posthumous Fragments of Karl Barth's Ethics of the Doctrine of Reconciliation." In *Theological Essays I*, translated by John Webster, 154–72. Edinburgh: T. & T. Clark, 1989.

———. *Karl Barth: A Theological Legacy*. Translated by Garrett E. Paul. Philadelphia: Westminster, 1986.

———. "Keine Menschenlosigkeit Gottes: Zur Theologie Karl Barths zwischen Theismus und Atheismus." In *Barth-Studien*, 332–47. Zürich: Benziger, 1982.

Kant, Immanuel. *Critique of Practical Reason*. Edited and translated by Mary Gregor. Cambridge Texts in the History of Philosophy. Cambridge: Cambridge University Press, 1997.

———. *Critique of Pure Reason*. Edited and translated by Paul Guyer and Allen W. Wood. The Cambridge Edition of the Works of Immanuel Kant. Cambridge: Cambridge University Press, 1998.

———. *Groundwork of the Metaphysics of Morals*. Edited and translated by Mary Gregor. Cambridge Texts in the History of Philosophy. Cambridge: Cambridge University Press, 1998.

———. *Religion within the Boundaries of Mere Reason*. Edited and translated by Allen W. Wood and George di Giovanni. Cambridge Texts in the History of Philosophy. Cambridge: Cambridge University Press, 1998.

Krötke, Wolf. "The Humanity of the Human Person in Karl Barth's Anthropology." In *The Cambridge Companion to Karl Barth*, edited by John Webster, 159–76. Cambridge Companions to Religion. Cambridge: Cambridge University Press, 2000.

Kuzmic, Rhys. "*Beruf* and *Berufung* in Karl Barth's *Church Dogmatics*: Toward a Subversive Klesiology." *International Journal of Systematic Theology* 7.3 (2005) 262–78.

Laats, Alar. *Doctrines of the Trinity in Eastern and Western Theologies: A Study with Special Reference to K. Barth and V. Lossky*. Frankfurt am Main: Peter Lang, 1999.

Macken, John. *The Autonomy Theme in the Church Dogmatics: Karl Barth and His Critics*. Cambridge: Cambridge University Press, 1990.

Małysz, Piotr J. *Trinity, Freedom, and Love: An Engagement with the Theology of Eberhard Jüngel*. T & T Clark Studies in Systematic Theology 18. London: T. & T. Clark, 2012.

Mangina, Joseph L. *Karl Barth on the Christian Life: The Practical Knowledge of God*. Issues in Systematic Theology 8. New York: Lang, 2001.

McCormack, Bruce L. "Election and the Trinity: Theses in Response to George Hunsinger." *Scottish Journal of Theology* 63.2 (2010) 203–24.

———. "Grace and Being: The Role of God's Gracious Election in Karl Barth's Theological Ontology." In *The Cambridge Companion to Karl Barth*, edited by John Webster, 92–110. Cambridge Companions to Religion. Cambridge: Cambridge University Press, 2000.

———. *Karl Barth's Critically Realistic Dialectical Theology: Its Genesis and Development 1909–1936*. Oxford: Oxford University Press, 1995.

———. "Karl Barth's Historicized Christology: Just How 'Chalcedonian' Is It?" In *Orthodox and Modern: Studies in the Theology of Karl Barth*, 201–33. Grand Rapids: Baker Academic, 2008.

———. "Participation in God, Yes, Deification, No: Two Modern Protestant Responses to an Ancient Question." In *Denkwürdiges Geheimnis: Beiträge zur Gotteslehre. Festschrift für Eberhard Jüngel zum 70. Geburtstag*, edited by Ingolf U. Dalferth, Johannes Fischer, and Hans-Peter Großhans, 347–74. Tübingen: Mohr/Siebeck, 2004.

———. "Seek God Where He May Be Found: A Response to Edwin Chr. van Driel." *Scottish Journal of Theology* 60.1 (2007) 62–79.

McDowell, John C. *Hope in Barth's Eschatology: Interrogations and Transformations Beyond Tragedy*. Ashgate New Critical Thinking in Theology & Biblical Studies. Aldershot, UK: Ashgate, 2000.

———. "'Openness to the World:' Karl Barth's Evangelical Theology of Christ as the Pray-er." *Modern Theology* 25.2 (2009) 253–83.

Migliore, Daniel L. "Freedom to Pray: Karl Barth's Theology of Prayer." In *Prayer*, by Karl Barth. Edited by Don E. Saliers. Translated by Sara F. Terrien, 95–113. Louisville: Westminster John Knox, 2002.

Molnar, Paul D. "Can the Electing God Be God without Us? Some Implications of Bruce McCormack's Understanding of Barth's Doctrine of Election for the Doctrine of the Trinity." *Neue Zeitschrift für Systematische Theologie und Religionsphilosophie* 49.2 (2007) 199–222.

———. *Divine Freedom and the Doctrine of the Immanent Trinity: In Dialogue with Karl Barth and Contemporary Theology*. London: T. & T. Clark, 2002.

———. "The Trinity, Election, and God's Ontological Freedom: A Response to Kevin W. Hector." *International Journal of Systematic Theology* 8.3 (2006) 294–306.

Moltmann, Jürgen. *The Trinity and the Kingdom of God: The Doctrine of God*. Translated by Margaret Kohl. London: SCM, 1981.

Neder, Adam. *Participation in Christ: An Entry into Karl Barth's "Church Dogmatics."* Louisville: Westminster John Knox, 2009.

Nimmo, Paul T. *Being in Action: The Theological Shape of Barth's Ethical Vision*. London: T. & T. Clark, 2007.

———. "Barth and the Trinity-Election Debate: A Pneumatological View." In *Trinity and Election in Contemporary Theology*, edited by Michael T. Dempsey, 162–81. Grand Rapids: Eerdmans, 2011.

———. "Karl Barth and the *concursus Dei*—A Chalcedonianism Too Far?," *International Journal of Systematic Theology* 9.1 (2007) 58–72.

———. "The Orders of Creation in the Theological Ethics of Karl Barth." *Scottish Journal of Theology* 60.1 (2007) 24–35.

Ochs, Peter. "Judaism and Christian Theology." In *The Modern Theologians: An Introduction to Christian Theology since 1918*, edited by David F. Ford with Rachel Muers, 645–62. 3rd ed. The Great Theologians. Oxford: Blackwell, 2005.

Parker, T. H. L. *Karl Barth*. Grand Rapids: Eerdmans, 1970.

Pinkard, Terry. *German Philosophy 1760–1860: The Legacy of Idealism*. Cambridge: Cambridge University Press, 2002.

Pippin, Robert. "You Can't Get There from Here: Transition Problems in Hegel's *Phenomenology of Spirit*." In *The Cambridge Companion to Hegel*, edited by Frederick C. Beiser, 52–85. Cambridge: Cambridge University Press, 1993.

Polanyi, Michael. *Personal Knowledge: Towards a Post-Critical Philosophy*. 2nd ed. London: Routledge and Kegan Paul, 1962.

Preece, Gordon. "Barth's Theology of Work and Vocation for a Postmodern World." In *Karl Barth: A Future for Postmodern Theology?*, edited by Geoff Thompson and Christiaan Mostert, 147–70. Hindmarsh: Australian Theological Forum, 2000.

Prenter, Regin. "Karl Barths Umbildung der traditionellen Zweinaturlehre in lutherischer Beleuchtung: Einige vorläufige Beobachtungen zu Karl Barths neuester Darstellung der Christologie." *Studia Theologica* 11.1 (1957) 1–88.

Quash, Ben. *Found Theology: History, Imagination and the Holy Spirit*. London: Bloomsbury, 2013.

———. *Theology and the Drama of History*. Cambridge Studies in Christian Doctrine 13. Cambridge: Cambridge University Press, 2005.

Rahner, Karl. "Dogmatic Questions on Easter." In *Theological Investigations Volume IV: More Recent Writings*, 121–33. Translated by Kevin Smith. London: Darton, Longdon & Todd, 1966.

———. *The Trinity*. Translated by Joseph Donceel. New York: Herder & Herder, 1970.

Reath, Andrews. Introduction to Kant, *Critique of Practical Reason*, edited and translated by Paul Guyer, and Allen W. Wood, vii–xxxi. Cambridge: Cambridge University Press, 1998.

Rendtorff, Trutz. "Radikale Autonomie Gottes: Zum Verständnis der Theologie Karl Barths und ihrer Folgen." In *Theorie des Christentums: Historisch-theologische Studien zu seiner neuzeitlichen Verfassung*, 161–81. Gütersloh: Gütersloher, 1972.

Reuter, Hans-Richard. Afterword to Bonhoeffer, *Act and Being: Transcendental Philosophy and Ontology in Systematic Theology*, edited by Hans-Richard Reuter and Wayne Whitson Floyd Jr., translated by H. Martin Rumscheidt, 162–83. Dietrich Bonhoeffer Works 2. Minneapolis: Fortress, 2009.

Rogers Eugene F., Jr. "The Eclipse of the Spirit in Karl Barth." In *Conversing with Barth*, edited by John C. McDowell and Mike Higton, 173–90. Barth Studies. Aldershot, UK: Ashgate, 2004.

Rosato, Philip J. *The Spirit as Lord: The Pneumatology of Karl Barth*. Edinburgh: T. & T. Clark, 1981.

Sherman, Franklin. "Act and Being." In *The Place of Bonhoeffer: Problems and Possibilities in His Thought*, edited by Martin E. Marty, 83–111. London: SCM, 1962.

Smail, Thomas A. "The Doctrine of the Holy Spirit." In *Beyond Christendom: Essays on the Centenary of the Birth of Karl Barth, May 10, 1886*, edited by John Thompson, 87–110. Allison Park, PA: Pickwick Publications, 1986.

———. *The Giving Gift: The Holy Spirit in Person*. London: Hodder & Stoughton, 1988.

Sonderegger, Katherine. "Barth and Feminism." In *The Cambridge Companion to Karl Barth*, edited by John Webster, 258–73. Cambridge Companions to Religion. Cambridge: Cambridge University Press, 2000.

———. "On Style in Karl Barth." *Scottish Journal of Theology* 45 (1992) 65–83.

———. *Systematic Theology: Volume 1, The Doctrine of God*. Minneapolis: Fortress, 2015.

Tanner, Kathryn. *Christ the Key*. Current Issues in Theology. Cambridge: Cambridge University Press, 2010.

———. "Creation and Providence." In *The Cambridge Companion to Karl Barth*, edited by John Webster, 111–26. Cambridge Companions to Religion. Cambridge: Cambridge University Press, 2000.

———. *Jesus, Humanity, and the Trinity: A Brief Systematic Theology*. Edinburgh: T. & T. Clark, 2001.

Taylor, Charles. *Hegel*. Cambridge: Cambridge University Press, 1975.

———. *Sources of the Self: The Making of Modern Identity*. Cambridge: Cambridge University Press, 1989.

Thiemann, Ronald F. *Revelation and Theology: The Gospel as Narrated Promise*. Notre Dame: University of Notre Dame Press, 1985.

Thomas Aquinas. *Summa Theologiae: Volume II; Existence and Nature of God*. Translated by Timothy McDermott. London: Blackfriars, 1964.

Thompson, John. *The Holy Spirit in the Theology of Karl Barth*. Princeton Theological Monograph Series 23. Allison Park, PA: Pickwick Publications, 1991.

Torrance, Alan J. *Persons in Communion: An Essay on Trinitarian Description and Human Participation with Special Reference to Volume One of Karl Barth's "Church Dogmatics."* Edinburgh: T. & T. Clark, 1996.

———. "The Trinity." In *The Cambridge Companion to Karl Barth*, edited by John Webster, 72–91. Cambridge Companions to Religion. Cambridge: Cambridge University Press, 2000.

Torrance, Thomas. F. *Karl Barth: An Introduction to His Early Theology, 1910–1931*. Edinburgh: T. & T. Clark, 2000.

———. *Karl Barth: Biblical and Evangelical Theologian*. Edinburgh: T. & T. Clark, 1990.

Volf, Miroslav. *Work in the Spirit: Toward a Theology of Work*. New York: Oxford University Press, 1991.

Webster, John. *Barth*. 2nd ed. London: Continuum, 2004.

———. *Barth's Ethics of Reconciliation*. Cambridge: Cambridge University Press, 1995.

———. *Barth's Moral Theology: Human Action in Barth's Thought*. Edinburgh: T. & T. Clark, 1998.

———. "'Eloquent and Radiant': The Prophetic Office of Christ and the Mission of the Church." In *Barth's Moral Theology: Human Action in Barth's Thought*, 125–50. Edinburgh: T. & T. Clark, 1998.

———. "Freedom in Limitation: Human Freedom and False Necessity in Barth." In *Barth's Moral Theology: Human Action in Barth's Thought*, 99–123. Edinburgh: T. & T. Clark, 1998.

Welker, Michael. "Barth und Hegel: Zur Erkenntnis eines methodischen Verfahrens bei Barth." *Evangelische Theologie* 43 (1983) 307–28.

Werpehowski, William. "Karl Barth on Politics." In *The Cambridge Companion to Karl Barth*, edited by John Webster, 228–42. Cambridge Companions to Religion. Cambridge: Cambridge University Press, 2000.

———. "Narrative and Ethics in Barth." *Theology Today* 43.3 (1986) 334–53.

West, Charles C. *Communism and the Theologians: Study of an Encounter*. London: SCM, 1958.

Williams, Rowan. "A Common Word for the Common Good." http://rowanwilliams.archbishopofcanterbury.org/articles.php/1107/a-common-word-for-the-common-good.

———. "Barth on the Triune God." In *Karl Barth: Studies of His Theological Method*, edited by S. W. Sykes, 147–93. Oxford: Clarendon, 1979.

———. *The Edge of Words: God and the Habits of Language*. London: Bloomsbury, 2014.

———. "Faith and Science." http://rowanwilliams.archbishopofcanterbury.org/articles.php/1366/archbishops-holy-week-lecture-faith-science.

———. *Faith in the Public Square*. London: Bloomsbury, 2012.

———. *Lost Icons: Reflections on Cultural Bereavement*. Edinburgh: T. & T. Clark, 2000.
———. "Triumph of the Will: Can We Ever Be in Charge of Our Own Lives?" *New Statesman*, May 1–6, 2015.
Willimon, William H. *The Early Preaching of Karl Barth: Fourteen Sermons with Commentary by William H. Willimon*. Translated by John E. Wilson. Louisville: Westminster John Knox, 2009.
Willis, Robert E. *The Ethics of Karl Barth*. Leiden: Brill, 1971.
Wingren, Gustaf. *Theology in Conflict: Nygren, Barth, Bultmann*. Translated by Eric H. Wahlstrom. Edinburgh: Oliver & Boyd, 1958.
Wright, Terry J. "Witnessing Christians from Karl Barth's Perspective." *Evangelical Quarterly* 75.3 (2003) 239–55.
Yocum, John. *Ecclesial Mediation in Karl Barth*. Barth Studies. Aldershot, UK: Ashgate, 2004.
Zahrnt, Heinz. *The Question of God: Protestant Theology in the Twentieth Century*. Translated by R. A. Wilson. London: Collins, 1969.

INDEX

Act and Being (Bonhoeffer), 21
action, freedom for, 207–12
actualism in Barth's theology
  Being-in Becoming and, 57–65
  in *Church Dogmatics* IV/3, 130–43
  contemporary interpretations of, 8
  development of, 10–12
  divine-human unity and, 120–21
  doctrine of election and, 6
  freedom and, 17–19, 54, 218–19
  God's sovereign relationality and, 39–42
  Hegel's influence on, 147–61
  Holy Spirit and, 184–89
  human flourishing in, 178–79
  Sabbath and, 101–4
actus purus et singularis, God as, 63–65
Adams, Nicholas, 9n28, 25, 148n4, 151, 156–57, 160n59
ad extra being of God, 46, 49, 108
  in Chalcedonian Christology, 115
  doctrine of election and, 67–73
  Molnar's discussion of, 74–78
  trinitarian doctrine and, 62–65
agency
  Christ's subjectivity and, 135–43
  ethical abstraction and, 213–15
  human freedom and, 88–89, 99–102
Alexandrian Christology, 113–15
analogia entis, 57
  Barth's resistance to, 46
analogia relationis, 62–65

Anselm text, Barth's actualism and, 39–42
Antiochene Christology, 113–15
anti-Pelagianism, 123n59
  in Barth's theology, 13, 142–43, 177–78
anxiety, Barth on overcoming, 221–22
apokatastasis, Christ's covenantal truth and, 137–38
Apollinarian Christology, 113–14
aporia, theology and, 21, 25–28
Archimedes, Barth's references to, 222
arts, Barth's theology and, 224–25
asymmetrical reciprocity
  divine-human mediation and, 128–43
  invocation to freedom and, 208–12
  oppositional logic and, 162–66
atheism, Barth's discussion of, 85n159
autonomy
  freedom and, 34–35, 52–53
  moral responsibility and, 197–98
  prayerful responsibility and, 100–104
Axt-Piscalar, Christine, 19n4

Balthasar, Hans Urs von, 224
Barmen declaration of 1934, 220
Barth, Karl
  Being-Act tradition and, 35–39
  legacy of, 1–2, 217–19
  liberal theology and, 28–35
  "strong" and "weak" interpretations of, 75–78

Begbie, Jeremy, 225
being-act tradition
  a-historical Word and, 46–53
  ambiguity in God's relation to, 44–46
  Barth's theology and legacy of, 19–39, 35–39, 218–19
  doctrine of election and, 67–73
  Holy Spirit and, 183–85
  Kant's philosophy and, 22–28
  knowledge of God and, 58–65
  liberal theology and, 28–35
  trinitarianism and, 42–44
being-in-becoming
  Barth's actualism and, 57–65
  Christocentrism, 97–102
  doctrine of election and, 65–78, 78–80
  human freedom as, 78–104
  prayer and, 210–12
  prayerful responsibility and, 100–104
being-knowing tradition
  in Barth's theology, 9–11, 133, 166–67, 217–19
  in Hegel and, 14, 147–61
Bible
  Barth's study of, 20–21
  Corinthians, 186, 213
  Ephesians, 213
  freedom as gift in, 3–5
  Gospel of John, 134, 136, 168–72, 203–6
  Gospel of Matthew, 212
  human liberation accounts in, 51
biblical exposition, Barth's emphasis on, 1–2
Biggar, Nigel, 196n87, 197–98
Bloesch, Donald G., 125–26
body imagery, in *Church Dogmatics* IV/3, 122–28
Bonhoeffer, Dietrich, 17, 21, 37–38, 61, 81n135, 126, 222, 224
Bowie, Andrew, 154
Bultmann, Rudolf, 21, 123n59, 134, 183, 201
Busch, Eberhard, 34
Butin, Phil, 124n61

Calvin, John, 124n61, 214
capitalism, Barth's criticism of, 220
causal determinism, human freedom and, 83–96
Chelcedonian Christology, 111–17
Christianity
  Hegel's discussion of, 159–61
  vocation for freedom in, 198–201
The Christian Life (Barth), 183, 195–96, 207–12
Christocentrism
  Barth's actualism and, 39–42, 58
  in Barth's freedom theology, 17–19, 56, 218–19
  object-subject schema and, 75–78, 109–10
Christology of Barth
  Chelcedonian Christology and, 111–17
  in *Church Dogmatics* IV/3, 110–17
  historical simultaneity of divinity and humanity in, 117–21
  Holy Spirit and, 182–89
  soteriology in, 9
Christomonism, 5, 14, 187
Church, klesis (calling) and, 205–7
Church, Christ as foundation of, 186–89
Church Dogmatics (Barth)
  exegetical method in, 4n15
  freedom theology in, 1–5, 217–19
  human freedom and determinism in, 84–85
  legacy of, 220–30
  Registerband for, 220
Church Dogmatics I
  actualism in, 18
  freedom theology in, 11, 39–44, 50–53
  trinitarian doctrine in, 11, 42–44
Church Dogmatics II, 6
  actualism in, 18, 57–65
  divine ontology in, 56
  doctrine of election in, 11–12
  "double-structure" of God's being in, 61–65
  Holy Spirit in, 192

Church Dogmatics II/2, divine freedom in, 118
Church Dogmatics IV/1 and 2, *munus propheticum,* 110–11
Church Dogmatics IV/3
  actualism in, 7–8
  Chalcedonian Christology in, 111–17
  Christocentric theology in, 12–13
  criticism of, 5–6, 121–28
  divine-human unity in, 117–21
  freedom as witness in, 204–7
  freedom in, 107–10
  Hegelian influence in, 161–72
  Holy Spirit in, 189–92
  human flourishing in, 177–215
  Hunsiger's interpretation of, 113–15
  munus propheticum in, 108
  object-subject schema in, 9–10, 12–13, 121, 128–43
  participative logic of, 145–76
  reassessment of, 110–17
  theology of freedom in, 18–19
  trinity-election debate and, 172–76
Cocksworth, Ashley, 103n258
Colwell, John, 58
command and obedience, human freedom and, 80–83
"A Common Word Between Us and You" initiative, 227
communicatio idiomatum, Chalcedonian Christology and, 114
communism, Barth and, 220
compatibilist conception of freedom, 96n210, 197–98
concursus Dei doctrine, 100–104
confession, Barth's discussion of, 102–4
"Copernican Revolution," Kant and, 22–28
correspondence, language of, Barth's use of, 126n74
cosmos, human freedom and order of, 85–96
Couenhoven, Jesse, 96n210
covenant
  asymmetrical reciprocity and, 169–72
  Barth's object-subject schema and, 130–43, 145–47, 181–82
  Christian vocation for freedom and, 198–201
  freedom as witness in, 202–7
  Holy Spirit and consumation of, 182–92
creation
  human freedom and, 85–96
  non-necessity to God of, 44–46
critical realism, Barth's discussion of, 53–54
Critique of Practical Reason (Kant), 22, 27–28
Critique of Pure Reason (Kant), 22, 27–28

Descartes, René 21, 25–26
  Hegel and, 155, 158–61
Desmond, William, 150–51
determinism, human freedom and, 83–96
Deus pro nobis
  in Barth's Christology, 111, 113
  divine and human freedom and, 54, 127–28
  doctrine of election and, 68–72, 73n87
  objectivity of God and, 62–64
dialectical theology, Being-Act tradition and, 35–39
Die Christliche Welt, 29
Diller, Kevin, 20–21
di-polarity
  of God's being, 61–65
  trinitrianism and election and, 66–67
divine-human unity
  Chalcedonian Christology and, 114–17
  in *Church Dogmatics* IV/3, 109–10
  in Hegel's work, 148–61
  historical subjectivity and, 117–21, 182
  Holy Spirit and, 183–89
Hunsinger, George *(continued)*

divine-human unity *(continued)*
  participative theology of freedom
    and, 146–47, 218–19
divine identity, a-historicity of, 46–53,
  56
divine ontological risk, Barth's discussion of, 141–43
docetism, Barth's theology and,
  112–13, 124n60
doctrine of election
  in *Church Dogmatics* II/2, 11–12
  in *Church Dogmatics* IV/3, 172–76
  divine freedom and, 67–78
  Holy Spirit and, 192–95
  human freedom and, 78–80
  Hunsinger's interpretation of,
    73–78
  McCormack's interpretation of,
    67–73
  Molnar's interpretation of, 73–78
  "strong" and "weak" interpretations
    of Barth on, 75–78
  trinitarianism and, 65–78
dogmatism, Hegel's discussion of, 156
"double-structure" of God's being,
  61–65
Drewes, Hans-Anton, 208–9
Driel, Edwin Chr. van, 150n9
dualism, Barth's rejection of, 86–96,
  104
dynamic teleology, in *Church Dogmatics* IV/3, 136–43

ecclesiology
  actualism and, 178
  in Barth's theology, 7, 122n56, 225
  freedom and, 202–5
  promise of the Holy Spirit and,
    179–89, 193
The Eclipse of Grace (Adams), 9n28
empirical realism, Kant and, 22n21
Enlightenment
  Barth's separation from, 28–29,
    52–53, 80
  Kant's philosophy and, 25–28
Epistle to the Romans
  Barth's commentary on, 30–35,
    43–44, 59, 149, 213

divine freedom in, 118–19
spatial distance discussed in,
  161–62
Erkenntnisweg von oben nach unten,
  ("way of knowledge from above
  to below"), 35n103
eternity
  being-in-act and, 75–78
  human freedom and, 83–84
  time and, 92–96
ethical abstraction, freedom and,
  212–15
eudaimonia, Barth's perspective on,
  197
Evangelicalism, witness and, 206–7
existentialism, Barth's rejection of,
  87n166
extra Calvinisticum, 48, 68–69

fear, freedom from, 219–30
Fergusson, David, 160n59
Fichte, Johann Gottlieb, 81–83
Ford, David, 4n15, 52, 204, 224–25,
  227
freedom
  Christian vocation for, 198–201
  determinism and, 83–96
  ethical abstraction and, 212–15
  from fear, 219–30
  for invocation, 207–12
  moral space and, 196–98
  prayer and, 103–4
  as witness, 202–7
freedom, Barth's theology of
  Being-Act tradition and, 19–39
  Christocentrism in, 1–5, 8, 12,
    97–102
  in *Church Dogmatics* I, 11, 39–44
  in *Church Dogmatics* II, 57–65
  development of, 55–56
  divine love as, 59–65
  doctrine of election and, 67–78,
    78–80
  in early Barthian theology, 17–19,
    44–53
  Kant's discussion of, 22, 27–28
  promise of the Spirit in, 179–95

Index

rejection of liberal theology and, 31–35
speech-act of God and, 39–42
Frei, Hans, 84–85, 224
Gnosticism, 190–92
God, freedom and, 3–5
God as the Mystery of the World (Jüngel), 21
God is the Mystery of the World (Jüngel), 225n23
God-man
  actuality of Christ as, 108–9
  Barth's Christology and, 12, 139–43
  Barth's use of, 111n10
  divine-human unity and, 119–21
  munus propheticum and, 110–11
  prayerful responsibility and, 100–104
Godself, ambiguity in being and act of, 44–46
Gogarten, Friedrich, 46n167
Gorringe, Timothy, 1n2, 2, 97, 111n10, 222–23, 228
grace, freedom and, 197–98
Greggs, Tom, 93, 201n117, 226–27
Gunton, Colin
  on Barth's Christology, 139–40
  on Barth's pneumatology, 179–82, 188
  on Barth's theology, 224
  on *Church Dogmatics,* 110n6, 122, 124n63, 125n65
  on Hegel and Barth, 161–62, 163n69

Hardy, Daniel, 164–65, 223–24, 226–27
Harnack, Adolf von, 29
Hauerwas, Stanley, 224
Healy, Nicholas, 204
Hegel, G. W. F.
  Adams's interpretation of, 9n28
  Barth's theology and, 8–9, 12–13, 147–61, 212, 218–19
  being and knowing in, 147–61
  on Kant, 13–14, 22, 25–28, 37n119, 152–61
  on logic of spatial distance, 161–66

on truth, 145
Heidegger, Martin, 87n166, 220
Hendry, George S., 64n45
Herrmann, Wilhelm, 29, 53
historicity
  a-historical Word of God and, 47–53, 108
  asymmetric reciprocity with God and, 133–43
  of Christ, 111n10
  subjectivity and, 204–7
  of truth, 166–72
Holy Spirit
  election and trinity and, 192–95
  human freedom and promise of, 179–80, 189–95
  Pentecostal promise of, 189–92
  pneumatology in Barth's theology and, 179–82
  subjectivity and, 182–89
hospitality, theology of, 228–29
Houlgate, Stephen, 153
How to Read Karl Barth (Hunsinger), 115n27, 123n59
human freedom
  Barth's discussion of, 51–53
  as Being-in Becoming, 78–104
  command and obedience and, 80–83
  determinism and, 83–96
  doctrine of election and, 78–80
humanity
  asymmetric reciprocity with God and, 128–43
  doctrine of election and, 69–73
  "double-structure" of God's being and, 62–65
  God in relation to, 44–46, 56, 59–60
  historical simultaneity of divinity and, 117–21
"The Humanity of God" (Barth), 117–21
Hunsinger, George, 12
  on Barth's Christology, 112–15
  on Barth's ontology, 175–76
  on Barth's soteriology, 123n59
  on ethics of abstraction, 214–15

Hunsinger, George *(continued)*
  on freedom and witness, 202–3
  on Hegel and Barth, 150n9
  interpretations of Barth by, 73–78, 110n6, 224
  on revelation doctrine, 131–32

idealism, Barth's discussion of, 35, 61–65
in se, God's identity as, 47–53, 63–65
  in Chalcedonian Christology, 115
  doctrine of election and, 67–73
  Molnar's discussion of, 74–78
  object-subject schema and, 108
inter-faith relations, Barth's eschatology of hope and, 226–27
invocation *(Anrufung)*
  freedom for, 207–12
  reconciliation and, 195–96
Israel, Christ as fulfilment of history of, 131–32

Jenson, Robert, 30–31, 71–72, 179–81, 183, 224
Jesus Christ. *See also* Christocentrism; Christology of Barth; Christomonism
  doctrine of election and, 58–60, 67–73
  as foundation of the Church, 186–89
  as freedom, Barth's declaration of, 1–3, 220–30
  illuc et tunc vs. hic et nunc in life of, 178–79
Johannine lexicon, in *Church Dogmatics IV/3*, 122n56, 168–72
Jones, Paul Daffyd, 8, 47n168, 48n173, 65
  on Chalcedonian Christology, 113, 116–17
  on *munus propheticum*, 145
Judaism, Barth's theology and, 227n29
Jüngel, Eberhard, 21, 24–26
  on Barth's freedom theology, 1–2, 42–44, 53, 224–25
  on "being-in-becoming," 58–65, 79–80

Christocentrism and freedom and, 98–100
  on Hegel and Barth, 150
  on object-subject schema in in *Church Dogmatics IV/3*, 109, 130–31
  on prayer, 208, 212
  on reconciliation ethics, 208–9
  trinitarianism and, 65n46
  trinity-election debate in *Church Dogmatics IV/3*, 173–75
justification, doctrine of, 199–201

Kant, Immanuel, 8n27
  aporia and, 21
  Barth's analysis of, 18–19, 33–35, 218–19
  concept of God, 10–11, 35–39
  Hegel's critique of, 13–14, 22, 25–28, 37n119, 152–61
  influence on Barth of, 22–28, 53, 57
  liberal theology and, 29
  on prayer, 208, 212
"Karl Barth's Christology: Its Basic Chalcedonian Character," 112
kerygma, 123n58
  absence of witness to, 4n15
  Barth's interpretation of, 135–43
  freedom and, 200–201
Kirschbaum, Charlotte von, 148n4, 219–20
Kittel, Gerhard, 190
klesis (calling), Barth's discussion of, 205–7
knowledge
  in *Church Dogmatics IV/3*, 122n56, 140–43
  God as object of, 56–65
  Hegel's discussion of, 161–66
  Kant's discussion of, 23–28
Krötke, Wolf, 89n173, 92n186
Küng, Hans, 224

Laats, Alar, 48
language, freedom and, 88n172
Laplace, Pierre-Simon, 89
laws of nature, human freedom and, 89–96

Lectures on the Philosophy of Religion
  (Hegel), 159–61
liberal theology
  Barth's discussion of, 19n4
  Barth's separation from, 30–35,
    48–50
  Being-Act tradition and, 28–29
liberum arbitrium doctrine, 142–43
logos asarkos, 48, 66, 68, 77–78, 194
logos ensarkos, 48, 66, 68, 77–78
logos incarnandus, 68, 77–78
love, God's being as, 59–65
Luther, Martin, 4n15
Lutheranism
  Barth's discussion of, 48, 68–69,
    91, 214
  Jüngel's discussion of, 224–25

Macken, John, 197, 220n4
Mackinnon, Donald, 224
Mangina, Joseph L., 126n74, 213
martyrdom, Barth's discussion of, 203
materialism, determinism and, 88–96
Maury, Pierre, 56, 65
McCormack, Bruce, 6, 8, 31–33, 58
  on *actus purus et singularis* of God,
    63–64
  on *Anselm* text, 39n129
  on Barth's theology, 224
  on Chalcedonian Christology,
    113–14
  Christocentrism and, 100
  on divine-human unity, 127–28
  on Hegel and Barth, 149n7, 150n9
  interpretation of *Church Dogmatics*
    II/2, 65–66
  on trinity, election and divine free-
    dom, 67–73
McDowell, John C., 126n68, 141
mechanical reductionism, human
  freedom and, 90
mediation
  Barth's theology of, 6
  in *Church Dogmatics* IV/3, 7,
    145–47
  Hegel's analylsis of, 158–61
  oppositional logic and, 163–66
  triadic interpretation of, 9–10

ministerium Verbi divini, 203
modernity, Barth's rejection of, 52–53
Molnar, Paul, 12, 62–63, 73–78
  on Barth's ontology, 175–76
  on Hegel and Barth, 150n9
Moltmann, Jürgen, 49n180, 224
moral space
  freedom and, 102–4
  human freedom and, 81–83
  reconciliation ethics and, 196–98
Mozart, Wolfgang Amadeus, Barth
  on, 224–25
munus propheticum
  asymmetric reciprocity and, 172
  Barth's discussion of, 5
  in *Church Dogmatics* IV/3, 108,
    110–17
  divine-human truth and, 166–72
  Holy Spirit and, 182–89
  object-subject schema and, 128–43
  self-witness and, 203–7
  truth of Christ and, 182
munus triplex, 111, 124n61k
music, Barth on worship and, 224–25

natural theology, 88n172
  Barth's critique of, 18
Nayed, Aref, 227
neo-Kantian liberalism, Barth and,
  18–19
neo-Protestant theology
  Barth's break from, 28–29
  Being-Act tradition and, 19–39
Nestorianism
  Barth's theology and, 112–14
  in *extra Calvinisticum*, 68
New Testament
  Barth's discussion of, 221–22
  Holy Spirit in, 181n23
Nimmo, Paul, 6, 8, 75, 78, 183n25,
  192–95, 213–14
noetic mediation
  Holy Spirity and, 140–43, 183–89,
    219
  prayer and, 210–12
noumena
  Hegel's analysis of, 153–61
  Kant's concept of, 23–28

objectivity. *See also* secondary objectivity
  actualism and, 11–12, 57–65
  a-historical Word of God and, 47–53
  in Barth's theology, 7–10, 17–19
  Being-Act tradition and, 20, 31–35
  "double-structure" of God's being and, 61–65
  freedom and, 43–44
  of God, 57–65
  Kant and, 22–28
object-subject schema. *See also* subjectivity
  in Barth's soteriological objectivism, 123–28
  Christocentrism and, 75–78
  in *Church Dogmatics* IV/3, 9–10, 12–13, 109, 121, 128–47
  criticism of, 121–28
  in Hegel's work, 148–61
  Holy Spirit and, 184–89
  invocation to freedom and, 211–12, 215–16
  in se identity of God and, 108
Ochs, Peter, 227
O'Donovan, Oliver, 224
Oepke, Albrecht, 190–91
"oneness," divine-human unity and Barth's concep tof, 121
ontic foundations
  Holy Spirit and, 184–89
  prayer and, 210–12
oppositional logic, Barth's emphasis on, 161–66

Pannenberg, Wolfhart, 224
parousia
  Barth's conception of, 190–92
  doctrine of election and, 193–95
participative theology of freedom, Hegel and Barth on, 145–47
Pauline theology
  Barth's interpretations of, 32–35, 213–15, 221–22
  in *Church Dogmatics* IV/3, 122n56
  Jüngel's discussion of, 225n23

Pentecost, *parousia* and promise of, 190–92
perichoretic movement, trinitarian doctrine and, 62–65
Phenomenology of Spirit (Hegel), 154–61
phenomenon
  Hegel's analysis of, 153–61
  Kant's discussion of, 23–28
philosophy
  Barth's analysis of, 20–21
  theology and, 85–86
physicalism, 88n172
Platonic humanity, 220
  Barth's Christology and, 124–26
pneumatology
  Barth's Christology and, 5, 178–79, 182n23
  criticism of Barth's work in, 179–82, 215–16
  doctrine of election and, 192–95
  ethics of abstraction and, 214–15
  object-subject relation and, 188–89, 219
Polanyi, Michael, 161–62
prayerful responsibility, 100–104
  freedom and, 207–12
prophetic office, in *Church Dogmatics* IV/3, 130–43
providence
  human freedom and, 85–96
  prayerful responsibility and, 101104
Przywara, Erich, 46

Quash, Ben, 225
quasi-Kantian criticism, Barth's theology and, 8, 10–11, 18–19, 34–35, 59, 149, 218–19

Rade, Martin, 29
Rahner, Karl, 123n58
"Rahner's rule," 67n52
Rashkover, Randi, 227
reality
  Barth's discussion of, 35, 61–65
  Hegel's discussion of, 155–61
  Kant's discussion of, 22–28

reason
　Hegel's discussion of, 156–61
　Kant on, 22–28
Reath, Andrews, 27
reconciliation, Barth's ethic of
　asymmetrical reciprocity with God and, 128–43
　Chalcedonian Christology and, 112–17
　criticism of, 121–28, 219
　divine-human unity in, 118–21
　moral field and, 196–98
　noetic aspects of, 183–89
　oppositional logic and, 163–66
　prayerfulness and, 208–12
　triadic interpretation of, 9–10
　vocation and invocation, 195–96
Reformed tradition, Barth's theology and, 91, 219–20
Registerband, 220
Rendtorff, Trutz, 52–53
resurrection
　absence of witness to, 4n15
　in *Church Dogmatics* IV/3, 135–43
revelation
　Barth's doctrine of, 11, 42–44, 48–53
　reconciliation and, 130–43
Ritschl, Albrecht, 29
Rogers, Eugene, 179–81
Roman Catholic ecclesiology, Barth's perceptions of, 183
Rosato, Philip, 179–82, 189–90

Sabbath (day of rest), actualism and, 101–4
salvation
　in *Church Dogmatics* IV/3, 123–28, 134–43
　for non-Christians vs. Christians, 200–201
　parousia and Pentecost and, 190–92
　role the Spirit in, 183–89
sanctification, doctrine of, 199–201
　confession and, 102–4
　human activity, 99–102
Sartre, Jean-Paul, 87n166
Schleiermacher, Friedrich, 29

The Science of Logic (Hegel), 154n30
Scriptural Reasoning, 227
secondary objectivity, God's being, 62–65
self-determination
　doctrine of election and, 79–80
　freedom as, 41–42, 84–96, 121
service, Barth's discussion of, 202–7
Sherman, Franklin, 39
Smail, Thomas, 179, 181–82
Sonderegger, Katherine, 223, 226
soteriological objectivism, 5, 12–13
　Barth's eschatology and, 189–92
　Chalcedonian Christology and, 116–17
　Christ's subjectivity and, 132–43
　human freedom and, 98–100
　invocation to freedom and, 211–12
　reconciliation doctrine and, 122–28, 163–66
　theological epistemology and, 170–72
　trinitarianism and, 70–73
sovereign relationality of God
　Barth's actualism and, 39–42
　human freedom and, 100
spatial distance, Hegel on logic of, 161–66
speech-act, God's Word as, 39–42
　"double-structure" of God's being and, 61–65
　trinitarian doctrine and, 42–44
spirit, Hegel's discussion of, 160–61
status exaltationis, 111
status exinanitionis, 111
Strauss, David Friedrich, 29
subjectivity. *See also* object-subject schema
　actualism and, 11–12
　a-historical Word of God and, 47–53
　in Barth's theology, 7–10, 17–19, 219
　Being-Act tradition and, 20, 31–35
　in *Church Dogmatics* IV/3, 124–28, 132–43, 182–89
　divine-human unity and, 117–21, 182

subjectivity *(continued)*
  divine ontology and, 57–65
  God's freedom and, 43–44
  Holy Spirit and, 183–89
  Kant and, 22–28
  prayer and, 210–12
  witness and, 204–7
Sykes, Stephen, 35, 224
synergism, freedom and, 5

Tanner, Kathryn, 85n161, 91–92, 226
Taylor, Charles, 81n128
theological confidence, Barth's discussion of, 220–30
theological epistemology, Barth's concepts of freedom and, 31–35
theology
  Kant's discussion of, 23–28
  philosophy and, 21
Thompson, John, 188–89
Thurneysen, Eduard, 20
time, eternity and, 92–96
Torrance, Alan, 42
transcendental idealism
  Barth's discussion of, 35–39
  Kant and, 22n21, 23–28
triadic interpretation of mediation, 9–10, 13
  in *Church Dogmatics* IV/3, 135–43, 145–47, 151–52
  Hegel's analylsis of, 158–61
  humanity's asymmetric reciprocity with God and, 128–43
  oppositional logic and, 163–66
trinitarian doctrine
  Barth's freedom theology and, 48–53
  Barth's pneumatology and, 180–82
  in *Church Dogmatics* 1, 11
  in *Church Dogmatics* IV/3, 172–76
  divine freedom and, 65–78
  doctrine of election and, 67–78
  "double-structure" of God's being and, 61–65

  God's Being-in-Act and, 42–44
  Holy Spirit and, 192–95
  "strong" and "weak" interpretations of Barth on, 75–78
trinity-election debate, 12
*Troeltsch, 29
truth
  in *Church Dogmatics* IV/3, 122n56, 135–43, 166–72
  freedom and, 212
  Hegel's discussion of, 155–61
  historicity of, 166–72

unity-in-distinction, freedom and, 201–2, 211–12

Verbum incarnandum, 194–95
vestigium trinitatis, Barth's resistance to, 46
vocation *(Berufung)*
  for freedom, in Christianity, 198–201
  freedom as witness and, 203–7
  reconciliation and, 195–96

Ward, Graham, 224
Waller, Giles, 4n15
Webster, John, 5, 81–82, 92, 110, 133, 184–85, 196–99
Welker, Michael, 148n4
Williams, Rowan, 40–51, 88–89, 90n177, 224–25, 227–28
Willis, Robert E., 126, 169n85, 199–200
Wingren, Gustaf, 47–51
Wissenschaft, liberal theology and, 29
witness, freedom as, 202–7
Wording a Radiance (Hardy), 226
Word of God, as a-historical, 46–53
Wright, Terry J., 200

Zoloth, Laurie, 227

www.ingramcontent.com/pod-product-compliance
Lightning Source LLC
Chambersburg PA
CBHW030823230426
43667CB00008B/1354